Where to Stay in Northern California

WHERE TO STAY
IN
NORTHERN
CALIFORNIA

Phil Philcox

HUNTER
PUBLISHING INC
MPC

Hunter Publishing, Inc.
300 Raritan Center Parkway
Edison NJ 08818
(908) 225 1900
Fax (908) 417 0482

ISBN 1-55650-572-8

Published in the UK by
Moorland Publishing Co. Ltd.
Moor Farm Rd, Airfield Estate
Ashbourne, Derbyshire DE6 1HD
England

ISBN (UK) 0 86190 254 8

Cover photograph: Lake Tahoe (Steve Vidler/Leo de Wys Inc.)

Contents

Introduction

If you're California-bound for business or pleasure, this is the ultimate guide to finding a place to bed down for the night. **More places to stay are described here – over 3,000 in Northern California from Ahwahnee to Yuba City – than in any other guide.** Need a convenient downtown hotel with free airport transportation, exercise equipment, lighted tennis courts and meeting facilities? Prefer a waterfront apartment, a roadside motel or a high-rise condo with boat dock, completely equipped for move-in living? If elbow room is important, how about a rental home in Lake Tahoe? Or would a bed & breakfast near Mendocino fill the bill? If you have special needs, this guide explains everything from where to find properties offering wheelchair access and rooms for the disabled to accommodations that provide free local telephone calls or allow pets.

Included are the names and telephone numbers of regional rental sources that handle an assortment of accommodation options – from private homes to apartments. These agencies are excellent sources of information on what's available in each area in different price ranges and most have toll-free numbers you can call for information. You will also find, for the first time in any accommodations guide, toll-free and fax numbers you can call to request literature, rate cards and reservations. Many properties will fax their literature directly to your machine.

As of press time, the rates were current, based on interviews with the property owners. Rates are constantly changing and vary considerably with location and season, so use the rates listed to determine the price range of the property but always call to make reservations and confirm the price. Use the toll-free number where available when calling from the U.S. and Canada. Most toll-free numbers listed are valid from all states but some properties have outside-California or California-only numbers. If you reach an invalid number, check with the toll-free operator at 800-555-1212.

Properties in popular vacation areas often offer special discounts and programs for vacationers with children, seniors, frequent travelers and government employees. A list of chains with their California locations is included. Some resorts offer free shuttle transportation in and around areas with major attractions, discounts on admission tickets and other incentives. Call for further information.

After the abbreviations section below, you'll find a list of chain hotels and motels with special deals and offers available.

Abbreviations Used In This Guide

LS - low season – usually the lowest rates of the year.
MS - mid-season.
HS - high season – usually the highest rates of the year.
SGL - single room – rate for one person.
DBL - double room – rate for two people sharing one room.
EFF - efficiency – usually one room with kitchen or kitchenette.
STS - suites.
1BR, 2BR, 3BR - one- , two- or three-bedroom condo, apartment, villa or townhouse, usually with full kitchen facilities and washer/dryer.
No-smoking rooms - rooms available for non-smokers.
No-smoking - smoking not permitted on the property.
Child care - babysitting services available.
Complimentary breakfast - a free continental or full American breakfast is included in the room rate.
Airport courtesy car - free transportation to and from local airports.
Airport transportation - transportation is available to and from local airports for a fee.
Meeting facilities - the property can provide facilities for meetings and conferences.
$00-$000 - daily rate span.
$000W-$000W - weekly rate span.
$00/$000W - daily rate followed by weekly rate.

Chain Hotels

Locations and Special Deals

BEST WESTERN Box 10203, Phoenix AZ 85064; 602-957-4200, Reservations 800-528-1234

Most locations offer a 10% discount to senior travelers on a space-available basis with advanced reservations. The Government-Military Travel Program provides discounts to federal employees and military personnel. The Gold Crown Club provides points toward free stays and special amenities.

California Locations: Alturas, Anaheim, Anderson, Antioch, Arcadia, Arroyo Grande, Atascadero, Auburn, Azusa, Bakersfield, Barstow, Beaumont, Benicia, Bishop, Blythen, Bodega Bay, Bridgeport, Buena Park, Camarillo, Cambria, Cameron Park, Canoga Park, Carlsbad, Carpinteria, Carmel, Chico, Chino, Clearlake, Concord, Corona, Coronado, Corte Madera, Costa Mesa, Crescent City, Davis, Dunnigan, El Cajon, Escondido, Eureka, Fairfield, Fallbrook, Fillmore, Fort Bragg, Fremont, Fresno, Fullerton, Garberville, Gilroy, Glendale, Gress Valley, Hanford, Hayward, Healdsburg, Hemet, Hollister, Hoopa, Huntington Beach, Jackson, Kettleman City, King City, La Hambra, Laguna Beach, Lake Tahoe, Lancaster, Lee Vining, Lemoore, Lodi, Lompac, Lone Pine, Long Beach, Los Angeles, Los Osos, Madera, Manteca, Maricopa, Merced, Modesto, Monterey, Morgan Hill, Morro Bay, Mount Shasta, Mountain View, Napa, Needles, Newport Beach, Oakland, Oceanside, Ojai, Ontario, Oroville, Pacific Grove, Palm Springs, Palo Alto, Pasadena, Paso Robles, Petaluma, Pismo Beach, Placerville, Rancho Cordova, Rancho Cucamonga, Redding, Redlands, Redondo Beach, Redwood City, Rialton, Riverside, Roseville, Rowland Heights, Sacramento, Salinas, San Bernadino, San Diego, San Francisco, San Jose, San Juan Capistrano, San Luis Obispo, San Mateo, San Pedro, Santa Barbara, Santa Clara, Santa Cruz, Santa Maria, Santa Monica, Santa Nella, Santa Rosa, Scotts Valley, Seaside, Selma, Smith River, Soledad,

Solvang, Sonoma, Sonora, Stockton, Sunnyvale, Sunset Beach, Susanville, Tehachapi, Temecula, Thousand Oaks, Three Rivers, Truckee, Tulare, Turlock, Twentynine Palms, Ukiah, Union City, Vacaville, Valencia, Ventura, Victorville, Visalia, Walnut Creek, Watsonville, Westminster, Whittier, Willows, Yountville

BUDGET HOST INNS 2601 Jackboro Highway, Fort Worth TX 76114; 817-626-7064, Reservations 800-BUD-HOST

California locations: *Banning, Beaumont, Blythe, Eureka, Inglewood, Los Angeles, Maywood, Midpines, Pico Rivera, South Gate*

CLARION-CHOICE HOTELS 10750 Columbia Pike, Silver Spring MD 20901; 301-593-5600, Fax 301-681-7478

Reservation Numbers: Sleep Inn 800-62-SLEEP; Friendship Inn 800-453-4511, Econo Lodge 800-55-ECONO, Rodeway Inn 800-229-2000, Comfort Inn 800-228-5150, Quality Inn 800-228-5151, Clarion Hotels 800-CLARION.

Clarion and Choice Hotels consist of Sleep Inn, Comfort Inns, Friendship Inns, Econo Lodges, Rodeway Inns, Quality Inns and Clarion Hotels and Resorts. The Family Plan allows children to stay free when sharing a parents' room. Prime Time and Prime Time Senior Saver for people over age 60 offers a 10% discount at all hotels year-round and a 30% discount at limited locations when you call 800-221-2222 and ask for the Prime Time Senior Saver rate.

Special discounts of 10%-20% are available at participating locations for members of AAA and businesses with 100 employees or fewer enrolled in the Small Organizations Savings (SOS) Program. SOS-enrolled companies receive a 10% discount off the first 15 rooms used by company employees. The Weekender Rate Program offers special room rates of $20, $30 or $35 per night with an advanced reservation. All local, state and federal government employees and military personnel receive special per diem rates and upgrades when available at participating hotels.

California Locations: Anaheim, Arcata, Bakersfield, Barstow, Blythe, Calistoga, Calpine, Canoga Park, Carson, Castaic, Costa Mesa, Downey, El Monte, El Toro, Fontana, Fremont, Glendora, Hayward, Hemet, Hollywood, Huntington Beach, Indio, Industry, La Mesa, Laguna Hills, Lancaster, Lawndale, Lompoc, Long Beach, Los Angeles, Mammoth Lake, Manhattan Beach, Marina, Millbrae, Milpitas, Monterey, Moreno Valley, Mountain View, Napa, National City, Norwalk, Novato, Oakland, Oceanside, Ontario, Pacific Grove, Palm Springs, Pasadena, Petaluma, Pismo Beach, Placentia, Rancho Cordova, Redwood City, Sacramento, Salinas, San Bernardino, San Clemente, San Diego, San Dimas, San Francisco, San Gabriel, San Jose, San Luis Obispo, Santa Ana, Santa Barbara, Santa Clara, Santa Cruz, Santa Monica, Sepulveda, Simi Valley, Stanton, Sunnyvale, Temecula, Torrance, Upland, Vacaville, Vallejo, Ventura, West Covina, Williams, Wilmington, Woodland

CO-Z 8 MOTELS Reservations 800-882-1985

California Locations: Mountain View, Palo Alto, Redwood City, Santa Clara, Sunnyvale

DAYS INN 2751 Buford Highway, Atlanta GA 30324; 404-329-7466, Fax 404-325-7731, Reservations 800-325-2525

The September Days Club offers travelers over the age of 50 up to 40% discounts on rooms, 10% discounts on food and gifts, a quarterly club magazine, seasonal discounts and special tours and trips. The Inn Credible Card is designed for business travelers and provides up to 30% savings on room rates, free stays for spouses and other benefits. The Days Gem Club is a free travel club for military personnel and government employees that offers up to 30% savings on room rates. School Days Club for academic staff and educators offers a minimum of 10% savings on room rates, special group rates and additional benefits. The Sport Plus Club is designed for coaches and team managers who organize team travel and offers 10% discounts on room rates, special team rates and late check-outs.

California Locations: Adelanto, Anaheim, Bakersfield, Banning, Corning, Guerneville, Lompoc, Los Angeles, Monterey, Needles, Ontario, Palmdale, Palm Springs, Placerville, Redding, Riverside, Sacramento, San Diego, San Francisco, San Jose, Santa Clara, Santa Monica, Santa Rosa, Ventura, Victorville, Westley, Yosemite

DOUBLETREE HOTELS 555 Madison Avenue, Suite 815, New York NY 10022; 212-754-7800, Fax 212-754-7846, Reservations 800-528-0444

Doubletree operates 38 hotels in the United States, including Doubletree Club Hotels that provide oversized rooms, complimentary, cooked-to-order breakfasts, club rooms and hosted evening receptions. Family Plans allow up to two children under the age of 18 to stay free when they share the rooms with their parents. For the business traveler, most hotels offer secretarial services, photocopying, fax machines and computer hook-up capabilities. A special discounted rate is available to seniors. A Corporate Plus Program is available at all business center locations.

California Locations: Burlingame, Los Angeles, Monterey, Ontario, Orange, Santa Ana, Palm Springs, Pleasanton, San Diego, Santa Clara, Santa Rosa, Temecula, Ventura, Walnut Creek

ECONOMY INNS OF AMERICA 755 Raintree Drive, Suite 200, Carlsbad CA 92009; 619-438-6661, Fax 407-396-4979, Reservations 800-826-0778

California Locations: Bakersfield, Barstow, Carlsbad, Fairfield, Fresno, Lost Hills, Madera, Milpitas, San Diego, San Ysidro, Rancho Cordova, Tulare

EMBASSY SUITES 222 Las Colinas Blvd., Irving TX 75039; 214-556-1133, Fax 214-556-8222, Reservations 800-528-1100
California Locations: Anaheim, Arcadia, Brea, Buena Park, Burlingame, Covina, Downey, El Segundo, Irvine, Lompac, Los

Angeles, Milpitas, Napa Valley, San Diego, San Francisco, San Rafael, Santa Ana, Santa Clara, Walnut Creek

GUEST QUARTERS SUITE HOTELS 30 Rowes Wharf, Boston MA 02110; 617-330-1440, Fax 716-737-8752, Reservations 800-424- 2900

California Locations: Santa Monica

HAMPTON INNS 6800 Poplar, Memphis TN 38138; 901-758-3100, Fax 901-756-9479, Reservations 800-426-7866

California Locations: Fairfield, Fresno, Los Angeles, Oakland, Palm Springs, Riverside, San Diego, Santa Barbara

HILTON HOTELS 9336 Civic Center Drive, Beverly Hills CA 90209; 213-278-4321, Fax 213-205-4599, Reservations 800-HILTON

Zip-Out/Quick Check-Out is available to travelers using major credit cards. An itemized statement of charges is provided the night before departure. Many Hilton locations have hotels-within-hotels, Tower and Executive accommodations offering room upgrades, use of a private lounge, access to business services, complimentary cocktails and continental breakfast and use of telex, fax machines and photocopying equipment.

The HHonors Guest Reward Program is a free program that earns points toward free or discounted stays at participating properties and members-only privileges that include rapid check-ins, free daily newspaper, free stay for spouse and free use of health club facilities when available.

The Corporate Rate Program offers business travelers guaranteed rates annually, speed reservations, Tower and Executive accommodations and Quick Check-Out facilities.

Hilton's Senior HHonors offers special amenities to travelers over the age of 60. Included are room discounts up to 50%, a 20% dinner discount and money-back guarantee, a private toll-free reservation number and automatic enrollment in Hilton's Guest Reward Programs. BounceBack Weekend offers a free, daily continental breakfast, children free in parents' rooms and special rates for Thursday to Sunday with a Saturday stay. During the summer, these discounted rates apply Monday to Wednesday when a Saturday stay is included.

Hilton Leisure Breaks includes packages for honeymooners and special occasions with special rates. Hilton Meeting 2000 is a network of business meeting facilities available at some locations and includes special meeting room, audiovisual systems, refreshments and assistance in planning meetings and programs.

California Locations: Baldwin Park, Beverly Hills, Fremont, Los Angeles, Oakland, Oxnard, Pasadena, Pleasanton, San Bernardino, San Diego, San Francisco, Sunnyvale, Valencia

HOLIDAY INN 1100 Ashwood Parkway, Atlanta GA 30338; 404-551-3500, Reservations 800-HOLIDAY

When sharing a parent's room, children 12 and under stay free at all locations; cribs are also free and, in some participating hotels, the age limit is extended to 18. The Forget Something Program provides complimentary shaving cream, razor, comb, toothbrush and toothpaste. Holiday Inn Preferred Senior Travelers Program and other Senior Savings Programs offer a 20% savings on rooms and a 10% discount at participating Holiday Inn restaurants. Great Rates provide up to 10% off the standard room rate with advance reservation.

Government-Military Rates are available to government employees, military personnel and contractors. Room upgrades, special room rates and a 10% dinner discount with free continental breakfast is available at participating locations. The Priority Club offers frequent travelers special rates, points toward free stays and additional benefits.

California Locations: Barstow, Belmont, Brentwood-Bel Air, Buena Park, Burbank, Chico, Costa Mesa, Fairfield, Foster City, Fresno, Fullerton, Glendale, Half Moon Bay, Hollywood, Hunt-

ington Beach, Irvine, Laguna Hills, Livermore, Long Beach, Los Angeles, Marin, Milpitas, Modesto, Monrovia, Montebello, Monterey, Oakland, Ontario, Palm Desert, Palmdale, Palm Springs, Palo Alto, Pasadena, Pleasanton, Redondo, Redding, Riverside, Sacramento, San Clemente, San Diego, San Jose, San Francisco, San Simeon, Santa Barbara, Santa Cruz, Santa Monica, Santa Nelle, Solvang, Stockton, Sunnyvale, Thousand Oaks, Torrance, Union City, Vallejo, Van Nuys, Ventura, Victorville, Visalia, Walnut, Walnut Creek, West Covina, Woodland Hills

HOMEWOOD SUITES 3742 Lamar Avenue, Memphis TN 38195; 901-362-4663, Fax 901-362-4663, Reservations 800-225-5466

California Locations: San Jose

HOSPITALITY INTERNATIONAL INNS 1152 Spring Street, Suite A, Atlanta GA 30309; 404-873-5924, Reservations 800-251-1962

Hospitality International consists of Red Carpet Inns, Scottish Inns, Passport Inns and Downtowner Motor Inns

The Identicard Program provides room discounts at participating inns and resorts.

California Locations: Anaheim, Indio, Mohave, San Bernardino, Victorville

HOWARD JOHNSON 3838 East Van Buren, Phoenix AZ 85038; 201-256-9030, Fax 201-890-3051, Reservations 800-654-2000
The Howard Johnson Road Rally Program offers discounts to senior travelers over the age of 60 and members of AARP and other national seniors' organizations. With advanced reservations, a 30% discount is available at some locations. The Family Plan lets children under the age of 12 stay free at all locations with some properties extending the age limit to 18.

Government Rate Programs offer special rates to federal employees, military personnel and government contractors. The Corporate Rate Program offers special rates to companies and business travelers. Howard Johnson Executive Section offers guests special rooms, complimentary wake-up coffee and newspapers and snacks. Kids Go Hojo provides children with free FunPacks filled with toys, puzzles, coloring books and games.

California Locations: *Anaheim, Baldwin Park, Barstow, Claremont, Colton, Corta Madera, Culver City, Dublin, Fresno, Hollywood, Huntington Beach, Long Beach, Los Angeles, Mill Valley, Monrovia, Norco, Ontario, Orange, Palm Desert, Pomona, Redwood City, Reseda, Riverside, Sacramento, San Bernardino, San Diego, San Francisco, San Jose, San Luis Obispo, Santa Anna, Santa Clara, Santa Maria, Sepulveda, Thousand Oaks, Torrance*

HYATT HOTELS INTERNATIONAL Madison Plaza, 200 West Madison, Chicago IL 60606; 312-720-1234, Fax 312-750-8579, Reservations 800-228-9000

Hyatt Gold Passport provides earned credits for free stays, a private toll-free reservation number, express check-in, special members-only rooms, free newspaper daily, complimentary morning coffee and use of fitness centers when available. Hyatt Reserved Upgrade coupon booklets are available for confirmed room upgrades. Hyatt Gold Passport At Leisure is available at over 155 locations worldwide and includes invitations to private receptions, room amenities, priority room and dining reservations and a quarterly newsletter with member-only offers.

The Regency Club is a hotel within a hotel offering VIP accommodations. Located on the topmost floors of participating hotels, the rooms are reached by special elevators requiring a passkey. Also included is a free morning paper, complimentary breakfast, afternoon hors d'ouevres, wine and cocktails.

Camp Hyatt is for children and their parents. Upon arrival at any Hyatt hotel or resort, children receive a free cap, frequent travel passport and a registration card. The program offers special children's menus in the dining room, room discounts, kitchen tours and other pastimes.

California Locations: Anaheim, Burlingame, Garden Grove, Hollywood, Indian Wells, Irvine, Long Beach, Los Angeles, Monterey, Newport Beach, Oakland, Palm Springs, Palo Alto, Sacramento, San Diego, San Francisco, San Jose, Westlake Village

LA QUINTA INNS 10010 San Pedro, San Antonio TX 78279; 512-366-6000, 800-531-5900, Fax 512-366-6100, Reservations 800-531-5900

La Quinta has 200 inn locations around the United States. In addition to standard guest rooms, some properties offer King Plus and Executive King rooms with king-size beds, two telephones, remote-control television and other amenities. Most properties offer free local telephone calls, complimentary morning coffee in the lobby, a complimentary issue of the current *Newsweek* magazine, same-day laundry and dry cleaning service and free parking.

Rooms for the disabled are available at some locations and consist of lower dresser vanities, low-pile carpeting, portable shower heads, upper and lower closet racks, bath area railings and remote-control TV.

All active U.S. military and government employees receive special room rates at most locations. Children 18 and under stay free at all locations when sharing their parent's room. Cribs are available at no cost and roll-away beds are available at an extra charge.

Senior citizens age 55 and over receive a discount on room rates and many locations offer special rates on weekends. La Quinta Senior Class for travelers over the age of 60 provides a 20% discount at all Inns nationwide, no additional charge for a third or fourth person in a room, credits toward free night stays and guaranteed reservations. Upon applying for membership ($10), you receive a certificate good for $20 off the regular room rate.

La Quinta Per Diem Preferred offers credits and discounts to military personnel, U.S. government workers and cost-reimbursable contractors. La Quinta Returns earns credits for free nights, special room rates, guaranteed reservations for late arrivals, account summaries and $50 check-cashing privileges.

California Locations: Bakersfield, Fresno, Chula Vista, Costa Mesa, Irvine, Rancho Penasquitos, Sacramento, San Bernardino, San Francisco, Stockton, Ventura, Vista

MARRIOTT Marriott Drive, Washington DC 20058; 301-380-9000. Reservations: 800-228-2800; 800-321-2211 (Courtyard); 800-331-3131 (Residence Inns); 800-228-9290 (Fairfield Inns)

Marriott consists of Marriott Hotels and Resorts, Marriott Suites, Courtyard by Marriott, Residence Inns and Fairfield Inns.

SuperSaver rates offer discounts on weekday and weekend stays at participating hotels. Discounts range from 10% and up. The TFB program (Two for Breakfast) offers discounts for weekend stays for two adults that include complimentary breakfasts.

Advance Purchase Rates are discounts up to 50% for advance, prepaid, non-refundable reservations 7, 14, 21 and 30 days in advance. Senior Citizen discounts for members of AARP and other senior groups are available at all participating hotels.

The Marriott Honored Guest Award offers special upgrades to members at participating hotels. After staying 15 nights during a 12-month period, members receive express checkout services, complimentary newspapers, check cashing privileges, free luggage tags and discounts.

California Locations: Anaheim, Arcadia, Bakersfield, Campbell, Pleasant Hill, Costa Mesa, Fountain Valley, Fremont, Irvine, La Jolla, Livermore, Long Beach, Manhattan Beach, Mountain View, Ontario, Orange, Placentia, San Diego, Sacramento, San Mateo, San Ramon, Sunnyvale, Torrance

MOTEL 6 14651 Dallas Parkway, Dallas TX 75240; 214-386-6161, Fax 214-991-2976, Reservations 800-437-7486

California Locations: Anaheim, Arcata, Atascadero, Bakersfield, Barstow, Bermuda Dunes, Big Bear, Blythe, Buellton, Buena Park, Buttonwillow, Camarillo, Carlsbad, Carpenteria, Chico, Chino, Coalinga, Corona, Davis, El Cajon, Escondido, Eureka, Fairfield, Fontana, Fremont, Fresno, Gilroy, Indio, King City, Lake Tahoe, Lompac, Los Angeles, Lost Hills, Mammoth Lakes, Manhattan Beach, Monterey, Merced, Modesto, Mojave, Morro Bay, Napa, Needles, Newark, Oakland, Oceanside, Ontario, Oroville, Palmdale, Palm Springs, Palo Alto, Petaluma, Pinole, Pismo Beach, Pittsburg, Porterville, Rancho California, Red Bluff, Redding, Redlands, Ridgecrest, Riverside, Rohnert Park, Sacramento, Salinas, San Bernardino, San Diego, San Jose, San Luis Obispo, Santa Ana, Santa Barbara, Santa Clara, Santa Maria, Santa Nella, Santa Rosa, San Ysidro

NATIONAL 9 INN 2285 South Main, Salt Lake City UT 84115; 801-466-9820, Fax 801-466-9856, Reservations 800-524-9999

California Locations: Fresno, Lawndale, Livermore, Lone Pine, Redding

OMNI HOTELS 515 Madison Avenue, New York NY 10022; 212-308-4700, Fax 603-926-9122, Reservations 800-THE-OMNI

The Omni Club Program is available at selected hotels and offers concierge service, private lounge facilities, complimentary breakfast, evening cocktails and hors d'oeuvres and specially-appointed rooms.

The Omni Hotel Select Guest Program provides special services, priority room availability, accommodations upgrade, complimentary coffee and morning newspaper and a newsletter announcing additional programs. The Omni Hotel Executive Service Plan is available to corporate members and includes a variety of special benefits. For planning and scheduling meetings, the Omni Hotels Gavel Service and Omni-Express Programs provide assistance by experienced meeting planners. City'scapes is a special weekend package that offers discounts and special amenities.

California Locations: San Diego

PARK INN RESORTS 4425 West Airport Freeway, Irving TX 75062; 214-714-0095, Reservations 800-437-PARK

The Silver Citizens Club offers a 20% room discount and 10% food discount at participating hotels, free morning paper and coffee, special directory, all-night emergency pharmacy telephone number and personal check cashing.

California Locations: Palm Springs

RADISSON HOTELS INTERNATIONAL Carlson Parkway, Minneapolis MN 55459; 612-540-5526, Fax 612-449-3400, Reservations 800-333-3333

Radisson operates 270 hotels and affiliates worldwide. Plaza Hotels are usually located in the city center or suburban locations. Suite Hotels offer oversized rooms with living room, mini-bar and kitchenettes. Resort Hotels usually are near beaches, golf courses and recreational facilities.

California Locations: City of Commerce, Fullerton, Irvine, Long Beach, Los Angeles, Oxnard, Rancho Bernardo, Sacramento, San Diego, San Francisco, San Jose, Santa Ana, Simi Valley, Sunnyvale, Visalia

RAMADA INN Box 52106, Phoenix AZ 85072; 602-389-3800, Reservations 800-2-RAMADA

Ramada Inn has 700 locations world-wide consisting of Ramada Inns, Ramada Hotels and Ramada Renaissance Hotels. The Hotels are designed to five-star international standards and include convention and banquet facilities, restaurants, 24-hour room service, entertainment and lounges. Most Renaissance

Hotels offer a club floor with concierge services, upgraded room amenities and lounge.

Membership in the Ramada Business Card Program earns points for trips and merchandise based on dollars spent at Ramada properties. The card is available free. Membership includes favorable rates, automatic room upgrade when available, express check-in and check-out, free newspaper on business days, free same-room accommodations for your spouse when you travel together, extended check-out times, newsletter and points redeemable for hotel stays, air travel, car rentals and over 10,000 Service Merchandise catalog items.

Participating Ramada Inn properties offer SuperSaver Weekend discounts. These rates apply on Friday, Saturday and Sunday for one- , two- and three-night stays. Extra person rates may apply for a third or fourth person in the room. Because some hotels limit availability on some dates, reservations are recommended.

When traveling with family or friends, the Ramada 4-for-1 Program permits up to four people to share the same room and pay the single rate. At participating properties, the Best Years Seniors Program provides travelers over the age of 60 who are members of AARP, the Global Horizons Club, Catholic Golden Age, The Golden Buckeye Club, Humana Seniors Association, The Retired Enlisted Association, The Retired Officers Association and United Airlines Silver Wings Plus with a 25% discount off regular room rates.

The Ramada Per Diem Value Program is available at more than 350 locations. Properties honor the maximum lodging per diem rates set by the U.S. General Services Administration. Federal employees, military personnel and employees of Cost Reimbursable Contractors traveling on official government business are eligible. In addition to the per diem limits for lodging, the single person room rate at participating locations includes full American breakfast and all applicable taxes. All Ramada properties provide corporate customers favorable rates. Companies need a minimum of ten travelers with a combined total of 100 room nights per year.

California Locations: Agoura Hills, Anaheim, Antioch, Artesia, Bakersfield, Buelton, Buena Park, Burbank, Burlingame, Carlsbad, Carson, Chatsworth, Chula Vista, Claremont, Commerce, Compton, Culver City, Cypress, Davis, El Centro, El Montes, Fresno, Garden Grove, Hawthorne, Hemet, Hollywood, Long Beach, Los Angeles, Modesto, Monterey, Moreno Valley, Oakdale, Orange, Palmdale, Palm Springs, Salinas, San Bernardino, San Clemente, San Diego, San Francisco, Santa Ana, Santa Maria, Solano Beach, Sunset Beach, Temecula, Vallejo

RITZ CARLTON HOTELS 3414 Peachtree Rd. NE, Atlanta GA 30326; 404-237-5500, Fax 404-261-0119, Reservations 800-241-3333

California Locations: Laguna Beach, Rancho Mirage, Marina del Rey, San Francisco

SHERATON HOTELS, INNS AND RESORTS 60 State Street, Boston MA 02109; 617-367-3600, Fax 617-367-5676, Reservations 800-325-3535

Sheraton Club International is a frequent guest program that provides free stays based on points earned. Membership includes upgraded accommodations, late check-outs and other benefits. The Sheraton Executive Traveler Plan offers guaranteed room rates year-round, earned credits, free newspaper daily, automatic upgrades, family plans, express check-outs and other benefits.

California Locations: Anaheim, Bakersfield, Burlingame, Cerritos, City of Industry, Concord, Fresno, La Jolla, Long Beach, Los Angeles, Milpitas, Monterey, Newport Beach, Norwalk, Pleasanton, Pomona, Rancho Cordova, Redondo Beach, Riverside, Rosemead, Sacramento, San Diego, San Francisco, San Jose, San Pedro, Sunnyvale, Santa Barbara, Santa Monica, Solvang, Universal City

SHILO INNS 11600 Southwest Barnes Rd., Portland OR 97225; 503-641-6565, Reservations 800-222-2244

California Locations: Corning, Delano, Mammoth Lakes, Oakhurst, Palm Springs, Pomona

SUNDOWNER MOTOR INNS Box 145, Goodlettesville TN 37072; 615-851-0942, Reservations 800-322-8029

Sundowner International consists of Best Value Inns, Superior Motels, Sundowner Inns and Travel Host Motels.

California Locations: Los Angeles, Palm Springs, San Francisco, San Simeon

SUPER 8 MOTELS 1910 8th Avenue NE, Aberdeen SD 57402; 605-225-2272, Fax 605-225-1140, Reservations 800-800-8000, 800-848-8888

California Locations: Alameda, Anaheim, Arcata, Arvin, Auburn, Bakersfield, Banning, Barstow, Blythe, Cameron Park, Costa Mesa, Fortuna, Gilroy, Hayward, Hemet, Hesperia, Indio, Inglewood, Martinez, Milpitas, Kettleman City, Modesto, Monterey, Ontario, Palm Springs, Palmdale, Pleasanton, Red Bluff, Redding, Riverside, Sacramento, San Bernardino, San Diego, San Francisco, San Luis Obispo, Santa Rosa, Selma, Truckee, Ukiah, Upper Lake, Vacaville, Willow, Yucca Valley

TRAVELODGE 1973 Friendship Drive, El Cajon CA 92020; 619-448-1884, Fax 619-562-0901, Reservations 800-255-3050

The Business Break Club Program provides a 10% discount off the lowest published room rate, express check-in and check-out, free local telephone call and morning coffee and a special 800-number for fast reservations. The Corporate Business Break Club provides a 10% room discount and special amenities. Classic Travel Club is available to travelers over the age of 50. Room discounts of 15% are available, a quarterly newsletter, check cashing privileges, free morning coffee, car rental discounts and express check-in, check-out services.

Under the Family Plan, there is no charge for children under the age of 17 when sharing a room with their parents. The Government Traveler-Value America Plan offers rates equal to or less than the prevailing per diem rates paid and is available to federal employees, military personnel and contractors on government business.

California Locations: Azusa, Bakersfield, Baldwin Park, Banning, Bellflower, Berkeley, Blythe, Buena Park, Burbank, Carlsbad, Castro Valley, Cerritos-Artesia, Chula Vista, Claremont, Compton, Corona, Costa Mesa-Newport Beach, Crescent City, Culver City, Duarte-Monrovia, Dunsmuir, El Cajon, El Toro, Encinitas, Escondido, Eureka, Fallbrook, Garden Grove, Harbor City, Hayward, Hemet, Hermosa Beach, Hollywood, Huntington Park, Imperial Beach, Indio, Inglewood, La Jolla, La Mesa, La Puente, Lake Elsinore, Lake Tahoe, Long Beach, Los Angeles, Lynwood, Mammoth Lakes, Merced, Millbrea, Mill Valley, Milpitas, Montebello, Monterey, Morena Valley, Morro Bay, Napa Valley, Novato, Oceanside, Ontario, Orange, Palm Springs, Palo Alto, Pasadena, Paso Robles, Pico Rivera, Poway, Rancho Bernardo, Redondo Beach, Rialto, Richmond, Riverside, Rosemead, Sacramento, San Bernardino, San Carlos, San Clemente, San Diego, San Francisco, San Jose, San Juan Capistrano, San Luis Obispo, San Marcos, San Ysidro, Santa Barbara, Santa Clara, Santa Clarita, Santa Cruz, Santa Monica, Santa Nella, Santa Paula, Santa Rosa, Simi Valley, Spring Valley, Tehachapi, Torrance, Ukiah, Vacaville, Vallejo, Van Nuys, Ventura, Victorville, Westminster, Whittier

VAGABOND INNS 5405 Morehouse Drive, San Diego CA 92121; 619-455-1800, Fax 552-8214, Reservations 800-522-1555

Vagabond Inns offer free continental breakfasts, free coffee, free weekday newspapers, free local telephone calls and a free toiletry pack with toothbrush, shampoo, etc. Children under 18 stay free in the same room with adult. Stay nine nights at any location and get the tenth night free.

California Locations: Bishop, Chula Vista, Costa Mesa, Fresno, Glendale, Hayward, Long Beach, Los Angeles, Modesto,

Oxnard, Palm Springs, Palmdale, Pasadena, Redding, Redondo Beach, Rosemead, Sacramento, San Diego, Salinas, San Francisco, San Jose, San Luis Obispo, San Pedro, Santa Barbara, Santa Clara, Stockton, Sunnyvale, Ventura, Whittier, Woodland Hills

WESTIN HOTELS AND RESORTS The Westin Building, Seattle WA 98121; 206-443-5096, Fax 206-443-5096, Reservations 800-228-3000

At Westin hotels or resorts there is no charge for children under the age of 18 when they share the same room with parents or guardians. If more than one room is required to accommodate a family, the single guest room rate will apply to each room, regardless of the number of people occupying the room.

California Locations: Costa Mesa, Los Angeles, Rancho Mirage, San Francisco

WYNDHAM HOTELS AND RESORTS 2001 Bryan Street, Suite 2300, Dallas TX 75210; 214-978-4500, Reservations 800-822-4200

California Locations: Los Angeles, Commerce, Palm Springs, San Diego, Sunnyvale

Accommodations Directory

Ahwahnee

Area Code 209

Ol' Nip Gold Town Bed and Breakfast (Box 245, 93601; 683-2155) 7 rooms, bed & breakfast, complimentary breakfast, wheelchair access, no-smoking rooms. LS SGL/DBL$45-$65; HS SGL/DBL$59-$89.

Alameda

Area Code 415
Alameda Chamber of Commerce
2314 Central Avenue,
Alameda CA 94501
522-0414

Alameda Royal Motel (1925 Webster Street, 94501; 521-8400) 52 rooms, swimming pool, wheelchair access, no-smoking rooms. SGL$46-$60, DBL$52-$65.

Garratt Mansion (900 Union Street, 94501; 521-4779) 6 rooms, bed & breakfast, complimentary breakfast. SGL/DBL$65.

Marina Village Inn (Pacific Marina, 94501; 523-9450, 800-345-0304) 51 rooms and suites, restaurant, outdoor heated swimming, children under 12 free, in-room refrigerators, complimentary breakfast, airport transportation, valet laundry, free parking, wheelchair access, no-smoking rooms, no pets allowed. SGL$60, DBL$68, STS$85-$95.

Royal Motel (1925 Webster Street, 94501; 521-8400) 52 rooms. SGL/DBL$46-$60.

Albion

Area Code 707

Albion River Inn (37901 North Highway 1, 95410; 937-1919, 800-479-7944 in California) 20 rooms, restaurant, complimentary breakfast, wheelchair access, free parking. SGL/DBL$79-$175.

Fensalden Inn (33810 Navarro Ridge Rd., 95410; 937-4042) 8 rooms, bed & breakfast, complimentary breakfast, restaurant, wheelchair access, free parking. SGL/DBL$90-$135.

The Wool Loft (32751 Navarro Ridge Rd., 95410; 937-0377) 2 rooms, bed & breakfast, complimentary breakfast. SGL/DBL$65-$100.

Alleghany

Area Code 916

Kenton Mine Lodge (Box 942, 95910; 287-3212, 800-634-2002 in California) 20 rooms, bed & breakfast, complimentary breakfast. SGL$35, DBL$45.

Alturas

Area Code 916
Alturas Chamber of Commerce
522 South Main Street,

Alturas CA 96010
233-2819

Best Western Trailside Inn (343 North Main Street, 96101; 233-4111, 800-528-1234) 39 rooms, restaurant, swimming pool, airport courtesy car, no-smoking rooms, no pets. SGL$33-$40, DBL$38-$60.

Hacienda Motel (201 East 12th Street, 96101; 233-3459) 20 rooms, airport courtesy car, no-smoking rooms, pets allowed. SGL$/DBL$27-$45.

Amador City

Area Code 209

Imperial Hotel (Box 195, 95601; 267-9172) 6 rooms, bed & breakfast, complimentary breakfast. SGL/DBL$50.

Anderson

Area Code 916
Anderson Chamber of Commerce
2086 Balls Ferry Rd.
Anderson CA 96007
365-8095

Best Western Knight's Inn (2688 Gateway Drive, 96007; 916-365-2753, 800-528-1234) 40 rooms, restaurant, lounge, swimming pool, airport courtesy car, wheelchair access, free local telephone calls, pets allowed. SGL/DBL$40-$52.

The Plantation House (1690 Ferry Street, 96007; 365-2827) 8 rooms, bed & breakfast, complimentary breakfast. SGL$35, DBL$45.

Valley Inn (2861 Murray Drive, 96007; 365-2566) 62 rooms, swimming pool, wheelchair access, no-smoking rooms, free local telephone calls, tours, airport courtesy car. SGL/DBL$55-$75.

Angels Camp

Area Code 209
Calaveras County Chamber of Commerce
753 South Main Street,
Angels Camp CA 95222
736-4444

Cooper House Bed and Breakfast Inn (1184 Church Street, 95222; 736-2145) 3 rooms, bed & breakfast, complimentary breakfast. SGL/DBL$90.

Gold Country Inn (720 South Main Street, 95222; 736-4611) 28 rooms, pets allowed, no-smoking rooms. SGL/DBL$46-$56.

Jumping Frog Motel (330 Murphys Grade Rd., 95221; 736-2191) 15 rooms. SGL/DBL$43-$50.

Utica Mansion Inn (Box 1, 95222; 736-4209) 3 rooms, bed & breakfast, complimentary breakfast. SGL$80, DBL$90.

Angwin

Area Code 707
Angwin Chamber of Commerce
Box 111,
Angwin CA 94508
965-2130

Forest Manor (415 Cold Springs Rd., 94508; 965-3538) 3 rooms, bed & breakfast, complimentary breakfast, swimming pool. SGL/DBL$50+.

Antioch

Area Code 518
Antioch Chamber of Commerce
Box 399, Antioch CA 94509
757-1800

Best Western Heritage Inn (32110 Delta Fair Blvd., 94509; 510-778-2000, Fax 778-2000, 800-528-1234) 75 rooms, restaurant, lounge, complimentary breakfast, swimming pool, children under 12 free, in-room refrigerators, whirlpool, fax service, pets allowed. SGL/DBL$52-$74.

Lexington Inn (2436 Mahogany Way, 94509; 415-754-6600, Fax 415-754-6828) 119 rooms, complimentary breakfast, swimming pool, wheelchair access, airport transportation. SGL$65-$75, DBL$73-$115.

Ramada Inn (2436 Mahogany Way, 94509; 754-6600, Fax 754-6828, 800-2-RAMADA) 117 rooms and suites, restaurant, complimentary breakfast, heated swimming pool, whirlpool, in-room refrigerators, children under 16 free, free parking, wheelchair access, no-smoking rooms, airport transportation. SGL/DBL$50-$70.

Aptos

Area Code 408
Aptos Chamber of Commerce
9099 Soquel Drive
Aptos CA 95001
688-1467

RENTAL SOURCES: Bob Bailey Property Management (106 Aptos Beach Drive, 95003; 688-7009, Fax 688-1523) rental condos and private homes. **Cheshire Rio Realty** (107 Aptos Beach Drive, 95003; 688-2041, Fax 688-0702) rental condos. LS

$400W-$3500W; HS $500W-$3500W. **Kendall and Potter Realtors** (793 Rio Del Mar Blvd., 95003; 688-3511) rental condos and homes.

Apple Lane Inn (6265 Soquel Drive, 95003; 475-6868) 5 rooms, bed & breakfast, complimentary breakfast. SGL/DBL$85-$125.

Bayview Hotel (8041 Soquel Drive, 95003; 688-8654) 7 rooms, bed & breakfast, complimentary breakfast. SGL/DBL$75-$115.

Best Western Seacliff Inn (7500 Old Dominion Court, 95003; 688-7300, Fax 685-3603, 800-528-1234) 140 rooms and suites, restaurant, lounge, swimming pool, beach, room service, fax services, meeting facilities, no-smoking rooms, hot tubs, kitchenettes, no pets. LS SGL/DBL$59-$79; HS SGL/DBL$84-$119, STS$165-$190.

Mangels House (570 Aptos Creek Rd., 95003; 688-7982) 5 rooms, bed & breakfast, complimentary breakfast, balconies, fireplaces, meeting room, private baths, free parking. SGL/DBL$94-$120.

Rio Sands Motel (116 Aptos Beach Drive, 95003; 688-3207, 800-826-2077 in California) 50 rooms and efficiencies, swimming pool, free parking. LS SGL/DBL$50-$80; HS SGL/DBL$70-$100.

Seacliff Inn (7500 Old Dominion Court, 95003; 688-7300, Fax 365-3603, 800-367-2003 in California) 140 rooms, restaurant, swimming pool, wheelchair access. LS SGL/DBL$59-$140; HS SGL/DBL$79-$165.

Arcata

Area Code 707
Arcata Chamber of Commerce
1062 G Street
Arcata CA 95521
822-3619

Best Western Arcata Inn (4827 Valley West Rd., 95521; 826-0313, 800-528-1234) 37 rooms, restaurant, complimentary breakfast, heated indoor swimming pool, spa, whirlpool, no-smoking rooms, pets allowed. SGL$48-$58, DBL$52-$62.

Fairwinds Motel (1674 G Street, 95521; 822-4824) 27 rooms, no-smoking rooms. SGL$32-$60, DBL$42-$70.

Holiday Gardens Motel (2255 Alliance Rd., 95521; 822-4651) 36 apartments, no pets. SGL/DBL$34-$80.

The Lady Ann Inn (902 14th Street, 95521; 822-2797) 5 rooms, bed & breakfast, complimentary breakfast. SGL$55, DBL$60.

Mad River Quality Inn (3535 Janes Rd., 95521; 822-0409) 64 rooms, restaurant, lounge, swimming pool, valet laundry, fax service, exercise equipment, meeting facilities, no-smoking rooms. SGL/DBL$38-$57.

Motel 6 (4755 Valley West Blvd., 95521; 891-6161) 81 rooms. SGL/DBL$29-$35.

North Coast Inn (4975 Valley West Blvd., 95521; 822-8888, 800-233-0903) 78 rooms, restaurant, lounge, indoor heated swimming pool, sauna, exercise equipment, fax service, meeting facilities, gift shop, laundry room, airport courtesy car, free parking, free local telephone calls, no-smoking rooms, pets allowed. SGL$64-$78, DBL$72-$78.

Plough And The Stars (1800 27th Street, 95521; 822-8236) 5 rooms, bed & breakfast, complimentary breakfast. SG/DBL$76-$100.

Super 8 Motel (4887 Valley West Blvd., 95521; 822-8888, Fax 822-2513, 800-800-8000) 62 rooms, restaurant, spa, complimentary breakfast, fax service, valet laundry, no-smoking rooms, pets allowed. SGL/DBL$33-$38.

Arnold

Area Code 209

RENTAL SOURCES: Barry Ward Realty (1122 Highway Four, 95223; 795-1662) rental homes and cabins, two night minimum. SGL/DBL$210-$225. **Century 21 Sierra Properties** (2038 Highway Four, 95223; 795-4485) cabins rentals, two night minimum. SGL/DBL$176-$247. **Don Fry Realty** (1027 Highway Four, 95223; 795-4441) cabin rentals, two night minimum. SGL/DBL$155-$220. **Sierra Vacation Rentals** (908 Moran Rd., 95223; 795-2422) cabin rental, two night minimum. SGL/DBL$180$220.

Ebbetts Pass Lodge (1173 Highway Four, 95223; 795-1563) 15 rooms, kitchenettes. SGL/DBL$38-$60.

The Lodge At Manuel Mill (Box 998, 95223; 795-2633) 5 rooms, complimentary breakfast. SGL/DBL$85-$105.

Wehe's Meadowmont Lodge (2011 Highway 4, 95223; 795-1394) 19 rooms, pets allowed. SGL/DBL$47-$58.

Auburn

Area Code 916
Auburn Area Visitors and Convention Bureau
1101 High Street
Auburn CA 95603
885-5616

Auburn Chamber of Commerce
601 Lincoln Way
Auburn CA 95603
885-5616

Auburn Inn (1875 Auburn-Ravine Rd., 95603; 885-1800, Fax 888-6424, 800-272-1444) 81 rooms and suites, complimentary breakfast, heated swimming pool, children under 12 free, wheelchair access, laundry room, meeting facilities for 130, airport courtesy car, wheelchair access, no-smoking rooms, no pets. SGL$52, DBL$58-$62, STS$100-$120.

Best Western Golden Key Motel (13450 Lincoln Way, 95603; 885-8611, 800-528-1234) 68 rooms, restaurant, heated swimming pool, laundry room, wheelchair access, pets allowed, no-smoking rooms. SGL/DBL$42-$60.

The Dry Creek Inn (13740 Dry Creek Rd., 95603; 878-0885) bed & breakfast, complimentary breakfast. SGL/DBL$65-$70.

The Lincoln House (191 Lincoln Way, 95603; 885-8880) 4 rooms, bed & breakfast, complimentary breakfast, swimming pool, no smoking, no pets. SGL/DBL$50-$75.

Powers Mansion Inn (164 Cleveland Avenue, 95603; 885-1166) 13 rooms, bed & breakfast, complimentary breakfast, no pets. SGL/DBL$65-$150.

Super 8 Motel (140 East Hillcrest Drive, 95603; 888-8808, Fax 885-3588, 800-800-8000, 800-848-8888) 52 rooms, restaurant, complimentary breakfast, outdoor swimming pool, spa, free local telephone calls, meeting facilities, kitchenettes, jacuzzis, in-room refrigerator and microwave, wheelchair access, no-smoking rooms, no pets. SGL$40-$49, DBL$45-$55.

Victorian Hill House (Box 9097, 95604; 885-5879, 800-348-9768 in California) 4 rooms, bed & breakfast, complimentary breakfast, swimming pool. SGL/DBL$65-$85.

Avery

Area Code 209

Avery Hotel (4573 Moran Rd., 95224; 795-9935) 6 rooms, restaurant. SGL/DBL$55.

Balboa

Area Code 714

Balboa Inn On The Sand At Newport (105 Main Street, 92661; 675-3412) 34 rooms and suites, restaurant, swimming pool. SGL/DBL$65-$73.

Bass Lake

Area Code 209
Bass Lake Chamber of Commerce
54432 North Shore Rd.
Bass Lake CA 93604
642-3676

Ducey's On The Lake (Box 326, 93604; 642-3131, Fax 642-3902, 800-350-7463) 104 chalets and suites, two restaurants, lounge, outdoor heated swimming pool, jacuzzis, sauna, exercise equipment, tennis, children under 16 free, in-room refrigerators, kitchenettes, fax service, meeting facilities for 200, gift shop, free parking, wheelchair access, no-smoking rooms, no pets. LS STS$88-$128; HS STS$125-$165.

Fork's Resort (39150 Rd. 222, 93604; 642-3737) 11 rooms and efficiencies, pets allowed. SGL/DBL$65-$105.

The Pines Resort (54432 North Shore Rd., 93604; 642-3121, Fax 642-3902, 800-350-7463) 104 rooms and suites, restaurant, lounge, swimming pool, spa, meeting facilities, fireplaces, exercise equipment, tennis, no pets. LS SGL/DBL$88-$128; HS SGL/DBL$125-$160.

Bear Valley

Area Code 209

Bear Valley Lodge (Highway Four and Bear Valley Rd., 95223; 753-2327) 55 rooms and suites, lounge. SGL/DBL$79-$209.

Belmont

Area Code 415
Belmont Chamber of Commerce
1365 Fifth Avenue, Belmont CA 94002
595-8696

Belmateo Motel (803 Belmont Avenue, 94002; 591-0748) 30 rooms. SGL$32, DBL$35.

Belmont Palms Motel (700 El Camino Real, 94002; 593-3957) 14 rooms. SGL$33, DBL$39.

Holiday Inn (1101 Shoreway Rd., 94002; 591-1471, Fax 593-6415, 800-752-6162) 195 rooms, restaurant, lounge, swimming pool, exercise equipment, wheelchair access, children under 12 free, airport transportation, meeting facilities for 200, no-smoking rooms, pets allowed. SGL$65-$75, DBL$75-$85.

Benicia

Area Code 707
Benicia Chamber of Commerce
831 First Street
Benicia CA 94510
745-2120

Best Western Heritage Inn (1955 East 2nd Street, 94510; 746-0410, Fax 745-0842, 800-528-1234) 100 rooms, restaurant, swimming pool, whirlpool, in-room refrigerators, fax service, wheelchair access, children under 12 free, no-smoking rooms, pets allowed. LS SGL$50-$60, DBL$57-$67; HS SGL$57-$67, DBL$75-$100.

Captain Dillingham's Inn (145 East D Street, 94510; 746-7164, 800-544-2278 in California) 9 rooms, complimentary breakfast, pets allowed. SGL/DBL$70-$125, STS$160+.

Union Hotel (401 First Street, 94510; 746-0100, Fax 746-6458) 12 rooms, restaurant, complimentary breakfast. SGL/DBL$70-$120.

Ben Lomond

Area Code 408

Tyrolean Inn and Cottages (Box 372, 95005; 336-5188) 7 cottages, restaurant, free parking. LS SGL/DBL$41-$56; HS SGL/DBL$43-$56.

Berkeley

Area Code 415
Berkeley Chamber of Commerce
1834 University Avenue
Berkeley CA 94701
549-7000

Berkeley Marina Marriott (200 Marina Blvd., 94710; 548-7920, 800-228-9290) 375 rooms, restaurant, swimming pool, wheelchair access, meeting facilities, in-room refrigerators, exercise equipment, free parking. SGL/DBL$115-$145.

Campus Motel (1619 University Avenue, 94703; 841-3844) 23 rooms and efficiencies, free parking. SGL/DBL$45-$75.

The Durant Hotel (2600 Durant Avenue, 94704; 845-8981, Fax 486-8336, 800-238-7268) 140 rooms and suites, restaurant, lounge, complimentary breakfast, children under 16 free, fax service, valet laundry, airport transportation, wheelchair access, no-smoking rooms, no pets. SGL/DBL$75-$125, STS$180-$240.

Elmwood House (College Avenue, 94709; 540-5123) 4 rooms, bed & breakfast, complimentary breakfast, free parking. SGL$55, DBL$65.

Flamingo Hotel (1761 University Avenue, 94704; 841-4242) 29 rooms, no-smoking rooms, wheelchair access, free parking. SGL/DBL$45+.

The French Hotel (1538 Shattuck Avenue, 94709; 548-9930) 18 rooms, restaurant, complimentary breakfast, airport transportation, wheelchair access, free parking. SGL$68-$125, DBL$85-$95.

Golden Bear Motel (1620 San Pablo Avenue, 94702; 525-6770) 42 rooms, restaurant, free parking. SGL/DBL$35-$45.

Grandma's Inn Hotel and Gardens (2740 Telegraph Avenue, 94705; 549-2145, Fax 549-1085) 30 rooms, complimentary breakfast, wheelchair access, no-smoking rooms. SGL/DBL$85-$125.

Hotel Durant (2600 Durant Avenue, 94704; 845-8981, Fax 486-8336) 140 rooms and suites, restaurant, complimentary breakfast, meeting facilities, wheelchair access, airport transportation, no-smoking rooms. SGL$85-$95, DBL$95-$105.

Marriott Berkeley Marina (200 Marina Blvd., 94710; 548-7920, Fax 548-7944) 375 rooms, restaurant, swimming pool, exercise equipment, wheelchair access, no-smoking rooms, pets allowed. SGL/DBL$160, STS$675.

Shattuck Hotel (2086 Allston Way, 94704; 845-7300, Fax 644-2088, 800-BERKELY, 800-742-8825) 175 rooms, restaurant, lounge, complimentary breakfast, meeting facilities, free parking, wheelchair access, no-smoking rooms, airport transportation. SGL$72-$89, DBL$87-$104.

TraveLodge (1820 University Avenue, 94703; 510-843-4262, Fax 510-848-1480, 800-255-3050) 30 rooms, restaurant, tours, tennis, no pets, free parking. SGL/DBL$55-$82.

Blythe

Area Code 619
Blythe Chamber of Commerce
201 South Broadway
Blythe CA 92225
922-8166 .

Astro Motel (801 East Hobson Way, 92225; 922-4246) 24 rooms, swimming pool, pets allowed, no-smoking rooms. SGL/DBL$27-$40.

Best Western Sahara Motel (825 West Hobson Way, 92225; 922-7105, Fax 916-922-5836, 800-528-1234) 47 rooms, restaurant, lounge, complimentary breakfast, swimming pool, whirlpool, children under 12 free, in-room refrigerators and microwaves, jacuzzis, fax service, no-smoking rooms, pets allowed. SGL/DBL$47-$64.

Best Western Tropics Motor Hotel (9274 East Hobson Way 92225; 922-5101, Fax 922-2833, 800-528-1234) 57 rooms, restaurant, lounge, swimming pool, whirlpool, fax service, no-smoking rooms, pets allowed. SGL/DBL$47-$60.

Budget Host Motel (9820 East Hobsonway, 92225; 922-4126) 30 rooms. SGL/DBL$35-$45.

Comfort Inn (903 West Hobson Way, 92225; 922-4146, 800-221-2222) 48 rooms, restaurant, swimming pool, whirlpool, in-room refrigerators, exercise equipment, no pets. LS SGL$38-$52, DBL$49-$59; HS SGL$70-$80, DBL$80-$85.

Comfort Suites (545 West Hobson Way, 92225; 922-9208, 800-221-2222) 64 rooms, complimentary breakfast, swimming pool, wheelchair access, no pets. LS SGL$56-$76, DBL$66-$86; HS SGL$129-$139, DBL$139-$149.

Desert Inn Motel (850 Hobson Way, 92225; 922-5145) 50 rooms and efficiencies, restaurant, swimming pool, pets allowed. SGL$35, DBL$37.

Econo Lodge (1020 West Hobson Way, 92225; 922-3161, 800-424-4777) 46 rooms, restaurant, swimming pool, no pets. LS $30-$35, DBL$45-$50; HS SGL$80-$85, DBL$85-$90.

E-Z 8 Motel (900 West Rice Street, 92225; 922-9191, 800-326-6835) 66 rooms. SGL/DBL$22-$32.

Motel 6 (500 West Donion Street, 92225; 922-6666, 505-891-6161) 126 rooms. SGL/DBL$25-$35.

Rodeway Inn (401 East Hobson Way, 92225; 922-2198, 800-424-4777, 800-228-2000) 62 rooms, restaurant, swimming pool, meeting facilities, in-room refrigerators, children under 18 stay free, pets allowed. SGL$35-$45, DBL$39-$60.

Super 8 Motel (550 West Donlon Street, 92225; 922-8881, 922-8881, 800-800-8000) 80 rooms and suites, restaurant, outdoor heated swimming pool, meeting facilities, in-room refrigerators and microwaves, free local telephone calls, wheelchair access, no-smoking rooms, pets allowed. SGL/DBL$40-$47.

TraveLodge (850 West Hobson Way, 92225; 922-5145, 800-255-3050) 50 rooms, restaurant, lounge, swimming pool, in-room refrigerators, laundry room, tennis, no pets. LS SGL/DBL$44-$60; HS SGL/DBL$48-$68.

Bodega Bay

Area Code 707
Bodega Bay Chamber of Commerce

555 Highway 1
Bodega Bay CA 94923
875-3422

RENTAL SOURCES: Bodega Bay And Beyond (Box 129, 94923; 875-2814, 800-888-3565) rents private homes, two-night minimum. SGL/DBL$375-$550/$900-$1500. **Vacation Rentals International** (Box 38, 94923; 875-4000, 800-548-7631) rents one- to five-bedroom private homes in Bodega Bay. 1BR$120-$160, 2BR$135-$350.

Bay Hill Mansion (3919 Bay Hill Rd., 94923; 875-3577, 800-526-5927) 6 rooms, bed & breakfast, complimentary breakfast, private bath, free local telephone calls, no smoking, no pets. SGL/DBL$80-$150.

Best Western Bodega Bay Lodge (103 Coast Highway 1, 94923; 875-2428, Fax 875-2428, 800-368-2468, 800-528-1234) 78 rooms, restaurant, complimentary breakfast, swimming pool, spa, whirlpool, children under 12 free, balconies, beach, fax services, exercise equipment, wheelchair access, no-smoking rooms. SGL/DBL$108-$188.

Bodega Bay Lodge (103 Coast Highway 1, 94923; 875-3525) 78 rooms, complimentary breakfast, ocean view, swimming pool, exercise equipment. LS SGL/DBL$85; HS SGL/DBL$96-$126, STS$155.

Bodega Coast Inn (521 Coast Highway 1, 94923; 875-2217, 800-346-6999 in California) 45 rooms and suites, restaurant, meeting facilities, children under 12 free, in-room refrigerators, fireplaces, ocean view, wheelchair access, free parking. SGL$88-$140, DBL$95-$170.

Bodega Harbor Inn (Highway 1, 94922; 875-3594) 14 rooms and suites, kitchenettes, ocean view. SGL/DBL$65+.

Bay Hill Mansion (3939 Bay Hill Rd., 94923; 875-3577) 5 rooms, bed & breakfast, complimentary breakfast, water view. SGL/DBL$80-$150.

Inn At The Tides (800 Coast Highway; 875-2751, 800-541-7788) 88 suites, restaurant, complimentary breakfast, swimming pool, fireplaces, saunas, hot tubs, room service, children under 12 free, meeting facilities, wheelchair access, no-smoking rooms. SGL/DBL$110-$185.

Schoolhouse Inn (Box 136, 94922; 876-3257) bed & breakfast, 4 rooms, complimentary breakfast. SGL/DBL$76-$100.

Sea Horse Guest Ranch (2660 Highway One, 94922; 875-2721) 5 rooms. SGL/DBL$65-$75.

Boulder Creek

Area Code 408

Boulder Creek Lodge and Conference Center (16901 Big Basin Highway, 95006; 338-2111, Fax 338-7862) rental condominiums. SGL/DBL$75-$190.

Bridgeport

Area Code 619
Bridgeport Chamber of Commerce
Highway 395
Bridgeport CA 93517
932-7500

Best Western Ruby Inn (Box 475, 93517; 619-932-7241, 800-528-1234) 30 rooms, restaurant, whirlpools, children under 12 free, wheelchair access, airport transportation, no-smoking rooms, pets allowed. SGL/DBL$55-$75.

Cain House (Box 454, 93517; 932-7040, 932-7419, 800-433-CAIN) 6 rooms, bed & breakfast, complimentary breakfast, private bath, free local telephone calls, fax service, airport transportation, free parking, no smoking. SGL/DBL$80-$135.

Silver Maple (20 Main Street, 93517; 932-7383) 20 rooms, restaurant, wheelchair access, no-smoking rooms, pets allowed. SGL$40-$50, DBL$50-$55.

Walker River Lodge (One Main Street, 93517; 619-932-7021) 36 rooms, restaurant, swimming pool, whirlpool, in-room refrigerators, airport transportation, pets allowed, wheelchair access. SGL/DBL$60-$95.

Brookdale

Area Code
Brookdale Chamber of Commerce
105 Pacific Avenue
Brookdale CA 95007
335-2764

Brookdale Lodge (11570 Highway 9, 95007; 338-6433) 40 rooms and cottages, restaurant, lounge, swimming pool, hot tub, conference facilities, no-smoking rooms, laundry, convenience store, free parking, wheelchair access. LS SGL/DBL$40+; HS SGL/DBL$60+.

Burlingame

Area Code 415
Burlingame Chamber of Commerce
306 Lorton Avenue
Burlingame CA 94010
344-1735

Burlingame Hotel (287 Lorton Avenue, 94010; 344-6666, Fax 342-1161) 41 rooms and efficiencies, restaurant, lounge, fireplaces, SGL$25-$50, DBL$35-$75.

Country House Inn (217 Lorton Avenue, 94010; 344-6666) 27 rooms and efficiencies. SGL$45, DBL$50.

Crown Sterling Suites (150 Anza Blvd., 94010; 342-4600, Fax 343-8137, 800-433-4600) 344 suites, restaurant, complimentary breakfast, swimming pool, sauna, spa, meeting facilities, room service, fireplaces, airport transportation. SGL/DBL$149-$159.

Days Inn (777 Airport Blvd., 94010; 342-7772, Fax 342-2635, 800-325-2525) 200 rooms, restaurant, lounge, swimming pool, children under 12 free, fax service, wheelchair access, meeting facilities for 300, no-smoking rooms, pets allowed. SGL$49-$72, SGL$59-$82.

Doubletree Hotel Airport (835 Airport Blvd., 94010; 344-5500, Fax 340-8851, 800-528-0444) 291 rooms and suites, restaurant, room service, meeting facilities for 200, exercise equipment, airport courtesy car, free parking. SGL/DBL$129-$139, STS109-$119.

Embassy Suites (150 Anza Blvd., 94010; 342-4600, Fax 343-8137, 800-EMBASSY) 344 suites, restaurant, complimentary breakfast, swimming pool, meeting facilities for 550, beauty and barber shop, no-smoking rooms, wheelchair access, free parking. SGL$119, DBL$129.

Holiday Inn Crown-Plaza Airport (600 Airport Blvd., 94010; 340-8500, 800-HOLIDAY) 405 rooms and suites, restaurant, swimming pool, meeting facilities for 750, no-smoking rooms, exercise equipment, wheelchair access, airport transportation, no pets, free parking. SGL$89+, DBL$94+.

Hotel Ibis (835 Airport Blvd., 94030; 800-553-1580, 800-624-7702 in California) 305 rooms and suites, bay view, restaurant, meeting facilities for 180, free parking, wheelchair access, no-smoking rooms, airport courtesy car. SGL$76, DBL$86.

Hyatt Regency San Francisco Airport (1333 Old Bayshore Highway, 94010; 347-1234, Fax 696-2669, 800-233-1234) 791 rooms, restaurant, swimming pool, sauna, spa, airport courtesy car, exercise equipment, wheelchair access, meeting facilities for 2,000, child care, beauty and barber shop, gift shop, no-smoking rooms, free parking. SGL$140, DBL$160.

Marriott San Francisco Airport (1800 Old Bayshore Highway, 94010; 629-9100, 800-228-9290) 684 rooms, restaurant, swimming pool, meeting facilities for 1,800, gift shop, child care, beauty and barber shop, wheelchair access/room, no-smoking rooms, exercise equipment, pets allowed. SGL$140+, DBL$159+.

Ramada San Francisco Airport (1250 Old Bayshore Highway, 94010; 347-2381, Fax 348-8838, 800-227-2381) 151 rooms, restaurant, lounge, swimming pool, free parking, airport transportation, wheelchair access, children under 18 free, meeting facilities for 40, no-smoking rooms. SGL$69, DBL$140.

Sheraton San Francisco Airport (1177 Airport Blvd., 94010; 342-9200, 800-325-3535) 306 rooms, two restaurants, lounge, indoor and outdoor swimming pool, sauna, meeting facilities for 630, airport courtesy car, exercise equipment, pets allowed, meeting facilities for 750, beauty and barber shop, gift shop, wheelchair access, no-smoking rooms, free parking. SGL$89-$109, DBL$104-$214.

Vagabond Inn (1640 Bayshore Highway, 94010; 692-4040, Fax 692-5314, 800-522-1555) 91 rooms, restaurant, complimentary breakfast, laundry room, swimming pool, in-room refrigerators and microwaves, pets allowed, wheelchair access, airport transportation, free local telephone calls, no-smoking rooms, children under 18 free, fax service, complimentary newspaper. SGL$65-$75, DBL$70-$85.

Burney

Area Code 916
Burney Chamber of Commerce
Box 36
Burney CA 96013
335-2111

Charm Motel (37363 Main Street, 96013; 335-2254) 42 rooms and efficiencies, wheelchair access, in-room refrigerators. SGL/DBL$38-$64, EFF$$50-$70.

Clark Creek Lodge (Highway 89N, 96013; 335-2574) 6 cabins, restaurant. SGL/DBL$55.

Green Gables Motel (37385 Main Street, 96013; 335-2264) 23 rooms and efficiencies, swimming pool. SGL/DBL$36-$38.

Shasta Pines Motel (37386 Main Street,96013; 335-2201) 17 rooms and efficiencies, restaurant, swimming pool, no-smoking rooms. SGL/DBL$45-$52.

Calistoga

Area Code 707
Callstoga Chamber of Commerce
1458 Lincoln Avenue
Calistoga CA 94515
942-6333

RENTAL SOURCES: Bed and Breakfast Exchange (1458 Lincoln Avenue, 94515; 942-2924, 800-942-2924) reservation services for bed & breakfasts in Napa, Sonoma, Mendocino and San Francisco.

Brannan Cottage Inn (109 Wapoo Avenue, 94515; 942-4200) 6 rooms, bed & breakfast, complimentary breakfast, handicapped rooms. SGL/DBL$101-$125.

Calistoga Country Lodge (2883 Foothill Blvd., 94515; 942-5555) bed & breakfast, 6 rooms, complimentary breakfast, swimming pool. SG/DB$76-$100.

Calistoga Inn (1250 Lincoln Avenue, 94515; 942-4101, Fax 942-4914) 18 rooms, restaurant, complimentary breakfast, free parking. SGL/DBL$50-$55.

Calistoga Spa Hot Springs (1006 Washington, 94515; 942-6269) 57 rooms, restaurant, exercise equipment, swimming pool, spa, meeting facilities, jacuzzis, wheelchair access, free parking. SGL$51-$91, DBL$60-$100.

Calistoga Village Inn and Spa (1880 Lincoln Avenue, 94515; 942-4636) 32 rooms, restaurant, complimentary breakfast, swimming pool, wheelchair access, free parking. SGL$65-$95, DBL$65-$165.

Calistoga Wayside Inn (1523 Foothill Blvd., 94515; 942-0645, Fax 942-5357) 12 rooms, bed & breakfast, complimentary breakfast. SGL$65, DBL$75.

Comfort Inn (1865 Lincoln Avenue, 94515; 942-9400, Fax 942-5306, 800-221-2222) 55 rooms, restaurant, lounge, complimentary breakfast, swimming pool, whirlpool, sauna, wheelchair access, no-smoking rooms, no pets. SGL/DBL$58-$120.

Culver's A Country Inn (1804 Foothill Bboulevard, 94515; 942-4535) 6 rooms, bed & breakfast, complimentary breakfast, swimming pool, whirlpool, no-smoking. SGL/DBL$95-$115.

Dr. Wilkinson's Hot Springs (1507 Lincoln Avenue, 94515; 942-4102) 42 rooms, complimentary breakfast, three swimming pools, sauna, meeting facilities, in-room refrigerators, exercise equipment, free parking. SGL/DBL$49-$89.

Foothill House (3037 Foothill Blvd., 94515; 942-6933) 3 rooms, bed & breakfast, complimentary breakfast, no-smoking, fireplaces. SGL/DB$101-$125+.

Golden Haven Hot Springs (1713 Lake Street, 94515; 942-6703) 30 rooms, swimming pool, no children. SGL/DBL$45-$95.

Hideaway Cottages (1412 Fairway, 94515; 942-4108) 16 cottages. SGL/DBL$42-$85.

Hot Springs Motel (1507 Lincoln Avenue, 94515; 942-4102) 42 rooms. SGL/DBL$45-$100.

Inn On Cedar Street (1307 Cedar Street, 94515-942-9244) 3 rooms, bed & breakfast, complimentary breakfast, free parking. SGL/DBL$76-$100.

Lake Mead Country Inn (1103 Lakemead Lane, 94515; 942-9581) 9 rooms, bed & breakfast, complimentary breakfast. SGL/DBL$100-$165.

Meadowlark Country House (601 Petrified Valley Raod, 94515; 942-5651) 4 rooms, complimentary breakfast, swimming pool, no-smoking rooms. SGL/DBL$100-$130.

Mountain View Hotel (1457 Lincoln Avenue, 94515; 942-6877) 34 rooms, restaurant, complimentary breakfast, whirlpool, meeting facilities, swimming pool, free parking. SGL/DBL$75-$95.

The Pink Mansion (1415 Foothill Blvd., 94515; 942-0558) 5 rooms, bed & breakfast, complimentary breakfast, swimming pool, wheelchair access, no smoking. SGL/DBL$85-$155.

Quail Mountain (4455 North Street, 94515; 942-0316) 3 rooms and suites, bed & breakfast, complimentary breakfast, swimming pool. SGL/DBL$75-$110.

Roman Spa Resort (1300 Washington Street, 94515; 942-4441) 51 rooms, restaurant, swimming pool, wheelchair access, free parking. SGL/DBL$42-$90.

Scarlett's Country Inn (3918 Silverado Trail, 94515; 942-6669) 3 rooms, bed & breakfast, complimentary breakfast, swimming pool. SG/DB$95-$115.

Scott Courtyard (1443 Second Street, 94515; 942-0948) 6 rooms, bed & breakfast, complimentary breakfast. SGL$85, DBL$95.

The Silver Rose Inn (351 Rosedale Rd., 94515; 942-9581) 5 rooms, bed & breakfast, complimentary breakfast, swimming pool, no-smoking. SGL/DBL$100-$175.

Trailside Inn (4201 Silverado Trail, 945151; 942-4106) 3 rooms and suites, bed & breakfast, complimentary breakfast. SGL/DBL$76-$100.

Wayside Inn (1523 Foothill Blvd., 94515; 942-0645, 800-845-3532 in California) 3 rooms, bed & breakfast, complimentary breakfast, no-smoking rooms, free parking. SGL/DBL$65-$85.

Calpine

Area Code 707

Sierra Valley Lodge (Box 130, 96124; 994-3367) 12 rooms and efficiencies, restaurant. SGL/DBL$27-$34.

Cameron Park

Area Code 916

Best Western Inn (3361 Coach Lane, 95682; 677-2203, Fax 677-1412, 800-528-1234) 63 rooms, restaurant, lounge, complimentary breakfast, swimming pool, laundry room, airport courtesy car, pets allowed, kitchenettes, fax service, wheelchair access, no-smoking rooms. SGL$48-$58, DBL$53-$63+.

Super 8 Motel (3444 Coach Lane, 95682; 677-7177, 800-843-1991, 677-2235, 800-800-8000) 60 rooms and suites, complimentary breakfast, outdoor swimming pool, spa, free local telephone calls, fax service, wheelchair access, no-smoking rooms, pets allowed. SGL/DBL$42-$47.

Campbell

Area Code 408
Campbell Chamber of Commerce
54 North Central Avenue
Campbell CA 95008
378-6809

All Star Inn (1240 Camden Avenue, 95008; 371-8870) 33 rooms. SGL/DBL$37-$43.

Campbell Inn (675 East Campbell Avenue, 95008; 374-4300, 800-582-4300) 99 rooms, complimentary breakfast, swimming pool, exercise equipment, airport transportation, wheelchair access, no-smoking rooms, pets allowed. SGL$99, DBL$109-$119.

Courtside Tennis Club (14675 Winchester Blvd.; 395-7111) 116 rooms. SGL$80, DBL$72-$85.

Executive Inn Suites (1300 Campbell Avenue, 95008; 559-3600, Fax 371-0695, 800-888-3611) 39 rooms, restaurant, exercise equipment, wheelchair access. SGL/DBL$72-$85.

Marriott Residence Inn (2761 South Bascom, 95008; 559-1551, Fax 371-9808, 800-331-3131) 135 rooms and suites, restaurant, lounge, airport courtesy car, exercise equipment, wheelchair access, meeting facilities for 30, VCRs, bicycle rentals, pets allowed. SGL/DBL$104-$149.

Pruneyard Inn (1995 South Bascom Avenue, 95009; 559-4300, 800-582-4300) 116 rooms and suites, lounge, complimentary breakfast, outdoor heated swimming pool, jacuzzi, spa, free local telephone calls, free parking, valet laundry, meeting facilities for 100, wheelchair access, no-smoking rooms, no pets, airport transportation. SGL$89, DBL$99, STS$125-$130.

Canyon Country

Area Code 805
Canyon Country Chamber of Commerce
17956 Sierra Highway
Canyon Country CA 91351
252-4131

Country Inn (17901 Sierra Highway, 91351; 252-1722, 800-537-8930) 50 rooms and suites, outdoor heated swimming pool, spa, in-room refrigerators, fax service, free parking, wheelchair access, no-smoking rooms, no pets. SGL$33-$55, DBL$55-$77.

Capitola

Area Code 408
Capitola Chamber of Commerce
410 Capitola Avenue
Capitola CA 95010
475-6522

RENTAL SOURCES: Vacations By The Sea (215 Monterey Avenue, 95010; 479-9360; Fax 462-1697) rental cottages, condos and private homes.

Capitola Inn (822 Bay Avenue, 95010; 462-3004) 56 rooms and suites, three restaurants, heated swimming pool, balconies, fireplaces, meeting facilities, free parking, wheelchair access. LS SGL/DBL$55-$125; HS SGL/DBL$75-$160.

Capitola Venetian (1500 Wharf Rd., 95010; 476-6471) 20 rooms. SGL/DBL$60+.

El Salto Resort (620 El Salto Drive, 95010; 462-6365) 24 rooms and efficiencies, complimentary breakfast, free parking. LS SGL/DBL$65-$140; HS SGL/DBL$100-$160.

Harbor Lights Motel (5000 Cliff Drive, 95010; 476-0505) 10 rooms and efficiencies, balconies, fireplaces, ocean view, beach, free parking. LS SGL/DBL$70-$125; HS SGL/DBL$80-$145.

Inn At Depot Hill (250 Montgomery Avenue, 95010; 462-3376, Fax 458-0989) 8 rooms, bed & breakfast, complimentary breakfast, free parking. SGL/DBL$155-$250.

Summer House Bed and Breakfast (216 Montgomery Avenue, 95010; 475-8474) 2 rooms, bed & breakfast, complimentary breakfast, pets allowed. SGL/DBL$60+.

Carlotta

Area Code 707

Carlotta Hotel (136 Central; 768-3101) 21 rooms, restaurant. SGL/DBL$45-$48.

Carnelian Bay

Area Code 916

RENTAL SOURCES: Carnelian Bay Rentals (5193 North Lake Blvd., 96140; 546-5547) rents one- to five-bedroom condos. SGL/DBL$93. **R.Rent Realty** (6873 North Lake Blvd., 96140) rental condos and homes. SGL/DBL$125+. **Sierra Vacation Rentals** (7252 North Lake Blvd., 96140; 546-8222, 800-521-6656) rental studio apartments, condos and one-to five-bedroom private homes. SGL/DBL$112-$450.

Lakeside Chalets (5240 North Lake Blvd., 96140) 16 cottages, pets allowed. SGL/DBL$85+.

North Tahoe Guest House (5732 Uplands Rd., 96140) 11 rooms, complimentary breakfast, swimming pool. SGL/DBL$45.

Castro Valley

Area Code 510
Castro Valley Chamber of Commerce
21096 Redwood Rd.
Castro Valley CA 94546
537-5300

Econo Lodge (3954 East Castro Valley, 94546, 800-446-6900) 56 rooms, restaurant, swimming pool, whirlpool, wheelchair access, children under 18 free, no pets. SGL/DBL$45-$200.

TraveLodge (2532 Castro Valley Blvd., 94546; 538-9501) 59 rooms, restaurant, lounge, swimming pool, spa, laundry room, meeting facilities for 49, swimming pool, no pets. SGL$47-$54, DBL$59-$61.

Cathy's Valley

Area Code 707

Chibchas Inn (2751 Highway 140, 95306; 966-2940) 6 rooms, bed & breakfast, complimentary breakfast, restaurant. SGL$45, DBL$48.

La Daun's Bed and Breakfast (2093 Trower Rd., 95306; 374-3468) 8 rooms, bed & breakfast, complimentary breakfast. SGL/DBL$37-$48.

The Shadow Ranch (3086 Highway 140, 95306; 966-3132) 1 suite, bed & breakfast, complimentary breakfast. SGL/DBL$60.

Cave Junction

Area Code 707

Kerbyville Inn (4210 Holland Loop Rd.; 592-4688) 3 rooms, bed & breakfast, complimentary breakfast. SGL/DBL$49-$85.

Oregon Caves Chateau (2000 Caves Highway; 592-3400) 28 rooms, restaurant. SGL/DBL$53-$56.

Cazadero

Area Code 707

Cazanoma Lodge (Box 37, 95421; 632-5255) 5 rooms and suites, bed & breakfast, complimentary breakfast, swimming pool. SGL/DBL$65-$85, STS$85+.

Timberhill Ranch (35755 Hauser Bridge Rd., 95421; 847-3258) 20 rooms and cottages, bed & breakfast, restaurant, complimentary breakfast, swimming pool, spa, meeting facilities, room service, tennis, wheelchair access, no-smoking rooms. SGL$205-$250, DBL$285-$365.

Chester

Area Code 916
Chester Chamber of Commerce
Box 1198
Chester CA 96020
258-2426

RENTAL SOURCES: Coldwell Banker (Box 556, 96020; 258-2103) rental three- to five-bedroom private homes. **Keefer Realty** (Box 1103, 96020; 258-2148) rental two- to four-bedroom private homes.

Antlers Motel (Main Street, 96020; 258-2722) 12 rooms and apartments, restaurant. SGL/DBL$28-$38, 1BR$45/$275W.

Bidwell House (One Main Street, 96020; 258-3338) 13 rooms and one-bedroom cottages, bed & breakfast, complimentary breakfast. SGL/DBL$60-$90, 1BR$110.

Black Forest Lodge (Highway 36, 96020; 258-2941) 9 rooms. SGL/DBL$21-$38.

Chico

Area Code 916
Greater Chico Chamber of Commerce
500 Main Street
Chico CA 95927
891-5556

Best Western Heritage Inn (25 Heritage Lane, 95926; 894-8600, Fax 894-8600, 800-528-1234) 103 rooms, restaurant, lounge, complimentary breakfast, swimming pool, whirlpools, meeting facilities, fax service, wheelchair access, exercise equipment, no-smoking rooms. SGL$53-$69, DBL$57-$75.

Camelot Bed and Breakfast (2803 Eskin Maidu Trail, 95926; 345-1393) 6 rooms, bed & breakfast, complimentary breakfast. SGL/DBL$60+.

Deluxe Inn (2507 Esplanada, 95296; 342-8386) 30 rooms, swimming pool, airport transportation, wheelchair access, pets allowed. SGL/DBL$30-$45.

Econo Lodge (630 Main Street, 95928; 895-1323, Fax 343-2719) 43 rooms, swimming pool, children under 18 free, complimentary newspaper, wheelchair access, pets allowed. SGL$32-$40, DBL$34-$50.

Esplanada House (620 The Esplanada, 95926; 345-8084) 13 rooms, bed & breakfast, complimentary breakfast. SGL/DBL$50+.

Holiday Inn (685 Manzanita Court, 95926; 345-2491, Fax 893-3040, 800-HOLIDAY) 174 rooms, restaurant, exercise equipment, outdoor swimming pool, jacuzzi, meeting facilities for 250, room service, wheelchair access, airport courtesy car, exercise equipment, no-smoking rooms, pets allowed. SGL$60-$75, DBL$70-$85.

Matador Motel (1934 Esplanada, 95926; 342-7543) 26 rooms and efficiencies, swimming pool, pets allowed. SGL/DBL$30-$45.

Music Express Inn (1091 Monte Avenue, 95926; 345-8376) 16 rooms, bed & breakfast, complimentary breakfast, pets allowed. SGL/DBL$45-$60.

O'Flaherty House (1462 Arcadian, 95926; 893-5494) 4 rooms, bed & breakfast, complimentary breakfast. SGL/DBL$58-$100+.

Safari Garden Motel (2352 Esplanada, 95926; 343-3201) 22 rooms and efficiencies, swimming pool, pets allowed. SGL/DBL$30-$45.

Thunderbird Motel (715 Main Street, 95926; 343-7911) 28 rooms, swimming pool, pets allowed. SGL/DBL$30-$45.

Town House Motel (2231 Esplanada, 95926; 343-1621) 16 rooms, swimming pool, pets allowed. SGL/DBL$30-$45.

Chowchilla

Area Code 209
Chowchilla Chamber of Commerce
115 South Second Street
Chowchills CA 93610
665-5603

Safari Motel National Inn (220 East Robertson, 93610; 665-4821) 30 rooms and efficiencies, swimming pool, pets allowed. LS SGL/DBL$32-$38; HS SGL/DBL$35-$40+.

Clearlake and Clearlake Oaks

Area Code 707
Clearlake Chamber of Commerce
Box 629
Clearlake CA 95422
994-3600

Best Western El Grande Inn (15135 Lakeshore Drive, 95422; 994-2000, Fax 994-2042, 800-528-1234) 68 rooms, restaurant, lounge, indoor heated swimming pool, fax service, meeting facilities, wheelchair access, no pets. SGL$65-$76, DBL$71-$83.

Island Park (12840 Island Drive, 95423; 998-3940) 15 cottages. SGL/DBL$12-$15.

Lake Marina Resort Motel (10215 East Highway 20, 95423; 998-3787) 13 rooms and efficiencies, swimming pool. SGL/DBL$26-$48.

Surina's Ship-N-Shore Resort (13885 Lakeshore Drive, 95422; 994-6672) 19 cottages, swimming pool. SGL/DBL$65-$95.

Tamarack Lodge (13825 Lakeshore Drive, 95422; 995-2424) 10 cottages, swimming pool, no pets. SGL/DBL$35-$70.

Wiseda Lakeside Resort (14375 Lakeshore Drive, 95422; 994-2145, Fax 994-2151, 800-342-0323 in California) 15 rooms, restaurant, swimming pool, no-smoking rooms, pets allowed. SGL$34-$43, DBL$54-$57.

Clio

Area Code 916

White Sulphur Springs Ranch (Box 136, 96106; 836-2387, 800-854-1797 in California) 8 rooms and cottages, bed & breakfast, complimentary breakfast, swimming pool, free local telephone calls, free parking, wheelchair access, no-smoking, no pets. SGL/DBL$85-$140.

Cloverdale

Area Code 707
Cloverdale Chamber of Commerce
555 South Cloverdale Blvd.
Cloverdale CA 95425
894-2507

Abrams House Inn (314 Main Street, 95425; 894-2412) 4 rooms, bed & breakfast, complimentary breakfast. SGL/DBL$60-$100.

Vintage Towers (302 North Main Street, 95425; 894-4535, 800-858-3311 in California) 7 rooms, bed & breakfast, complimentary breakfast. SGL/DBL$80-$110.

Ye Olde Shelford House (29955 River Rd., 95425; 894-5956, 800-833-6479) 6 rooms, bed & breakfast, complimentary breakfast, swimming pool. SGL/DBL$85-$115.

Cobb

Area Code 707

Cobb Village Inn (7990 Highway 29, 95426; 928-5242) 13 rooms, no pets. SGL/DBL$33-$38.

Coffee Creek

Area Code 916

Coffee Creek Ranch (96091; 266-3343) 14 rooms, restaurant, complimentary breakfast, swimming pool, wheelchair access, airport transportation, pets allowed. SGL/DBL$45-$50.

Coleville

Area Code 619
Northern Mono County Chamber of Commerce
Box 227
Coleville CA 96107
387-2723

Andruss (Box 64, 96107; 495-2216) 12 rooms and efficiencies, restaurant, pets allowed. SGL/DBL$36-$45.

Meadowcliff (Box 126, 96107; 495-2255) 11 rooms and efficiencies, restaurant, swimming pool, pets allowed. SGL$30-$40, DBL$40-$45.

Columbia

Area Code 209
Columbia Chamber of Commerce
Box 1824
Columbia CA 95310
532-4301

City Hotel (Main Street, 95310; 532-1479) 23 rooms, restaurant, lounge, airport transportation, pets allowed, no-smoking rooms. SGL/DBL$60-$80.

Columbia Inn Motel (22646 Broadway Street, 95310; 533-0446) 24 rooms, swimming pool, airport transportation, pets allowed. SGL$32-$45, DBL$34-$56.

Fallon Hotel (Box 1870, 95310; 532-1470) 14 rooms, bed & breakfast, complimentary breakfast. SGL/DBL$50-$85.

Comptche

Area Code 707

RENTAL SOURCES: Robinson Properties Vacation Homes (18901 Bald Hills Rd., 95427; 895-2907, 800-359-4649) rental homes in the Comptche area. $100-$195.

Concord

Area Code 510
Concord Convention and Visitors Bureau
2151 Salvio Street
Concord CA 94520
685-1184

Best Western Heritage Inn (4600 Clayton Rd., 94521; 686-446, Fax 825-0581, 800-528-1234) 132 rooms and efficiencies, complimentary breakfast, swimming pool, whirlpools, fax service, in-room refrigerators, wheelchair access, no-smoking rooms, pets allowed. SGL/DBL$65-$71.

Concord Hilton Hotel (1970 Diamond Blvd., 94520; 415-827-2000, Fax 671-0984, 800-826-6688, 800-826-2644 in California) 330 rooms, restaurant, swimming pool, meeting facilities for 1500, exercise equipment, airport courtesy car. SGL/DBL$94-$119, DBL$104-$129.

El Monte Motor Inn (3555 Clayton Rd., 94519; 682-1601) 42 rooms, complimentary breakfast, swimming pool, wheelchair access, no-smoking rooms. SGL/DBL$43-$54.

Holiday Inn (1050 Burnett Avenue, 94520; 689-7055, Fax 687-5500, 800-465-4329) 198 rooms, restaurant, lounge, swimming pool, meeting facilities, fax service, free parking. SGL/DBL$75-$95.

Sheraton Concord Hotel and Conference Center (45 John Glenn Drive, 94520; 415-825-7700, Fax 415-674-9567, 800-325-3535) 333 rooms and suites, restaurant, lounge, indoor swimming pool, spa, exercise equipment, meeting facilities for 850, gift shop, airport courtesy car, wheelchair access, pets allowed, no-smoking rooms, free parking. SGL$75-$110, DBL$85-$115.

Trees Inn (1370 Monument Blvd., 94520; 827-8998) 47 rooms, swimming pool, wheelchair access, pets allowed. SGL/DBL$50-$90.

Copperopolis

Area Code 209

RENTAL SOURCES: California Properties (48 Copper Drive, 95228; 785-4500) rents private homes. SGL/DBL$150-$250/$900W-$1500W.

Poker Flat Resort (7260 O'Byrnes Ferry Rd., 95228; 785-2286) 32 rooms, restaurant, lounge, swimming pool. SGL/DBL$45-$55.

Cordelia

Area Code 707

Best Western Cordelia Inn (1420 East Monte Vista; 448-8453, 800-528-1234) 41 rooms, swimming pool, pets allowed. SGL/DBL$65-$85.

Economy Inn (4376 Central Place; 864-1728, 800-423-3018) 101 rooms, meeting facilities, swimming pool, spa, free parking, free local telephone calls, pets allowed. SGL/DBL$30-$36.

Hampton Inn (4441 Central Place; 864-1446, 800-426-7866) 60 rooms and suites, complimentary breakfast, indoor swimming pool, jacuzzi, exercise equipment, valet laundry, free parking, free local telephone calls. SGL/DBL$49-$59, STS$75-$100.

Overniter Lodge (4625 Central Way; 864-2426) 149 rooms, complimentary breakfast. SGL/DBL$65-$89.

Corning

Area Code 916
Corning Chamber of Commerce
1108 Solano Street
Corning CA 96021
824-5550

Bel Air Motel (2104 Solano Street, 96021; 824-5103) 12 rooms. SGL/DBL$35-$40.

Days Inn (3475 Highway 99 West, 96021; 824-2000, Fax 824-2736, 800-325-2525, 800-824-2000) 63 rooms, restaurant, swimming pool, laundry room, fax service, children under 12 free, pets allowed, wheelchair access, no-smoking rooms. SGL$32-$38, DBL$36-$42.

Corning Olive Inn Motel (2165 Solano Street, 96021; 824-2468, 800-247-2744 in California) 41 rooms, swimming pool, no-smoking rooms. SGL/DBL$45-$48.

Economy Inn (945 South Highway 99W, 96021; 824-4322, 800-423-3018) 18 rooms, swimming pool. SGL/DBL$35-$45.

Shilo Inn (3350 Sunrise Way, 96021; 824-2940, 800-222-2244) 78 rooms and suites, complimentary breakfast, outdoor swimming pool, spa, meeting and conventional facilities, spa, sauna, exercise equipment, in-room refrigerators and microwaves, laundry room, airport courtesy car, complimentary newspaper. SGL/DBL$52-$66.

Corte Madera

Area Code 415
Corte Madera Chamber of Commerce
498 Tamalpais Drive
Corte Madera CA 94929
927-5071

Best Western Inn (1815 Redwood Highway, 94925; 924-1502, Fax 924-5419, 800-528-1234, 800-777-9670) 110 rooms and suites, restaurant, lounge, complimentary breakfast, heated swimming pool, spa, meeting and reception facilities for 200, in-room refrigerators, transportation to local attractions, children under 18 free, fireplaces, whirlpools, exercise equipment, wheelchair access, airport transportation, no-smoking rooms, free parking. SGL$73-$91, DBL$83-$145.

Howard Johnson Lodge (1595 Casa Buena Drive, 94925; 924-3570, 800-654-2000) 18 rooms, restaurant, no-smoking rooms, no pets. LS SGL/DBL$49-$69; HS SGL/DBL$55-$79.

Madera Village Inn (45 Tamal Vista, 94925; 924-3608, 800-726-5600, 800-362-3372) 100 suites, outdoor heated swimming pool, children under 12 free, in-room refrigerators and microwaves, fax service, laundry room, free parking, wheelchair access, no-smoking rooms, no pets. 1BR$65-$75, 2BR$90-$105.

Coulterville

Area Code 209
Coulterville Chamber of Commerce
Box 333
Coulterville CA 95311
878-3148

The Hotel Jeffrey (One Main Street, 95311; 878-3471) 20 rooms, restaurant. SGL/DBL$55-$68.

Sherlock Holmes Bed and Breakfast (5006 Min Street, 95311; 878-3915) 3 rooms, complimentary breakfast. SGL$65, DBL$70.

Yosemite Americana Inn (10407 Highway 49, 95311; 878-3407) 9 rooms. SGL/DBL$41-$48.

Crescent City

Area Code 707
Crescent City-Del Norte County Chamber of Commerce
1001 Front Street
Crescent City CA 95531
464-3174

American Best Motel (685 US Highway 101 South; 464-4111) 49 rooms, restaurant, airport courtesy car, wheelchair access, no-smoking rooms. SGL/DBL$40-$53.

Best Western Northwoods Inn (655 Highway 101S, 95531; 464-9771, Fax 464-9461, 800-528-1234) 52 rooms, restaurant, lounge, whirlpool, fax service, wheelchair access, no-smoking rooms, no pets. SGL/DBL$47-$80.

Best Western Ship Ashore (Highway 101, 95567; 487-3141, 800-528-1234) 50 rooms. SGL/DBL$50-$80.

Cedar and Pine (Box 1173, 92325) 338-5866) 3 rooms, bed & breakfast, complimentary breakfast. SGL/DBL$50+.

Crescent Beach Motel (1455 Redwood Highway South, 95531; 464-5436) 27 rooms, restaurant. SGL/DBL$41-$48.

Curly Redwood Lodge (701 Redwood Highway, 95531; 464-2137) 40 rooms and suites, restaurant, no-smoking rooms. SGL/DBL$35-$40.

El Patio Budget Motel (655 H Street, 95531; 464-5114) 24 rooms and efficiencies. SGL/DBL$32-$55.

Fair Winds Inn (Box 333, 95531; 465-FAIR) 1 room, bed & breakfast, complimentary breakfast, ocean view. SGL/DBL$76-$100.

Pacific Motor Lodge (Box 595, 95531; 464-4141) 62 rooms, restaurant, airport courtesy car. SGL/DBL$40-$60.

TraveLodge (725 Highway 101 North, 95531; 464-6106, 800-255-3050) 52 rooms, restaurant, lounge, whirlpool, laundry room, no pets. LS SGL/DBL$37-$52; HS SGL/DBL$37-$57.

Valu Inn (353 L Street, 95531; 464-6124) 27 rooms. SGL/DBL$40-$80.

Wagon Wheel Motel (8280 Highway 199, 95531; 457-3314) 22 rooms and efficiencies, restaurant. SGL/DBL$24-$34.

Cupertino

Area code 408
Cupertino Chamber of Commerce
20455 Silverado Avenue
Cupertino CA 95014
252-7054

Courtyard by Marriott (10605 North Wolfe Rd., 95014; 252-9100, Fax 252-0632, 800-321-2211) 161 rooms. SGL/DBL$88+.

Cypress

Area Code 714
Cypress Chamber of Commerce
9471 Walker Street
Cypress CA 90630
827-2438

Friendship Inn Suites (6262 West Lincoln Avenue, 90630; 220-0900) 45 rooms and suites. SGL/DBL$35-$75.

Ramada Hotel (5865 Katella Avenue, 90630; 827-1010, Fax 220-0543, 800-2-RAMADA) 204 rooms, restaurant, lounge, outdoor heated swimming pool, spa, children under 18 free, airport transportation, free parking, wheelchair access, no-smoking rooms, exercise equipment. SGL/DBL$77-$87.

Woodfin Suites (5905 Corporate Avenue, 90630; 828-4000, Fax 229-0566, 800-237-8811) 124 rooms and suites. SGL/DBL$95-$139.

Daly City

Area Code 415
Daly City Chamber of Commerce
244 92nd Street
Daly City CA 94015
755-8526

Alpine Motel (560 Carter Street, 94014; 334-6969) 35 rooms. SGL/DBL$30.

El Camino Motel (7525 Mission Street, 94014; 755-8667, 800-426-1771) 37 rooms. SGL$42, DBL$46+.

Danville

Area Code 415
Danville Chamber of Commerce
665 South Hartz Avenue
Danville CA 94526
837-4400

Econo Lodge (803 El Camino Ramon, 94526; 838-8080) 59 rooms, restaurant, lounge, swimming pool, free local telephone calls, children under 18 free, airport courtesy car, wheelchair access. SGL/DBL$49-$57.

Dardanelle

Area Code 209

Dardanelle Resort (Highway 108, 95314; 965-4355) 12 rooms, restaurant, pets allowed. SGL/DBL$45-$65.

Davenport

Area Code 408

New Davenport (31 Davenport Avenue, 95017; 425-1818, 800-523-7830) 12 rooms, bed & breakfast, complimentary breakfast, free parking, wheelchair access. LS SGL/DBL$55-$90; HS SGL/DBL$55-$105.

Davis

Area Code 916
Davis Area Chamber of Commerce
228 B Street
Davis CA 95616
756-5160

Best Western University Lodge (123 B Street, 95616; 756-7890, Fax 756-0245, 800-528-1234) 53 rooms, restaurant, in-room refrigerators and microwaves, bicycles, complimentary newspaper, whirlpool, spa, fax service, kitchenettes, wheelchair access, exercise equipment, no-smoking rooms. SGL$48-$58, DBL$52-$62.

Motel 6 (4835 Chiles Rd., 95616; 753-3777) 63 rooms. SGL/DBL$31-$37.

Ramada Inn (110 F Street, 95616; 753-3600, Fax 785-2410, 800-2-RAMADA) 135 rooms, restaurant, lounge, swimming pool, free parking, no-smoking rooms. SGL/DBL$60-$66.

Rodeway Inn (110 F Street, 95616; 753-3600, Fax 758-8623, 800-221-2222) 36 rooms. SGL/DBL$40-$60.

Dorrington

Area Code 209

Dorrington Hotel (3431 Highway Four, 95223; 795-5800) 5 rooms, restaurant. SGL/DBL$75+.

Dorris

Area Code 916

Hospitality Inn (200 South California Street, 96023; 397-2097) 4 rooms. SGL/DBL$65.

Downieville

Area Code 209
Downieville Chamber of Commerce
Box 515
Downieville CA 95936
289-3560

Sierra County Chamber of Commerce
Box 473
Downieville CA 95936
289-3122

Dyer's Resort Motel (Box 406, 95936; 289-3308, 800-696-3308 in California) 14 rooms and efficiencies, swimming pool. SGL/DBL$49-$125.

The Lure (Box 84, 95936; 289-3465) 8 cabins and efficiencies. SGL/DBL$30-$108.

Saundra Dyer's Resort (Box 406, 95936; 289-3308, 800-696-3308 in California) 43 rooms, swimming pool. SGL/DBL$45-$75.

Dunnigan

Area Code 916

Best Western Country (Box 740, 95937; 724-3471, Fax 724-4233, 800-528-1234) 55 rooms and efficiencies, swimming pool, whirlpool, laundry room, fax service, children under 12 free, wheelchair access, no-smoking rooms, pets allowed. SGL$45-$58, DBL$55-$78.

Dunsmuir

Area Code 916
Dunsmuir Chamber of Commerce
Box 17
Dunsmuir CA 96025

Bavaria Motel (4601 Dunsmuir Avenue, 96025; 235-0766) 15 rooms and efficiencies. SGL/DBL$23-$55.

Cave Springs Resort (4727 Dunsmuir Avenue, 96025; 235-2721) 28 rooms and efficiencies, swimming pool. SGL/DBL$26-$80.

Cedar Lodge (4201 Dunsmuir Avenue, 96025; 235-4331) 19 rooms and efficiencies, pets allowed. SGL$28-$32, DBL$34-$44.

Dunsmuir Inn (5423 Dunsmuir Avenue, 96025; 235-4543) 16 rooms. SGL/DBL$30-$48.

Railroad Park Resort (100 Railroad Park Rd., 96025; 235-4440) 32 rooms and cottages, restaurant, swimming pool. SGL/DBL$23-$55.

Shasta View Inn (4221 Siskiyou Avenue, 96025; 235-4844) 31 rooms, swimming pool. SGL/DBL$27-$70.

Travelers Hotel (5815 Dunsmuir Avenue, 96025; 235-4465) 32 rooms. SGL/DBL$16-$24.

TraveLodge (5400 Dunsmuir Avenue, 96025; 235-4395, 800-255-3050) 18 rooms and suites, restaurant, lounge, SGL/DBL$35-$55.

El Cerrito

Area Code 510
El Cerrito Chamber of Commerce
6318 Fairmount Avenue
El Cerrito CA 94530
527-5333

Freeway Motel (11645 San Pablo Avenue, 94530; 234-5581) 16 rooms and efficiencies, wheelchair access, free parking, pets allowed. SGL$40-$48, DBL$42-$52.

Terrace Motel (10869 San Pablo Avenue, 94530; 234-8335, Fax 236-7101) 50 rooms, wheelchair access, no-smoking rooms. SGL$36-$45, DBL$45-$60.

TraveLodge (6009 Potrero Avenue, 94530; 232-0900, Fax 231-0209, 800-255-3050) 48 rooms and suites, restaurant, lounge, complimentary breakfast, whirlpool, fax service, meeting facilities for 40, wheelchair access, no pets, free parking. SGL/DBL$45-$65.

El Monte

Area Code 818
El Monte Chamber of Commerce
11333 Valley Blvd.
El Monte CA 91734
580-2049

Comfort Inn (10038 East Valley Blvd., 91731; 575-7997, 800-221-2222, 800-228-5150) 39 rooms and suites, restaurant, complimentary breakfast, outdoor swimming pool, laundry room, fax service, wheelchair access, no-smoking rooms, free parking, no pets. SGL$35-$75, DBL$40-$95.

Motel 6 (3429 Peck Rd., 91731; 575-7997) 100 rooms. SGL/DBL$28-$35.

Ramada Suites (1089 Santa Anita Avenue, 91733; 850-9588, Fax 350-3849, 800-685-2168) 126 suites, restaurant, lounge, complimentary breakfast, airport transportation, fax and business services, meeting facilities for 300, in-room microwaves, VCRs, computer hookups, wheelchair access, no-smoking rooms. SGL$79-$200, DBL$89-$210.

El Portal

Area Code 209

Cedar Lodge (9966 Highway 140, 95338; 379-2612, Fax 742-7189, 800-321-5261) 206 rooms and efficiencies, restaurant, swimming pool, free parking. SGL/DBL$63-$115.

Elk

Area Code 707

Elk Cove Inn (6300 South Highway 1, 95432; 877-3321) 7 rooms and cabins, bed & breakfast, complimentary breakfast. SGL/DBL$108-$148.

Greenwood Pier Inn (Box 36, 95432; 877-9997) 11 rooms, bed & breakfast, complimentary breakfast, ocean view. SGL/DBL$76-$125+.

Sandpiper House Inn (Box 49, 95432; 877-3587) 4 rooms, bed & breakfast, complimentary breakfast. SGL/DBL$101-$125+.

Etna

Area Code 916

JH Mountain Guest Ranch (8525 Homestead Lane, 96027; 467-3468) 10 rooms. SGL/DBL$45+.

Eureka

Area Code 707
Eureka-Humboldt County Convention and Visitors Bureau
1034 Second Street
Eureka CA 95502
443-5097

Humboldt Bay Harbor and Recreational District
Box 1030
Humboldt Bay CA 95502
433-0801

Eureka Chamber of Commerce

2112 Broadway
Eureka CA 95501
442-3738

All Star Inns (1934 Broadway, 95501; 445-9631) 98 rooms. SGL/DBL$27-$33.

An Elegant Victorian Mansion (1406 C Street, 95501; 444-3144) 4 rooms and suites, bed & breakfast, complimentary breakfast, no smoking, no children. SGL/DBL$50-$110.

Bay View Motel (2844 Fairfield, 95501; 444-1673) 14 rooms, pets allowed. SGL/DBL$38-$58.

Best Western Thunderbird Inn (5th and Broadway, 95501; 442-2234, Fax 443-3489, 800-528-1234) 115 rooms and suites, restaurant, heated swimming pool, spa, fax service, meeting facilities, laundry room, wheelchair access, no-smoking rooms, pets allowed. SGL/DBL$47-$79.

Broadway Motel (1921 Broadway, 95501; 443-3156) 29 rooms. SGL/DBL$45-$55.

Budget Host Inn Townhouse Motel (4th and K Street, 95501; 445-6888, 800-445-6888) 20 rooms and suites, free parking, no-smoking rooms, pets allowed. SGL/DBL$30-$40.

Camellia Cottage (1314 I Street, 95501; 445-1089) 3 rooms, bed & breakfast, complimentary breakfast, no smoking, no pets. SGL/DBL$50-$100+.

Carger House (301 L Street, 95501; 444-8062) 27 rooms, complimentary breakfast, handicapped access. SGL/DBL$76-$100.

Carson House Inn (1209 4th Street, 95501; 443-1601, 800-772-1622) 60 rooms and suites, restaurant, outdoor heated swimming pool, free local telephone calls, free parking, wheelchair access, no-smoking rooms, pets allowed. SGL/DBL$45-$75, STS$110.

Carter House And Hotel Carter (301 L Street, 95501; 444-8062) 27 rooms, restaurant, complimentary breakfast, airport courtesy car, wheelchair access, no-smoking rooms. SGL/DBL$79-$199.

Carter House Country Inn (301 3rd Street, 95501; 445-1390) 7 rooms, bed & breakfast, complimentary breakfast, wheelchair access, airport courtesy car, no-smoking rooms. SGL/DBL$80-$250.

Chin's Motel (4200 Broadway, 95501; 443-0615) 14 rooms. SGL$38, DBL$42.

Craddock Manor Bed and Breakfast (814 J Street, 95501; 444-8589) bed & breakfast, 2 rooms, bed & breakfast, complimentary breakfast. SGL/DBL$65-$75.

Daly Inn (1125 H Street, 95501; 445-3638, 800-321-9656) 5 rooms, bed & breakfast, complimentary breakfast, no pets, no-smoking rooms. SGL/DBL$65-$120.

The Downtowner Motel (424 8th Street, 95501; 443-5061) 70 rooms, swimming pool. SGL/DBL$38-$48.

Econo Lodge (1630 4th Street, 95501; 443-8041, Fax 443-9275, 800-424-4777) 41 rooms, restaurant, swimming pool, kitchenettes, complimentary newspaper, pets allowed, children under 18 free. SGL/DBL$36-$45.

The Eureka Inn (7th and F Streets, 95501; 442-6441, Fax 442-0637, 800-862-4906) 105 rooms and suites, restaurant, lounge, swimming pool, spa, jacuzzi, sauna, laundry room, child care, fireplaces, meeting facilities for over 200, wheelchair access, airport courtesy car, free parking, pets allowed. SGL$85-$115, DBL$120-$250.

Eureka Ranch Hotel (2109 Broadway, 95501; 443-6751) 43 rooms. SGL/DBL$42-$52.

Fern Hill (7540 Zanes Rd., 95501; 445-2125) one apartment, no pets. SGL/DBL$90/$400W.

Fireside Inn (5th and R Street, 95501; 443-6312) 64 rooms. SGL/DBL$30-$55.

Flamingo Motel-Friendship Inn (4255 South Broadway, 95501; 443-4556) 21 rooms. SGL/DBL$33-$38.

Fort Humboldt Motel (1503 McCullens Avenue, 95501; 442-0222) 12 rooms. SGL/DBL$30-$50.

Heuer's Victorian Inn (1302 E Street, 95501; 442-7334) bed & breakfast, 3 rooms, complimentary breakfast, no-smoking. SGL/DBL$65-$85.

The Iris Inn (1134 H Street, 95501; 445-0307) 5 rooms, bed & breakfast, complimentary breakfast, no pets, no-smoking rooms. SGL/DBL$60-$90.

Lamplighter Motel (4033 Broadway, 95501; 443-501) 20 rooms. SGL/DBL$35-$75.

Matador Motel (129 4th Street, 95501; 443-9751, 800-824-6630 in California) 25 rooms, spa, sauna, laundry room, no-smoking rooms, pets allowed. SGL$36-$44, DBL$40-$58.

National 9 Inn Seabreeze (2846 Broadway, 95501; 443-9381, 800-524-9999) 25 rooms, no-smoking rooms. SGL/DBL$38-$58.

Old Town Bed and Breakfast Inn (1521 Third Street, 95501; 445-3951) 5 rooms, bed & breakfast, complimentary breakfast, no pets, no-smoking. SGL/DBL$75-$95.

The Olympic Motel (2832 South Broadway, 95501; 443-4525) 45 rooms and apartments. SGL/DBL$65+.

Red Lion Motor Inn (1929 Fourth Street, 95501; 445-0844, Fax 445-2752, 800-547-8010) 180 rooms, restaurant, lounge, swimming pool, spa, room service, meeting facilities for over

200, airport courtesy car, pets allowed, wheelchair access, free parking. SGL/DBL$75-$175.

Royal Pacific Lodge (1304 4th Street, 95501; 443-3193, 800-235-3232 in California) 50 rooms, restaurant, swimming pool, no-smoking rooms. SGL/DBL$35-$100.

Safari Budget 6 Motel (801 Broadway, 95501; 443-4891) 21 rooms. SGL$38, DBL$40.

Sandpiper Motel (4055 Broadway, 95501; 443-7394) 20 rooms, swimming pool. SGL/DBL$50-$60.

Seafarer Motor Inn (270 5th Street, 95501; 443-2206, 800-233-3782) 40 rooms, spa, sauna, wheelchair access, no-smoking rooms. SGL$38-$65, DBL$53-$79.

Shannon House (2154 Spring Street, 95501; 443-8130) 3 rooms, bed & breakfast, complimentary breakfast, no-smoking, no pets. SGL/DBL$50-$70.

Silverside Motel (6800 Fields Landing Drive, Fields Landing, 95501; 445-5931) 13 rooms. SGL/DBL$44-$53.

Townhouse Motel (933 Fourth Street, 95501; 443-4536, 800-445-6888) 20 rooms and efficiencies, free local telephone calls, jacuzzis, in-room refrigerators, no-smoking rooms, free parking, pets allowed. SGL$32-$65, DBL$36-$75.

Tradewind Inn (201 Fourth Street, 95501; 444-0401, Fax 442-8145) 27 rooms, complimentary breakfast, wheelchair access, no-smoking rooms. SGL$36-$60, DBL$42-$70+.

TraveLodge Motel (4th and B Streets, 95501; 443-6345, 800-225-3050) 46 rooms, restaurant, swimming pool, pets allowed, no-smoking rooms. SGL$35-$45, DBL$45-$55.

Tradewind Inn (2014 Fourth Street, 95501-444-0401, Fax 442-8145, 800-654-8027) 30 rooms, free local telephone calls, children under 12 free, jacuzzis, fax service, free parking, wheelchair access, no-smoking rooms, no pets. SGL$45-$65, DBL$48-$70.

TraveLodge (4 Fourth Street, 95501; 443-6345) 46 rooms, restaurant, swimming pool. SGL/DBL$35-$45.

A Weaver's Inn (1440 B Street, 95501; 443-8119) 4 rooms, bed & breakfast, complimentary breakfast, no-smoking, pets allowed. SGL/DBL$45-$50, STS$85.

Fairfield

Area Code 707
Fairfield Chamber of Commerce
1111 Webster Street
Fairfield CA 94533
425-4625

Best Western Cordelia Inn (4373 Central Place, 94585; 864-2029, 800-528-1234) 60 rooms, restaurant, complimentary breakfast, swimming pool, laundry facilities, children under 12 free, no-smoking rooms, pets allowed. SGL/DBL$42-$68.

Economy Inns of America (4376 Central Place, 94585; 864-1728, 800-826-0778) 101 rooms, swimming pool. SGL/DBL$45-$52.

E-Z 8 Motel (3331 North Texas Street, 94533; 436-6161) 101 rooms. SGL/DBL$27-$39.

Hampton Inn (4441 Central Place, 94585; 864-1446, Fax 864-4288, 800-HAMPTON, 800-531-0202) 58 rooms and suites, complimentary breakfast, swimming pool, meeting facilities, exercise equipment. SGL/DBL$46-$56.

Holiday Inn (1350 Holiday Lane, 94533; 422-4111, 800-HOLI-DAY) 142 rooms and suites, restaurant, swimming pool, meeting facilities for 300, whirlpools, exercise equipment, airport transportation, wheelchair access, no-smoking rooms, pets allowed. SGL/DBL$40-$90.

Motel 6 (1473 Holiday Lane, 94533; 425-4565) 89 rooms, swimming pool, wheelchair access, no-smoking rooms, pets allowed. SGL/DBL$29-$35.

Motel 6 (2353 Masgelian Rd., 94533; 427-0800) 83 rooms. SGL/DBL$24-$30.

Town House Inn (2170 North Texas Street; 422-1333) 45 rooms, swimming pool. SGL/DBL$45-$48.

Felton

Area Code408
San Lorenzo Valley Chamber of Commerce
6257 Highway 9
Felton CA 95018 335-2764

Griffin's Fern River Resort (5250 Highway 9, 95018; 335-4412) 12 rooms, efficiencies and suites, balconies, fireplaces, beach, free parking, wheelchair access. LS SGL/DBL$44-$62; HS SGL/DBL$49-$69.

Ferndale

Area Code 707
Ferndale Chamber of Commerce
325 Frances Street
Ferndale CA 95536
786-4477

The Ferndale Inn (619 Main Street, 95563; 786-4307) bed & breakfast, 5 rooms, complimentary breakfast, no smoking. SGL$63, DBL$73.

Francis Creek Inn (577 Main Street, 95563; 786-9611) 4 rooms, complimentary breakfast, free parking. SGL/DBL$36-$58.

Gingerbread Mansion (400 Bering Street, 95563; 786-4000) 9 rooms, bed & breakfast, complimentary breakfast, no-smoking. SGL/DBL$101-$125+.

Grandmother's House (861 Howard Street, 95563; 786-9704) 3 rooms, bed & breakfast, complimentary breakfast, no smoking, no pets. SGL/DBL$55-$65.

The Old Rectory (563 Ocean Avenue, 95536; 786-4055) 1 room, bed & breakfast, complimentary breakfast. SGL/DBL$55-$75.

The Shaw House Inn (703 Main Street, 95563; 786-9958) bed & breakfast, 9 rooms, no-smoking, no pets. SGL/DBL$110-$175.

Forestville

Area Code 707

The Farmhouse Inn (7871 River Rd., 95436; 887-3300, 800-464-6642 in California) 8 rooms and suites, complimentary breakfast, swimming pool. SGL/DBL$105-$175.

Fort Jones

Area Code 916

Marble View Motel (12425 Main Street, 96032; 468-2394) 6 rooms. SGL/DBL$23-$33.

Fortuna

Area Code 707
Fortuna Area Chamber of Commerce
735 14th Street
Fortuna CA 95540
725-3959

Fortuna Motor Lodge (275 12th Street, 95540; 725-6993) 25 rooms, no pets. SGL/DBL$39-$48.

Foster City

Area Code 415
Foster City Chamber of Commerce
1125 East Hillsdale Blvd.
Foster City CA 94404
573-7600

Courtyard by Marriott (550 Shell Blvd., 94404; 377-0600, 800-321-2211) 147 rooms and suites, restaurant, swimming pool, meeting facilities for 40, wheelchair access, no-smoking rooms, exercise equipment. SGL/DBL$58-$74.

Holiday Inn Foster City (1221 Chess Drive, 94404; 570-5700, Fax 570-0549, 800-HOLIDAY) 238 rooms, restaurant, swimming pool, wheelchair access, exercise equipment, meeting facilities for 1000, gift shop, beauty and barber shop, airport transportation, no-smoking rooms. SGL$74-$104, DBL$84-$114.

Fountain Valley

Area Code 714
Fountain Valley Chamber of Commerce
10525 Slater Avenue

Fountain Valley CA 92708
962-4441

Courtyard by Marriott (9950 Slater Avenue, 92700; 968-5775, Fax 968-0112, 800-321-2211) 162 rooms. SGL/DBL$79+.

Econo Lodge (9125 Recreation Circle, 92708; 847-3388, 800-424-4777) 54 rooms, restaurant, swimming pool, whirlpool, kitchenettes, meeting facilities, wheelchair access, no pets. SGL/DBL$40-$70.

Marriott Residence Inn (9930 Slater Avenue, 92708; 965-8000, Fax 962-3439, 800-331-3131) 122 rooms, restaurant, meeting facilities for 30, complimentary breakfast, in-room microwaves and VCRs, wheelchair access, no-smoking rooms, pets allowed. SGL$120-$135, DBL$130-$145.

Fremont

Area Code 510
Fremont Chamber of Commerce and Visitors Bureau
39737 Paseo Padre Parkway
Fremont CA 94538
657-1355

Best Western Thunderbird Inn (5400 Mowry Avenue, 94538; 792-4300, Fax 792-2643, 800-528-1234) 125 rooms, restaurant, lounge, complimentary breakfast, swimming pool, spa, sauna, laundry room, meeting facilities, wheelchair access, no-smoking rooms, no pets. SGL$65-$70, DBL$75-$80.

Courtyard by Marriott (47000 Lakeview Blvd., 94538; 656-1800, Fax 656-2441, 800-321-2211) 146 rooms, restaurant, swimming pool, exercise equipment, meeting facilities, free local telephone calls, wheelchair access, no-smoking rooms. SGL/DBL$70-$87.

Econo Lodge (46019 Warm Springs Blvd., 94538; 656-2800, 800-424-4777) 49 rooms, wheelchair access, children under 18 free, free local telephone calls. SGL/DBL$35-$39.

Lord Bradley's Inn (43344 Mission Blvd., 94539; 490-0520) 8 rooms, bed & breakfast, complimentary breakfast, free parking, wheelchair access, no-smoking rooms. SGL$65, DBL$65+.

Marriott Residence Inn (5400 Farewell Place, 94536; 415-794-5900, Fax 415-793-6587, 800-331-3131) 80 rooms and suites, restaurant, swimming pool, airport transportation, wheelchair access, meeting facilities for 45, in-room microwaves and VCRs, no-smoking rooms, pets allowed. SGL/DBL$85-$130.

Motel 6 (34047 Fremont Blvd., 94536; 793-4848) 211 rooms. SGL/DBL$27-$31.

Motel 6 (46101 Research Avenue, 94539; 490-4528) 159 rooms. SGL/DBL$27-$33.

Quality Inn (47031 Kato Rd., 94539; 490-2900, 800-221-2222) 115 rooms, restaurant, lounge, complimentary breakfast, swimming pool, whirlpool, meeting facilities, wheelchair access, no pets. SGL/DBL$61-$125.

Thunderbird Inn (5400 Mowry Avenue, 94538; 792-4300, Fax 792-2643, 800-874-7750 in California) 121 rooms, restaurant, complimentary breakfast, swimming pool, wheelchair access, no-smoking rooms. SGL$61-$71, DBL$71-$81.

Fort Bragg

Area Code 707
Fort Bragg-Mendocino Coast Chamber of Commerce
332 North Main Street
Fort Bragg CA 95437
964-3153

Anchor Lodge (780 North Harbor Drive, 95437; 964-4283) 19 rooms, wheelchair access. SGL/DBL$45-$135.

Avalon House (561 Steward Street, 95437; 964-5555) 6 rooms, bed & breakfast, complimentary breakfast, free parking, wheelchair access. SGL/DBL$80-$125.

Beachcomber Motel (1111 North Main Street, 95437; 964-2402, 800-400-SURF in California) 23 rooms and efficiencies, wheelchair access. SGL/DBL$52-$150.

Best Western Vista Manor Lodge (1100 North Main Street, 95437; 964-4776, 800-528-1234) 55 rooms, indoor heated swimming pool, no-smoking rooms, no pets. SGL/DBL$93-$100.

City Motel (250 South Main Street, 95437; 964-5321, Fax 964-6730) 31 rooms, no-smoking rooms, pets allowed. SGL/DBL$38-$65.

Cleone Lodge Inn (24600 North Highway 1, 95437; 964-2788) 11 rooms and suites, wheelchair access. SGL/DBL$61-$108.

The Cottage (28400 Simpson Lane, 95437; 964-7851) 1 room. SGL$65, DBL$80.

Driftwood Motel (820 North Main Street, 95437; 964-4061) 50 rooms. SGL/DBL$30-$70.

Glass Beach Inn (736 North Main Street, 95437; 964-6774) 9 rooms. SGL/DBL$54-$84.

The Grace Vacation Home (28401 Simpson Lane, 95437; 964-4094) rental home. LS $125; HS $300.

Grey Whale Inn (615 North Main Street, 95437; 964-0640, 800-382-7244) 14 rooms and suites, bed & breakfast, complimentary breakfast, in-room refrigerators, free parking, wheelchair access, no-smoking, no pets. SGL$60-$132, DBL$82-$154.

Harbor Lite Lodge (120 North Harbor Drive, 95436; 964-0221, 800-643-2700 in California) 79 rooms, wheelchair access, beach. SGL/DBL$65-$94.

Hi Seas Beach Motel (1201 North Main Street, 95437; 964-5929) 14 rooms, wheelchair access. SGL/DBL$52-$72.

Jughandle Beach Country Inn (32980 Gibney Lane, 95437; 964-1415) 4 rooms, bed & breakfast, complimentary breakfast. SGL/DBL$75-$95.

Noyo River Lodge (500 Casa del Noyo Drive, 95437; 964-8045, 800-628-1126) 16 rooms and suites, complimentary breakfast, meeting facilities for 60, free parking, wheelchair access, no smoking, no pets. SGL/DBL$80-$115, STS$130-$140.

The Old Coast Hotel (101 North Franklin Street, 95437; 961-0775) 16 rooms, pets allowed, wheelchair access. SGL/DBL$48-$68.

Old Stewart House Inn (511 Stewart Street, 95437; 961-0775) 6 rooms, bed & breakfast, complimentary breakfast, pets allowed, wheelchair access. SGL/DBL$75-$85.

Orca Inn And Cottages By The Sea (31502 North Highway 1, 95437; 964-5585) 10 rooms, wheelchair access, no pets. SGL/DBL$65-$150.

Pine Beach Inn (Box 1173, 95437; 964-8045) 60 rooms, restaurant, tennis. SGL/DBL$65+.

Pudding Creek Inn (615 North Main Street, 95437; 969-9529) 10 rooms, bed & breakfast-inn, complimentary breakfast, no-smoking, no pets. SGL/DBL$55-$105.

Rendezvous Inn (647 Main Street, 95437; 964-8142) 7 rooms, bed & breakfast, complimentary breakfast. SGL/DBL$75+.

Roundhedge Inn (159 Whipple Street, 95437; 964-9605) 7 rooms, bed & breakfast, complimentary breakfast, wheelchair access. SGL/DBL$55-$85.

Seabird Lodge (191 South Street, 95437; 964-4731, 800-345-0022 in California) 65 rooms, wheelchair access. SGL/DBL$60-$80.

Surf Motel (1220 South Main Street, 95437; 964-5361, Fax 964-5361, 800-339-5361 in California) 54 rooms and efficiencies, no pets. SGL$40-$55, DBL$50-$63.

Surrey Inn (888 South Main Street, 95437; 964-4003) 53 rooms. SGL/DBL$50-$57+.

Sunshine Hill (27917 Highway 20, 95437; 964-4269) 2 rooms, bed & breakfast, complimentary breakfast, wheelchair access, free parking. SGL/DBL$150-$175.

Surf Motel (1220 South Main Street, 95437; 964-5361) 54 rooms and efficiencies. SGL$55, DBL$60.

Garberville

Area Code 707
Garberville-Redway Chamber of Commerce
Box 445
Garberville CA 95440
923-2613

Benbow Inn (445 Lake Benbow Drive, 95440; 923-2125) 55 rooms and suites, restaurant, swimming pool, airport courtesy car, golf. SGL/DBL$88-$250.

Best Western Humboldt House (701 Redwood Drive, 95440; 923-2771, 800-528-1234) 56 rooms, restaurant, lounge, complimentary breakfast, swimming pool, exercise equipment, balconies, meeting facilities, whirlpools, wheelchair access, no-smoking rooms, pets allowed. LS SGL/DBL$46-$54; HS $49-$57.

Brass Rail Inn (3188 Redwood Drive, 95440; 923-3931) 17 rooms, restaurant. SGL/DBL$45-$55.

Garberville Motel (948 Redwood Drive, 95440; 923-2451) 30 rooms, restaurant, pets allowed. SGL/DBL$40-$50.

Johnston's Motel (839 Redwood Drive, 95440; 923-2634) 10-rooms. SGL$38, DBL$40.

Motel Rancho (987 Redwood Drive, 95440; 923-2451) 22 rooms, restaurant, swimming pool, no pets, no-smoking rooms. SGL/DBL$32-$62.

Redway Inn (3223 Redwood Drive, 95440; 923-2660) 13 rooms. SGL/DBL$45-$59.

Sherwood Forest Motel (814 Redwood Drive, 95440; 923-2721) 33 rooms and suites, restaurant, swimming pool, airport courtesy car, no-smoking rooms, pets allowed. SGL$45-$75.

Gasquet

Area Code 707

Patrick Creek Lodge (13950 Highway 199, 95543; 457-3323) 15 rooms, restaurant. SGL/DBL$46-$76.

Georgetown

Area Code 916

American River Inn (Box 43, 95634; 333-4499, 800-245-6566 in California) 24 rooms, bed & breakfast, complimentary breakfast, swimming pool, wheelchair access. SGL/DBL$65-$85.

Geyserville

Area Code 707
Geyserville Chamber of Commerce
Box 276
Geyserville CA 95441

Wine Country Inns of Sonoma County (Box 51; 433-INNS, 800-354-4743) represents inns in the Geyserville area.

Campbell Ranch Inn (1475 Canyon Rd., 95441; 857-3476) 5 rooms, bed & breakfast, complimentary breakfast, swimming pool, tennis. SGL/DBL$90-$125.

Hope-Bosworth House (21239 Geyersville Avenue, 95441; 857-3356) 5 rooms, bed & breakfast, complimentary breakfast, swimming pool, meeting facilities, no-smoking rooms. SGL/DBL$60-$80.

The Hope-Merrill House (21253 Geyserville Avenue, 95441; 857-3356, 800-825-4BED) 7 rooms, bed & breakfast, complimentary breakfast, swimming pool, private baths, whirlpools, wheelchair access, no-smoking rooms. SGL/DBL$85-$115.

Isis Oasis Lodge (20889 Geyserville Avenue, 95441; 857-3524) 37 rooms, exercise equipment. SGL$65, DBL$85.

Gilroy

Area Code 408
Gilroy Chamber of Commerce
80 West Fifth Street
Gilroy CA 95020
842-6437
Best Western Inn (360 Leavesley Rd., 95020; 848-1467, Fax 848-1424, 800-528-1234) 42 rooms, restaurant, complimentary

breakfast, heated swimming pool, spa, laundry room, fax service, no-smoking rooms, pets allowed. SGL/DBL$42-$69.

Country Rose Inn (Box 1804, 95021; 842-0441) 5 rooms, bed & breakfast, complimentary breakfast. SGL/DBL$65-$85.

Leavesley Inn (8430 Murray Avenue, 95020; 847-550) 58 rooms, complimentary breakfast, swimming pool, wheelchair access, no-smoking rooms. SGL/DBL$35-$65.

Motel 6 (6110 Monterey Highway, 95020; 842-6061) 59 rooms. SGL/DBL$30-$35.

Super 8 Motel (8435 San Ysidro Avenue, 95020; 848-4108, 848-2651, 800-800-8000) 53 rooms and suites, restaurant, outdoor swimming pool, complimentary breakfast, fax service, free local telephone calls, wheelchair access, no-smoking rooms, pets allowed. SGL/DBL$34-$38.

Glen Avon

Area Code 714

Circle Inn Motel (9220 Granite Hill, 92509; 360-1132) 59 rooms, complimentary breakfast, swimming pool, wheelchair access, no-smoking rooms, pets allowed. SGL/DBL$40+.

Glen Ellen

Area Code 707

Gaige House (13540 Arnold Drive, 95442; 935-0237) 8 rooms, bed & breakfast, complimentary breakfast, swimming pool. SGL/DBL$76-$125+.

Grants Pass

Area Code 503
Grants Pass Visitors and Convention Bureau
1501 Northeast Sixth Street
Grants Pass CA 97526
476-5510

Best Western Grants Pass Inn (111 North Agness Avenue, 97526; 476-1117, 800-553-ROOM) 84 rooms and suites, restaurant, swimming pool. SGL/DBL$69-$82.

Golden Inn Motel (1950 Northwest Vine Street, 97526; 479-6611) 60 rooms, swimming pool, no-smoking rooms, pets allowed. SGL/DBL$40-$48.

Shilo Inn Grants Pass (1880 Northwest Sixth Street, 97526; 479-8391) 70 rooms, complimentary breakfast, swimming pool, no-smoking rooms. SGL/DBL$49-$54.

Grass Valley

Area Code 916
Nevada County Chamber of Commerce
248 Mill Street
Grass Valley CA 95945

Alta Sierra Resort Motel (1235 Tammy Way, 95949; 273-9102, 800-992-5300 in California) 26 rooms and suites, restaurant, swimming pool, spa, tennis, golf, no-smoking rooms. SGL$55, DBL$65, STS$85-$95.

Annie Horan's (415 West Main Street, 95945; 272-2418, Fax 273-7462) 5 rooms, bed & breakfast, complimentary breakfast. SGL/DBL$65+.

Best Western Gold Country Inn (11972 Sutton Way, 95945; 916-273-1393, Fax 916-273-4229, 800-528-1234) 84 rooms, restaurant, complimentary breakfast, swimming pool. SGL/DBL$45-$73.

Holbrooke Hotel (212 West Main Street, 95944; 273-1352, Fax 273-0434, 800-933-7077) 28 rooms and suites, restaurant, complimentary breakfast, lounge, children under 12 free, exercise equipment, gift shop, valet laundry, free parking, wheelchair access, no-smoking rooms, no pets. SGL/DBL$66-$76, STS$120-$145.

Holiday Lodge (1221 East Main Street, 95945; 273-4406, Fax 477-6305) 47 rooms, swimming pool, wheelchair access, no-smoking rooms, pets allowed. SGL/DBL$55-$65.

Groveland

Area Code 209

Buck Meadows Lodge (7647 Highway 120, 95321; 962-5281, Fax 962-5285, 800-253-YOSE) 21 rooms and suites, restaurant, lounge, free local telephone calls, wheelchair access, meeting facilities for 25, free parking, no-smoking rooms, pets allowed. SGL$48-$60, DBL$53-$65, STS$65.

Groveland Hotel (18767 Main Street, 95321; 962-4000) 17 rooms, bed & breakfast, complimentary breakfast, wheelchair access. SGL/DBL$55-$65.

Lee's Middle Fork Resort-Motel (11399 Cherry Oil Rd., 95321; 962-7408, 800-626-7408 in California) 65 rooms. LS SGL/DBL$49-$69; HS SGL/DBL$59-$89.

Gualala

Area Code 707

RENTAL SOURCES: Serenisea (36100 Highway One South, 95445; 884-3836) rental homes and cottages. $60-$140. **Beach Rentals** (Box 246, 95445; 884-4235) rental homes in the Gualala area. **Kennedy and Associates** (Box 900, 94923; 884-9601) rents private homes.

Gualala Inn (Highway One, 95445; 884-3303) 5 rooms, restaurant, airport transportation. SGL/DBL$35-$55.

North Coast Country Inn (34591 South Highway 1, 95445; 884-4537) 4 rooms, bed & breakfast-inn, complimentary breakfast, airport courtesy car, no-smoking. SGL/DBL$76-$125.

St. Orres Inn (36601 Highway One, 95445; 884-3303) 19 rooms and cottages, complimentary breakfast, restaurant. SGL/DBL$50-$180.

Whale Watch Inn (35100 Highway One, 95445; 884-3667, Fax 884-4815) 18 rooms, complimentary breakfast, no children, no smoking, wheelchair access. SGL/DBL$150-$235.

Guerneville

Area Code 707
Russian River Region
14034 Armstrong Woods Rd. Guerneville CA 95446
869-9009

RENTAL SOURCES: Country Inns of Russian River (Box 2416, 95446; 800-927-4667) represents bed & breakfasts in the Russian River region. **D&G Equity Management** (14080 Mill Street, 95446; 707-869-0623) rental homes in the Guerneville area. $325W-$950W. **Wine Country Inns of Sonoma Country** (Box 52, 95441; 707-433-INNS) reservation service for 13 area inns.

Brookside Lodge and Resort Motel (Box 382, 95446; 707-869-2874) 33 rooms, restaurant, swimming pool, no-smoking rooms. SGL/DBL$55-$80.

Camelot Resort (16484 Fourth Street, 95446; 707-869-2538) 17 rooms and suites, swimming pool. SGL/DBL$75-$125.

Creekside Inn and Resort (16180 Neeley Rd., 95446; 707-869-3623, 800-776-6586) 15 rooms and cottage suites, bed & breakfast, complimentary breakfast, outdoor heated swimming pool, in-room refrigerators, fax service, free parking, wheelchair access, no-smoking rooms. SGL/DBL$35-$65, STS$55-$150.

Days Inn (14100 Brookside Lane, 95446; 707-869-2874, Fax 707-869-0714, 800-325-2525) 32 rooms and suites, complimentary breakfast, swimming pool, spa, sauna, in-room refrigerators and microwaves, fax service, wheelchair access, no-smoking rooms. SGL$52-$70, DBL$69-$98.

The Estate Inn (13555 Highway 116, 95446; 707-869-9093) 10 rooms, bed & breakfast, restaurant, complimentary breakfast, swimming pool, spa, airport courtesy car, wheelchair access, no-smoking. SGL/DBL$101-$175.

Fern Grove Inn (16650 River Rd., 95446; 707-869-9083, 800-347-9083) 20 one- and two-bedroom cottages, complimentary breakfast, heated swimming pool, fireplaces, handicapped access. SGL/DBL$60-$150.

Johnson's Beach Resort (Box 386, 95446; 707-869-2022) 10 cabins, no pets. SGL/DBL$25-$30/$135W-$150W.

North Forty Resort (19445 Highway 116, 95446; 707-869-9695) 18 cabins, no pets. SGL/DBL$50+.

Ridenhour Ranch House Inn (12850 River Rd., 95446; 707-887-1033) 7 rooms, bed & breakfast, restaurant, complimentary breakfast, wheelchair access, no smoking. SGL/DBL$65-$115.

Rivers End (Highway One, 95446; 869-3252) 8 rooms, restaurant, complimentary breakfast, ocean view, SGL/DBL$65-$135.

Riverlane Resort (1st and Church Street; 869-2323) cabins, swimming pool. SGL/DBL$45-$140.

Santa Nella House (12130 Highway 16; 869-9488) 6 rooms, bed & breakfast, complimentary breakfast. SGL$60.

Gustin

Area Code 209
Gustin Chamber of Commerce
Box A
Gustin CA 95322
854-6471

Gustin Hotel (411 Fifth Street, 95322; 854-2622) 17 rooms, complimentary breakfast. SGL/DBL$45-$52.

Hacienda Heights

Area Code 818

All-Star Inn (1154 South Seventy Avenue, 91754; 968-9462) 26 rooms. SGL/DBL$30-$40.

Courtyard by Marriott (1905 Azusa Avenue, 91745; 965-1700, Fax 965-1367) 162 rooms. SGL/DBL$75+.

Half Moon Bay

Area Code 415
Half Moon Bay Coastside Chamber of Commerce
225 South Cabrillo Highway
Half Moon Bay CA 94019
726-5202

Best Western Half Moon Bay Lodge (2400 South Cabrillo Highway, 94019; 726-9000, Fax 726-7951, 800-528-1234) 82 rooms, restaurant, heated swimming pool, spa, meeting facilities, children under 12 free, fax service, golf, wheelchair access, no-smoking rooms. SGL$86-$108, DBL$98-$120.

Hamburg

Area Code 916

Rainbow Resort (3590 Highway 96, 96045; 496-3242) 4 cabins. SGL/DBL$58-$87.

Steelhead Lodge (36309 Highway 96, 96045; 496-3256) 3 rooms. SGL/DBL$45-$55.

Happy Camp

Area Code 916

Anglers Motel (61700 Highway 96, 96039; 493-5425) 15 rooms and efficiencies. SGL/DBL$38-$42.

Forest Lodge (63712 Highway 96, 96039; 493-5424) 15 rooms. SGL/DBL$36-$56.

Rustic Inn Motel (64105 Hillside Rd., 96039; 493-2658) 14 rooms and apartments, airport courtesy car. SGL/DBL$66.

Harbor City

Area Code 213
Harbor City Chamber of Commerce
Box 525
Harbor City CA 90710
212-6300

Motel 6 (820 West Sepulveda Blvd., 90710; 549-9560, 505-891-6161) 57 rooms. SGL/DBL$35-$45.

Pleasant Holiday Motel (1440 West Pacific Coast Highway, 90710; 326-3400) 31 rooms and suites, complimentary breakfast, in-room refrigerators and microwaves, kitchenettes, wheelchair access, no-smoking rooms, free parking. SGL/DBL$35-$100.

TraveLodge (1665 West Pacific Coast Highway, 90710; 326-9026, Fax 530-3546, 800-255-3050) 33 rooms, restaurant, lounge, complimentary breakfast, laundry room, valet laundry, pets allowed, wheelchair access. SGL/DBL$44-$49.

Hawthorne

Area Code 213
Hawthorne Chamber of Commerce
12427 Hawthorne Blvd.
Hawthorne CA 90250
676-1163

The Cockatoo Inn (4334 West Imperial Highway, 90250; 679-2291, 800-262-5286, 800-458-2800) 207 rooms, restaurant, complimentary breakfast, swimming pool, airport courtesy car, free parking. SGL/DBL$45-$55.

Ramada Inn (5250 Segundo Blvd., 90250; 536-9800, Fax 536-9535, 800-2-RAMADA) 209 rooms, restaurant, lounge, swimming pool, transportation to local attractions, wheelchair access, no-smoking rooms, free parking. SGL$79-$99, DBL$89-$119.

Hayward

Area Code 510
Hayward Chamber of Commerce
22300 Foothill Blvd.
Hayward CA 94541
537-2424

All Star Inn (30155 Industrial Parkway South, 94544; 489-8333) 26 rooms. SGL/DBL$27-$32.

Best Western Inn (360 West A Street, 94541; 785-8700, 800-367-BEST, 800-528-1234) 91 rooms, restaurant, complimentary breakfast, swimming pool, sauna, kitchenettes, free local telephone calls, exercise equipment, wheelchair access, no-smoking rooms, no pets. SGL$52-$57, DBL$57-$73.

Comfort Inn (24997 Mission Blvd., 94544; 538-4466, Fax 581-8029, 800-221-2222) 62 rooms, restaurant, complimentary breakfast, sauna, kitchenettes, wheelchair access, no pets. SGL/DBL$46-$75.

Executive Inn (20777 Hesperian Blvd., 94541; 732-6300, Fax 783-2265, 800-553-5083) 150 rooms and suites, complimentary breakfast, swimming pool, airport courtesy car, exercise equipment, wheelchair access, no-smoking rooms, pets allowed. SGL$60-$85, DBL$75-$85, STS$65-$90.

Heritage Inn (410 West A Street, 94541; 785-0260) 33 rooms, no pets. SGL/DBL$49-$59.

Super 8 Motel (2460 Whipple Rd., 94544; 415-489-3888, Fax 415-489-4070, 800-800-8000) 77 rooms, restaurant, complimentary breakfast, free local telephone calls, fax service, in-room microwaves, wheelchair access, no-smoking rooms, no pets. SGL/DBL$38-$45.

TraveLodge (21598 Foothill Blvd., 94541; 538-4380, Fax 889-0728, 800-255-3050) 72 rooms, restaurant, swimming pool, laundry room, tennis, meeting facilities. SGL/DBL$38-$42.

Vagabond Inn (20455 Hesperian Blvd., 94541; 785-5480, Fax 785-9142, 800-522-1555) 100 rooms and suites, restaurant, complimentary breakfast, swimming pool, meeting facilities, wheelchair access, pets allowed, airport transportation, free local telephone calls, no-smoking rooms, children under 18 free, fax service, complimentary newspaper. SGL$50-$53, DBL$55-$63.

Healdsburg

Area Code 707
Healdsburg Chamber of Commerce
217 Healdsburg Avenue
Healdsburg CA 95448
433-6935

RENTAL SOURCES: Aggie's Wine Country Homes (Box 1698, 95448; 415-695-0361, 800-729-8069) two-bedroom home and cottage rentals in the Sonoma area. SGL/DBL$350W-$900W.

Belle De Jour Inn (16276 Healdsburg Avenue, 95448; 707-433-7892) 4 rooms and cottages, complimentary breakfast, no smoking. SGL/DBL$115-$165.

Best Western Dry Creek Inn (198 Dry Creek Rd., 95448; 707-433-0300, Fax 707-433-1129, 800-222-5784, 800-528-1234) 104 rooms, restaurant, complimentary breakfast, swimming pool, spa, children under 12 free, whirlpools, wheelchair access, no-smoking rooms, pets allowed. SGL/DBL$55-$70.

Camellia Inn Bed and Breakfast (211 North Street, 95448; 707-433-8182) 9 rooms, bed & breakfast, complimentary breakfast, whirlpool tubs, fireplaces, swimming pool, handicapped access. SGL/DBL$65-$115.

Dry Creek Inn (198 Dry Creek Rd., 95448; 433-0300, 800-222-5784) 28 rooms. SGL/DBL$45-$80.

Fairview Motel (74 Healdsburg Avenue, 95448; 707-433-5548) 32 rooms, complimentary breakfast. SGL/DBL$40-$50.

Frampton House (489 Powell Avenue, 95448; 707-433-5084) Victorian hotel, 3 rooms, complimentary breakfast, swimming pool. SGL/DBL$70-$85.

Grape Leaf Inn (539 Johnson Street, 95448; 707-433-8140) 7 rooms, bed & breakfast, complimentary breakfast, private baths, whirlpool tubs, no smoking. SGL/DBL$80-$125.

The Haydon House (321 Haydon Street, 95448; 707-433-5228) 6 rooms and cottages, bed & breakfast, complimentary breakfast, wheelchair access, no-smoking. SGL/DBL$75-$135.

Healdsburg Inn On The Plaza (116 Matheson Street, 95448; 707-433-6991) 9 rooms, bed & breakfast, complimentary breakfast, private baths. SGL/DBL$65-$145.

Inn On The Plaza (116 Matheson Street, 95448; 433-6991) 9 rooms, bed & breakfast, complimentary breakfast, no-smoking. SGL/DBL$84-$145

Madrona Manor (Box 818, 95448; 707-433-4231) 21 rooms and cottages, bed & breakfast, restaurant, complimentary breakfast, swimming pool, wheelchair access, no-smoking rooms. SGL/DBL$125-$190.

Raford House (10630 Wohler Rd., 95448; 707-887-9573) 5 rooms, bed & breakfast, complimentary breakfast, no pets. SGL/DBL$55-$84.

Vineyard Valley Inn (178 Dry Creek Rd., 95448; 433-0101, 800-499-0103 in California) 25 rooms and suites, restaurant, complimentary breakfast. SGL/DBL$80-$110.

Homewood

Area Code 707

Granlibakken (Granlibakken Rd., 96145) 36 one- and two-bedroom condos, complimentary breakfast, swimming pool, tennis. SGL/DBL$80+.

Grubstake Lodge (5335 West Lake Blvd., 96141; 585-5505) 36 rooms and efficiencies. SGL/DBL$40+.

Homeside Motel (5205 West Lake Blvd., 96141; 525-9990) 18 rooms and cabins. SGL/DBL$50+.

Homewood Marina Lodge (5180 West Lake Lodge, 96141; 525-5505) 28 rooms and efficiencies. SGL/DBL$50.

River Run (135 Alpine Meadows Rd., 96145; 583-0137) 36 condos. SGL/DBL$70+.

Rockwood Lodge (5295 West Lake Blvd., 96141; 525-5273) 6 rooms, bed & breakfast, complimentary breakfast. SGL/DBL$100+.

Sunnyside Lodge (1850 West Lake Blvd., 96141; 583-7200) 23 rooms, restaurant, marina. SGL/DBL$75+.

Tahoe Lake Cottages (7030 West Lake Blvd., 96141) one- and two-bedroom cottages, pets allowed. SGL/DBL$55+.

Hoopa

Area Code 916

Best Western Tsewenaldin Inn (Highway 96, 95546; 916-625-4294, 800-528-1234) 22 rooms, restaurant, lounge, heated swimming pool, water view, children under 12 free, no-smoking rooms, no pets. SGL$35-$60, DBL$40-$95.

Hopland

Area Code 707
Hopland Chamber of Commerce
Box 509
Hopland CA 95449
744-1047

Thatcher Inn (13401 South Highway 101, 95449; 744-1890, Fax 744-1219) 20 rooms, bed & breakfast, complimentary breakfast, private baths, restaurant, swimming pool, free parking. SGL/DBL$75-$125.

Inverness

Area Code 415

Blackthorne Inn (Box 712, 94937; 663-8621) 5 rooms, bed & breakfast, complimentary breakfast, no-smoking rooms. SGL/DBL$95-$175.

Golden Hinde Inn and Marina (12938 Sir Francis Drake, 94937; 669-1389, 800-339-9398 in California) 35 rooms and efficiencies, restaurant, lounge, swimming pool, kitchenettes. SGL/DBL$69-$125.

Ten Inverness Way (Box 63, 94937; 669-1648) 3 rooms, bed & breakfast, complimentary breakfast, no-smoking. SGL/DBL$90-$100.

Ione

Area Code 209

The Heirloom (Box 322, 95640; 274-4468) 6 rooms, bed & breakfast, complimentary breakfast. SGL/DBL$85-$95.

Isleton

Area Code 916
Isleton Chamber of Commerce
Box 758
Isleton CA 95641
777-6503

Delta Daze Inn (Box 607, 95641; 777-7777) 12 rooms, bed & breakfast, complimentary breakfast. SGL$55, DBL$65.

Isthmus Cove

Area Code 213

Banning House Lodge (Box 50441, 90704; 510-0303) 11 rooms, bed & breakfast, complimentary breakfast, restaurant, airport transportation. SGL/DBL$65.

Jackson

Area Code 209
Amador County Chamber of Commerce
30 South Highway 49
Jackson CA 95642
223-0350

Best Western Inn (200 Highway 49, 95642; 223-0211, Fax 223-4836, 800-528-1234) 119 rooms, restaurant, lounge, swimming pool, kitchenettes, children under 12 free, fax service, meeting facilities, wheelchair access, no-smoking rooms, pets allowed. SGL$46-$72, DBL$60-$84.

The Gatehouse Inn (1330 Jackson Gate Rd., 95642; 223-3500) 5 rooms and suites, bed & breakfast, complimentary breakfast, swimming pool, no-smoking rooms. SGL/DBL$75-$105, STS$105+.

Jackson Holiday Lodge (850 Highway 49 North; 223-0486) 36 rooms swimming pool, no-smoking rooms, pets allowed. SGL$35-$50, DBL$40-$55.

Wedgewood Inn (11941 Narcissus Rd., 95642; 296-4300, 800-WEDGE-WD) 6 rooms, bed & breakfast, complimentary breakfast, free local telephone calls, no smoking, free parking, no pets. SGL/DBL$80-$110.

Jamestown

Area Code 209

Jamestown Hotel (Box 539, 95327; 984-3902) 8 rooms, restaurant, complimentary breakfast. SGL/DBL$55-$85.

National Hotel (Box 502, 95327; 984-3446) 11 rooms, restaurant, complimentary breakfast, airport courtesy car, pets allowed. SGL/DBL$65-$75.

Royal Hotel (Box 219, 95327; 984-5271) 19 rooms, bed & breakfast, complimentary breakfast. SGL/DBL$45+.

Sheets n'Eggs (Box 657, 95327; 984-0915) 3 rooms, bed & breakfast, complimentary breakfast. SGL$65, DBL$75.

Jenner

Area Code 707

Fort Ross Lodge (20705 Coast Highway One, 95450; 847-3333) 22 rooms, fireplaces, hot tubs, in-room refrigerators, ocean view. SGL/DBL$60-$175.

Murphy's Jenner Inn (Box 69, 95450; 865-2377, 800-732-2377) 11 rooms, bed & breakfast, complimentary breakfast, fireplaces, beach. SGL/DBL$65-$150.

Stillwater Cove Ranch (225555 Coast Highway One, 95450; 847-3227) 18 rooms and efficiencies. SGL/DBL$37-$70.

Timber Cove Inn (21780 North Coast Highway, 95450; 847-3231) 49 rooms, restaurant. SGL/DBL$45-$65.

June Lake

Area Code 619
June Lake-Loop Chamber of Commerce
Box 2
June Lake CA 93529
648-7584

Boulder Lodge (Box 68, 93529; 648-7533, Fax 648-7330) 32 rooms, suites and cottages, swimming pool, tennis, no-smoking rooms. SGL/DBL$50-$70, STS$80-$220.

Gull Lake Lodge (Box 25, 93529; 648-7516, 800-631-9081 in California) 14 rooms and efficiencies, pets allowed. SGL/DBL$53-$100.

June Lake (Box 98, 93529; 648-7547, 800-648-6835 in California) 20 rooms and cabins, restaurant, pets allowed. SGL/DBL$55.

Kelseyville

Area Code 707

Konocti Harbor Inn and Spa (8727 Soda Bay Rd., 95451; 279-4281, Fax 279-9205, 800-862-4930) 250 rooms, restaurant, swimming pool, sauna, spa, exercise equipment, tennis, child care, meeting facilities, airport transportation, wheelchair access, free parking. SGL/DBL$55-$175.

Soda Bay Inn (3397 Live Oak Lane, 95451; 279-4722, 800-924-7632 in California) 26 efficiencies, boat dock, beach. SGL/DBL$65-$75.

Kenwood

Area Code 707

Kenwood Inn (10400 Sonoma Highway; 833-1293) 5 rooms. SGL/DBL$53-$125.

Kings Beach

Area Code 707

RENTAL SOURCES: Scenic Properties (Box 1558, 96143; 546-3454) rental condos and homes. SGL/DBL$50-$300. **Brockway Springs** (101 Chipmunk Ave., 96143; 546-4210) rental one- to four-bedroom condominiums. SGL/DBL$115.

Blue Vue Lodge (8755 North Lake Blvd., 96143; 546-4833) 30 rooms, restaurant. SGL/DBL$40+.

Crown Motel (8200 North Lake Blvd., 96143; 546-3388) 26 rooms. SGL/DBL$40+.

Falcon Lodge (8258 North Lake Blvd., 96143; 546-2583) 45 rooms, restaurant, wheelchair access, in-room refrigerators. SGL/DBL$30+.

Goldcrest Motel (8194 North Lake Blvd., 96143; 546-3302) 22 rooms. SGL/DBL$43+.

Lake Air Motel (265 Beat Street, 96143; 546-2711) 16 rooms, no pets. SGL/DBL$40+.

North Lake Lodge (8716 North Lake Blvd., 96143; 546-2731) 36 rooms, pets allowed. SGL/DBL$35..

Penny's By The Bay (8141 North Lake Blvd., 96143; 546-2446) 16 rooms, pets allowed. SGL/DBL$42.

Stevenson's Holiday Inn (8742 North Lake Blvd., 96143; 546-2269) 45 rooms. SGL/DBL$40+.

Ta-Tel Lodge (8748 North Lake Blvd., 96143; 546-2411) 18 rooms. SGL/DBLS40+.

Kings Canyon National Park

Area Code 209

Montecito-Sequoia Lodge (Box 858, 93633; 565-3388) 30 rooms, bed & breakfast, complimentary breakfast, swimming pool, skiing. SGL/DBL$65-$85.

Kirkwood

Area Code 209

The Meadows At Kirkwood (1120 Kirkwood Meadows Drive, 95646; 258-7000, Fax 258-7400) 30 apartments, restaurant, lounge, spa, meeting facilities, child care, tennis, wheelchair access, no-smoking rooms. SGL/DBL$60-$250.

Klamath and Klamath River

Area Code 707
Klamath River Chamber of Commerce
Box 750
Klamath CA 96050
465-2224

Camp Marigold Motel (16101 Highway 101, 95548; 482-3585) 16 rooms and cottages. SGL/DBL$32-$55.

Motel Trees (15495 Highway 101, 95548; 848-2982) 23 rooms, restaurant. SGL/DBL$36+.

Requa Inn (451 Requa Rd., 95548; 482-8205) 10 rooms, bed & breakfast, complimentary breakfast, no-smoking. SGL/DBL$50-$75.

Trees Motel (Box 309, 95548; 482-3152, Fax 482-2005) 25 rooms, restaurant, tennis. SGL/DBL$34-$50.

Kneeland

Area Code 707

Chalet de France Wilderness Retreat (443-6512) 8 rooms, bed & breakfast, complimentary breakfast, no-smoking. SGL$65, DBL$75.

Lafayette

Area Code 510
Lafayette Chamber of Commerce
1003 Oak Hill Rd.
Lafayette CA 94549
284-7404

Best Western Inn Lafayette Park (3287 Mount Diablo Blvd., 94549; 283-3700, Fax 284-1621, 800-528-1234) 139 rooms and suites, restaurant, lounge, swimming pool, meeting facilities, fireplaces, airport transportation, exercise equipment, fax service. SGL/DBL$130-$150, STS$250.

Lakeport

Area Code 707
Lake County Chamber of Commerce
875 Lakeport Blvd.
Lakeport CA 95453
263-6131

Anchorage Inn (950 Main Street, 95453; 263-5417) 34 rooms, restaurant, swimming pool, airport courtesy car. SGL$35, DBL$45+.

Cove Resort Motel (2812 Lakeshore Blvd., 95453; 263-6833) 30 efficiencies, boat dock. SGL/DBL$45+.

Forbestown (825 Forbes Street, 95453; 263-7858) 4 rooms, bed & breakfast, complimentary breakfast, swimming pool. SGL/DBL$76-$100.

Rainbow Lodge Motel (2599 Lakeshore Blvd., 95453; 263-4309) 18 rooms and efficiencies. SGL/DBL$45-$65.

Skylark Motel-Resort (1120 North Main Street, 95453; 263-6151, Fax 263-7733) 45 rooms and efficiencies, swimming pool, wheelchair access, free parking. SGL$50-$53, DBL$58-$70.

Starlight Motel (5960 Highway 20, 95458, 274-5515) 24 efficiencies, swimming pool. SGL/DBL$45-$53.

Lakeshore

Area Code 209

Lakeshore Resort (61953 Huntington Lake Rd., 93534; 893-3193) 32 rooms, restaurant, lounge, child care. SGL$50-$60, DBL$75-$115.

Lake Tahoe and South Lake Tahoe

(See also Tahoe City)

Area Code 916
Lake Tahoe Visitors Authority
3050 Highway 50
Lake Tahoe CA 95706
544-5050

RENTAL SERVICES: BRAT Realty Management (Box 7101, Incline Village NV, 89450; 702-831-3318, Fax 702-831-8668, 800-869-8308, 800-468-2463) rents condos, chalets and private, lakefront homes in the Lake Tahoe and Squaw Valley areas. SGL/DBL$90-$750. **ERA Tahoe Escape** (245 North Lake Blvd., 95730; 800-488-2177) represents 150 cabin, condo and home rentals. SGL/DBL$65+. **Lake Tahoe Accommodations** (2048 Dunlap Drive, 96150; 544-3234, 96156; 800-228-6921, 800-544-3234) rents condos, cabins and chalets in Heavenly Valley area. $400W-$2625W. **Lake Tahoe Reservations** (2235 Lake Tahoe Blvd., 96156; 544-7757, 800-562-4743).

Alder Inn (1072 Ski Run Blvd., 95729; 544-4485, Fax 544-8119, 800-544-0056 in California) 24 rooms, swimming pool, no-smoking rooms, pets allowed. SGL/DBL$50-$85+.

Bell Court Lodge (Box 4130, 96151; 541-5400) 121 rooms and efficiencies, restaurant, swimming pool, pets allowed. SGL/DBL$65-$85.

Best Western Lake Tahoe Inn (4110 Lake Tahoe Blvd., 96150; 541-2010, Fax 542-1428, 800-528-1234) 400 rooms, restaurant, lounge, two swimming pools, hot tubs, transportation to local attractions, meeting facilities, no-smoking rooms, no pets. SGL/DBL$54-$99.

Best Western Station House Inn (901 Park Avenue, 96157; 542-1101, Fax 542-1714, 800-822-5953, 800-528-1234) 100 rooms, restaurant, lounge, complimentary breakfast, heated swimming pool, spa, whirlpool, meeting facilities, transportation to local attractions, no-smoking rooms, no pets. SGL/DBL$78-$98.

Best Western Timber Cove Lodge (3411 Lake Tahoe Blvd., 96150; 541-6722, Fax 541-7959, 800-528-1234) 262 rooms, restaurant, lounge, swimming pool, hot tub, meeting facilities, fax service, no-smoking rooms, no pets. LS SGL/DBL$54-$64; HS SGL/DBL$99-$109.

Beverly Lodge (3480 Lake Tahoe Blvd., 96150; 544-2857) 30 rooms, swimming pool. SGL/DBL$150+.

Blue Jay Lodge (Box 6320, 96151; 544-5232, 800-258-3529) 65 rooms and efficiencies, restaurant, swimming pool. SGL/DBL$38-$80.

Capri Motel (Box 4276, 96151; 544-3665) 25 rooms, restaurant, swimming pool. SGL/DBL$39-$86.
Cedar Lodge (4069 Cedar Avenue, 95729; 544-6453) 35 rooms, swimming pool, no-smoking rooms. SGL/DBL$40-$90.

Chamonix Inn (Box 5274, 96157; 544-5274, 800-447-5353) 32 rooms, restaurant, outdoor heated swimming pool, spa, free local telephone calls, fax service, airport transportation, free parking, wheelchair access, no-smoking rooms, pets allowed. SGL$38, DBL$55.

Embassy Suites (4130 Lake Tahoe Blvd., 95729; 544-5400, Fax 544-4900, 800-362-2779) 400 suites, restaurant and deli, swimming pool, concierge, wheelchair access, meeting facilities for 400, room service. SGL/DBL$100-$140.

Fantasy Inn (924 Park Avenue, 96151; 544-6767, 800-441-6610) 24 rooms, restaurant. SGL/DBL$78-$128.

Flamingo Lodge (3961 Lake Tahoe Blvd., 96150; 544-5288, 800-822-5922 in California) 90 rooms and suites, restaurant, swimming pool, wheelchair access, no-smoking rooms. SGL/DBL$65-$85, STS$115+.

Forest Inn (1101 Park Avenue, 95729; 541-6655, 800-822-5950) 124 rooms and one- and two-bedroom suites, two outdoor heated swimming pools, jacuzzi, spa, in-room refrigerators, free local telephone calls, laundry room, free parking, exercise equipment, wheelchair access, no-smoking rooms, no pets. SGL/DBL$59-$79, 1BR$97, 2BR$110.

Highland Inn (Box 4098, 96157; 544-3862) 30 rooms, restaurant, swimming pool, pets allowed. SGL/DBL$35+.

Inn By The Lake (3300 Lake Tahoe Blvd., 96150; 542-0330, Fax 541-6596, 800-777-1700) 100 rooms and efficiencies, complimentary breakfast, restaurant, swimming pool, child care, kitchenettes. SGL/DBL$98-$330+.

Lakeland Village Beach and Ski Resort (3535 Highway 50, 96156; 544-1686, Fax 541-6278, 800-822-5969) one- to four-bedroom townhouses, restaurant, complimentary breakfast, swimming pool, wheelchair access, no-smoking rooms. 1BR$135+, 2BR$185+.

Lamplighter Motel (Box 4057, 96157; 544-2936) 28 rooms, restaurant, pets allowed. SGL/DBL$35-$80.

The Matterhorn (2187 Lake Tahoe Blvd., 95731; 541-0367) 18 rooms and efficiencies, swimming pool, airport courtesy car, pets allowed. SGL/DBL$38-$58, EFF$48-$68.

Montgomery Inn (Box 18245, 96151; 542-2583, 800-624-8224) 24 rooms and efficiencies, restaurant, complimentary breakfast, swimming pool, airport transportation, wheelchair access, no-smoking rooms, pets allowed. SGL/DBL$25-$70.

Motel 6 (2375 Lake Tahoe Blvd., 96150; 542-1400) 140 rooms. SGL/DBL$30-$36.

Pacifica Lodge (931 Park Avenue, 95729; 544-4131) 67 rooms and suites, complimentary breakfast, swimming pool, no-smoking rooms. SGL/DBL$65-$80, STS$90-$150.

Pinewood Lodge (Box 4099, 96151; 544-3319) 28 rooms, swimming pool. SGL/DBL$32-$80.

Royal Valhalla Motor Lodge (4101 Lakeshore Blvd., 96157; 544-2233, Fax 544-1436, 800-999-4104) 80 rooms and efficiencies, complimentary breakfast, swimming pool, wheelchair access, no-smoking rooms. SGL/DBL$70-$90, EFF$70-$200.

South Shore Inn (3900 Pioneer Trail, 95729; 544-1000) 22 rooms, no-smoking rooms. SGL/DBL$50-$85.

Sun N'Ski Lodge (3530 Lake Tahoe Blvd., 96150; 544-3445) 44 rooms, restaurant, swimming pool. SGL/DBL$30-$80.

Tahoe Beach and Ski Club (3601 Lake Tahoe Blvd., 96150; 541-6220) 145 rooms and efficiencies, restaurant, swimming pool. SGL/DBL$70-$80.

Tahoe Chalet Inn (3860 Lake Tahoe Blvd., 96150; 544-3311, 800-821-2656) 66 rooms and efficiencies, complimentary breakfast, airport transportation, swimming pool, wheelchair access, no-smoking rooms. SGL/DBL$40-$200.

Tahoe Sands Inn (3600 Highway 50, 96151; 544-3476, Fax 542-4011, 800-237-8882) 110 rooms and suites, restaurant, swimming pool, no-smoking rooms, pets allowed. SGL/DBL$60-$70, STS$85-$190.

Tahoe Seasons Resort (Box 5656, 96157; 541-6010) 160 rooms, restaurant, swimming pool, airport transportation, tennis, wheelchair access, no-smoking rooms. SGL/DBL$95-$130+.

Tahoe Valley Motel (Box 2241, 96151; 541-0353, 800-669-7544) 21 rooms and efficiencies, restaurant, swimming pool, airport courtesy car, pets allowed. SGL/DBL$85.

Tahoe Villa (933 Poplar, 96157; 544-3041) 37 rooms. SGL/DBL$30-$80.

Timber Touch Lodge (3536 Lake Tahoe Blvd., 96151; 544-2036) 37 rooms, restaurant, swimming pool. SGL/DBL$30-$80+.

Torchlite Inn (Box 4335, 96151; 541-2363, 800-852-2363) 33 rooms, swimming pool, pets allowed. SGL/DBL$32-$48.

TraveLodge (3489 Lake Tahoe Blvd., 96156; 544-5266, Fax 544-6985, 800-255-3050) 59 rooms and suites, restaurant, lounge, swimming pool, transportation to local attractions, no pets. LS SGL/DBL$55-$86; HS SGL/DBL$92-$108.

TraveLodge (4003 Lake Tahoe Blvd., 96157; 541-5000, Fax 544-6910, 800-255-3050) 66 rooms and suites, restaurant, lounge, swimming pool, transportation to local attractions, no pets. LS SGL/DBL$55-$86; HS SGL/DBL$92-$108.

TraveLodge (4011 Lake Tahoe Blvd., 96157; 544-6000, Fax 544-6869, 800-255-3050) 50 rooms and suites, restaurant, lounge, swimming pool, no pets. LS SGL/DBL$55-$86; HS SGL/DBL$92-$108.

TraveLodge (455 North Lake Blvd., 95730; 583-3766, Fax 583-8045, 800-255-3050) 47 rooms, restaurant, swimming pool, whirlpool, no pets. LS SGL/DBL$44-$64; MS SGL/DBL$67-$93; HS SGL/DBL$94-$114.

Value Inn (2659 Lake Tahoe Blvd., 96150; 544-3959) 62 rooms, restaurant, pets allowed. SGL/DBL$30-$40.

La Palma

Area Code 714
La Palma Chamber of Commerce
Box 52777
La Palma CA 90622, 527-2621

Best Western (3 Centerpointe Drive, 90623; 670-1400, Fax 522-4698, 800-325-2525) 161 rooms, restaurant, swimming pool, wheelchair access, no-smoking rooms. SGL$49-$79, DBL$59-$85.

Days Inn (3 Centerpointe Drive, 90623; 948-4651, Fax 522-4698, 800-325-2525) 160 rooms and suites, restaurant, lounge, swimming pool, spa, transportation to local attractions, tours, children under 12 free, fax service, gift shop, exercise equipment. SGL/DBL$69-$89.

Larkspur

Area Code 415

Courtyard by Marriott (2500 Larkspur Landing Circle, 94939; 925-1800, Fax 925-1107) 146 rooms, restaurant, swimming pool, exercise equipment, wheelchair access, no-smoking rooms. SGL/DBL$88-$98.

La Selva Beach

Area Code 408

Manresa Lodge (1535 San Andreas Rd., 95076; 688-5047) 5 rooms, efficiencies and suites, free parking, no pets, beach. LS SGL/DBL$42-$72; HS SGL/DBL$46-$72.

Lee Vining

Area Code 619
Lee Vining Chamber of Commerce
Box 100
Lee Vining CA 93541
387-2723

Best Western Lake View Lodge (30 Main Street, 93541; 647-6543, Fax 647-6325, 800-528-1234) 47 rooms, restaurant, lounge, fax service, laundry room, no pets. LS SGL/DBL$63-$73; HS SGL/DBL$65-$75.

Gateway (Highway 396, 93541; 647-6467) 12 rooms, restaurant, no-smoking rooms. SGL/DBL$45-$75.

Little River

Area Code 707

Glendeven (8221 North Highway One, 95456; 937-0083) 10 rooms and suites, bed & breakfast, complimentary breakfast. SGL/DBL$75-$150.

Heritage House (5200 North Highway One, 95456; 937-5885) 74 rooms, restaurant. SGL/DBL$125-$335.

The Inn At Schoolhouse Creek (7051 North Highway One, 95465; 937-5525) 12 rooms, restaurant. SGL/DBL$50-$100.

Little River Inn (7751 North Highway One, 95456; 937-5942) 56 rooms, restaurant, lounge, meeting facilities, lighted tennis courts, golf, wheelchair access, free parking. SGL$75-$135, DBL$85-$235.

Rachel's Inn (8200 North Highway One, 95456; 937-0088) 8 rooms, bed & breakfast-inn, complimentary breakfast, beach, handicapped access. SGL/DBL$76-$125+.

The Victorian Farmhouse (7001 North Highway One, 95456; 937-0697) 10 rooms, bed & breakfast, complimentary breakfast. SGL/DBL$80-$100.

Livermore

Area Code 510
Livermore Chamber of Commerce
2157 First Street

Livermore CA 94550
447-1606

All-Star Inn (4673 Lassen Rd., 94550; 443-5300) 36 rooms, swimming pool, no pets. SGL/DBL$25-$35.

Holiday Inn (720 Las Flores Rd., 94550; 443-4950, Fax 449-9059, 800-HOLIDAY) 127 rooms, restaurant, swimming pool, meeting facilities for 225, children under 18 free, no-smoking rooms, pets allowed. SGL/DBL$55-$70.

Marriott Residence Inn (1000 Airway Blvd., 94550; 373-1800, Fax 373-7252, 800-331-3131) 86 rooms and suites, swimming pool, sauna, exercise equipment, meeting facilities for 60, in-room microwaves, whirlpool, no-smoking rooms. SGL/DBL$85-$105.

Springtown Motel (933 Bluebell Drive, 94550; 449-2211) 127 rooms, swimming pool, wheelchair access, no-smoking rooms, pets allowed. SGL/DBL$30-$45.

Lodi

Area Code 209
Lodi District Chamber of Commerce
215 West Oak Street
Lodi CA 95241
334-4773

Best Western Royal Host Inn (710 South Cherokee Lane, 95240; 369-8484, Fax 369-0654, 800-528-1234) 48 rooms, restaurant, lounge, swimming pool, fax service, children under 12 free, no pets. SGL$46-$56, DBL$51-$93.

Lodi Motor Inn (1140 South Cherokee Lane, 95240; 334-6422, Fax 368-7967) 95 rooms, complimentary breakfast, swimming pool, sauna, spa, meeting facilities, laundry room, exercise equipment, wheelchair access, no-smoking rooms. SGL/DBL$50-$55.

Wine and Roses Country Inn (2505 West Turner Rd., 95242; 334-6988) 9 rooms, bed & breakfast, complimentary breakfast, restaurant, lounge, wheelchair access, no-smoking rooms. SGL$70+, DBL$85-$105.

Los Gatos

Area Code 408
Los Gatos Chamber of Commerce
1628 West Campbell Avenue
Los Gatos CA 95030
378-6252

Courtside Tennis Club (14675 Winchester Blvd., 95030; 395-7111, Fax 354-5854) 20 rooms, restaurant, complimentary breakfast, swimming pool, tennis, exercise equipment, no-smoking rooms. SGL$85-$95, DBL$95-$105.

The Garden Inn Of Los Gatos (46 East Minst Street, 95030; 354-6446l) 28 rooms and efficiencies, restaurant, complimentary breakfast, swimming pool, exercise equipment. SGL/DBL$55-$65, EFF$110-$130.

La Hacienda Inn (18840 Saratoga Rd.; 354-9230, Fax 354-7590) 21 rooms and efficiencies, restaurant, complimentary breakfast, swimming pool. SGL$75-$115, DBL$85-$120.

The Lodge At Villa Felice (15350 Winchester Blvd., 95030; 395-6710, Fax 354-1826, 800-662-9229) 33 rooms and suites, restaurant, complimentary breakfast, swimming pool, wheelchair access, no-smoking rooms. SGL$95-$115, DBL$105-$130, STS$130-$220.

Los Gatos Lodge (50 Saratoga Avenue, 95032; 408-354-3300, Fax 354-5451) 125 rooms and suites, restaurant, complimentary breakfast, swimming pool, airport transportation, exercise equipment, pets allowed, no-smoking rooms. SGL/DBL$60-$70.

Los Gatos Motor Inn (55 Saratoga Avenue, 95030; 356-9191, Fax 356-7502, 800-642-7889) 60 rooms, restaurant, complimentary breakfast, wheelchair access, no-smoking rooms. SGL/DBL$60-$70.

Toll House Motel (140 South Santa Cruz Avenue, 95030; 395-7070, 800-238-6111, 800-821-5518 in California) 98 rooms, restaurant, complimentary breakfast, airport transportation, exercise equipment, wheelchair access, no-smoking rooms. SGL$90-$95, DBL$95-$199+.

Villa Felice Lodge (15350 Winchester Blvd., 95030; 395-6710) 33 rooms, restaurant. SGL$88, DBL$98.

Loyalton

Area Code 707

Clover Valley Mill House (Railroad Avenue, 96118; 993-4819) 6 rooms, bed & breakfast, complimentary breakfast, no pets. SGL/DBL$35-$45.

Country Cookin' Inn (Box 356, 96118; 993-1162) 3 rooms, bed & breakfast, restaurant. SGL/DBL$43-$46.

Golden West Saloon (Box 216, 96118; 993-4467) 14 rooms. SGL$31, DBL$38-$48.

Mammoth Lakes

Area Code 619
Mammoth Lakes Resort Association
Box 48
Mammoth Lakes CA 93546
934-2712

RENTAL SOURCES (All of the following rent condos and private homes in the Mammoth Lakes area): **Mammoth Reservations** (800-MAMMOTH); **All Seasons Reservations** (934-8593, 800-634-2828) $75-$105; **Mammoth Accommodations Center** (934-6262, 800-358-6262 in California) $36-$85; **Mammoth Lakes Accommodations** (934-3931, 800-843-6285) $50-$110; **Mammoth Lodging Connection** (934-5254, 800-468-6386) $70-$120; **Mammoth Properties Reservations** (934-4242, 800-227-7669) $60-$150; **Mammoth Reservation Bureau** (934-2528, 800-527-6273) $30-$135; **Mammoth Sierra Reservations** (800-325-8415) $50-$300; **Mammoth-Summitt Accommodations** (934-7062, Fax 934-2319); **Summit Accommodations** (934-7062, 800-262-7062 in California) $43-$115; **Sun Mountain Management** (934-3111, 800-468-5364 in Southern California) $80-$120.

A. Lee Inn (1548 Cavern Rd., 93546; 934-6709, 800-4-LEEINN) 36 rooms, swimming pool, children under 12 free, free parking, no smoking, no pets. SGL$29, DBL$34.

Alpenhof Lodge (Box 1157, 93546; 934-6330, 800-828-0371 in California) 66 rooms and efficiencies, swimming pool. SGL/DBL$51-$90.

Alpine Lodge (5209 Minaret Street, 93546; 934-8526, Fax 934-1911) 62 rooms and efficiencies. SGL/DBL$48-$90.

Asgard Chalet (Box 7498, 93546; 962-6773) dormitory accommodations. SGL$12-$15.

Austria Hof (924 Canyon Blvd., 93546; 934-2764, 800-922-2966 in California) 24 rooms and suites, restaurant, wheelchair access, no-smoking rooms, pets allowed. SGL$30-$65, DBL$75-$100+.

Best Western Wildwood (Box 568, 93546; 934-6855, Fax 934-5165) 32 rooms, complimentary breakfast, swimming pool, pets allowed. SGL$60-$85, DBL$65-$95.

Canyon Ski and Racquet Condominiums (Box 7296, 93546; 934-4747) 120 one- and two-bedroom condos. SGL/DBL$80-$150.

Chamonix Condominiums (803 Canyon Blvd., 93546; 934-6729, 800-421-9799 in California) 62 apartments, swimming pool. SGL/DBL$50-$225.

Chateau de Montagne (Box 8433, 93546; 934-6374, 800-242-8330 in California) 56 rooms, swimming pool. SGL/DBL$75-$125.

Crestview Condominiums (Box 7178, 93546; 934-9552, 800-446-1100 in California) 64 one-, two- and three-bedroom condos, tennis. SGL/DBL$75-$110.

Crystal Crag Lodge (Box 88, 93546; 923-2436) 18 cabins. SGL/DBL$45-$150.

Discovery Four Condominiums (Box 112, 93546; 934-6410, 800-538-4751 in California) 43 one-bedroom condos, swimming pool. SGL/DBL$75-$100.

1849 Condominiums (Box 65, 93546; 934-7525, 800-421-1849 in Southern California) 154 one- and two-bedroom condos, swimming pool, tennis, airport courtesy car. SGL/DBL$70-$125.

Englehof Lodge (Box 111, 93546; 934-2416) 45 rooms and suites, complimentary breakfast, pets allowed. SGL/DBL$35-$80.

Horizons Four Condominiums (Box 611, 93546; 934-6779, 800-423-2388 in California) 120 one- and two-bedroom condos, swimming pool, tennis. SGL/DBL$70-$95.

Innsbruck Lodge (Box 6, 93546; 934-3035) dormitory accommodations. SGL$12-$55.

Jagerhof Lodge (Old Mammoth Rd., 93546; 934-6162) 28 rooms, restaurant, complimentary breakfast, no-smoking rooms. SGL/DBL$70-$135.

Krystal Villa East Condominiums (Box 222, 93546; 934-2669, 800-237-6181 in Southern California) 65 one-bedroom condos. SGL/DBL$45-$70.

Mammoth Estates Condominiums (221 Canyon Blvd., 93546; 934-2884, 800-228-2884) 78 one- , two- , three- and four-bedroom condos, kitchenettes, outdoor swimming pool, jacuzzi, fax service, two-night minimum, laundry room, no pets. 1BR$95, 2BR$145, 3BR$190, 4BR$220.

Mammoth Mountain Inn ((One Minaret Rd., 93546; 934-2581, Fax 934-7594, 800-228-4947) 214 rooms and suites, two restaurants, lounge, jacuzzi, children under 16 free, free parking, wheelchair access, no pets, airport courtesy car. SGL/DBL$69-$295.

North Village Inn (2300 Old Mammoth Rd., 93546; 934-2525, 800-257-3781 in California) 23 rooms and efficiencies, complimentary breakfast, pets allowed. SGL/DBL$42-$96.

Quality Inn (3537 Main Street, 93546; 934-5114, 800-221-2222, 800-874-4949 in California) 59 rooms, complimentary breakfast, wheelchair access, no-smoking rooms, no pets. SGL$60-$119, DBL$79-$129.

Seasons Four (Box 6, 93546; 934-2030, 800-732-7664) 200 one- and two-bedroom condos, outdoor swimming pool, laundry room, free parking, wheelchair access, no-smoking rooms, no pets. 1BR$55-$132, 2BR$99-$247.

Shilo Inn (2963 Main Street, 93546; 934-4500, 800-222-2244) 71 rooms and suites, restaurant, complimentary breakfast, swimming pool, airport courtesy car, lighted tennis courts, wheelchair access, pets allowed. LS SGL/DBL$69-$115, STS$79-$120; HS SGL/DBL$90-$140, STS$100-$150.

Sierra Nevada Inn (164 Old Mammoth Rd., 93546; 934-2515, Fax 934-7319, 800-824-5132 in California) 140 rooms and suites, restaurant, swimming pool, airport transportation, lighted tennis courts, wheelchair access. SGL/DBL$65-105.

Snow Goose Inn (57 Forest Trail, 93546; 934-2660, 800-874-7368) 20 rooms, bed & breakfast, restaurant, complimentary breakfast, airport courtesy car. SGL/DBL$75-$170.

TraveLodge (Minaret Rd., 93546; 934-8576, Fax 934-8007, 800-255-3050) 61 rooms, restaurant, lounge, swimming pool, whirlpool, in-room refrigerators, no pets. SGL/DBL$68-$108.

Viewpoint Condominiums (Box 41, 93546; 934-3132, 800-826-6680 in Southern California) 45 one- and two-bedroom condos. $43-$70.

Viking Inn (Route 113 Center, 93546; 934-2873, 800-845-2873) 10 rooms, complimentary breakfast, jacuzzi, free local telephone calls, fax service, free parking, wheelchair access, no smoking, no pets. SGL$39, DBL$89.

Manchester

Area Code 707

RENTAL SOURCES: Irish Beach Rental Agency (Box 337, 95459; 800-882-8007 in California) rental homes. $60-$197.

Manteca

Area Code 209
Manteca District Chamber of Commerce
166 North Maple Street
Manteca CA 95336
823-6121

Best Western Inn (1415 East Yosemite Avenue, 95336; 825-1415, Fax 825-4251, 800-MANTECA, 800-528-1234) 101 rooms, restaurant, lounge, swimming pool, jacuzzis, spa, meeting facilities, exercise equipment, wheelchair access, no-smoking rooms. LS SGL/DBL$50-$62; HS SGL/DBL$60-$72.

Mariposa

Area Code 209
Mariposa County Chamber of Commerce
5158 Highway 140
Mariposa CA 95338
966-2456

RENTAL SOURCES: The Guest House (4962 B Triangle Rd., 95338; 742-6869). **Yosemite Motels** (742-7106, 800-321-5261 in California) reservation service for hotels near Yosemite National Park. SGL/DBL$45-$55.

Best Western Yosemite Way Station (4999 Highway 140, 95338; 966-7545, 800-528-1234) 78 rooms, restaurant, complimentary breakfast, outdoor swimming pool, spa, free parking. SGL/DBL$76.

Boulder Creek Bed and Breakfast (4572 Ben Hur Rd., 95338; 742-7720) 11 rooms, bed & breakfast, complimentary breakfast. SGL/DBL$60-$70.

Canyon View Bed and Breakfast (7117 Snyder Ridge Rd., 95338; 742-6268) 4 rooms, bed & breakfast, complimentary breakfast. SGL/DBL$65-$85.

The Clubb's Bed and Breakfast (5060 Charles Street, 95338; 966-2532) 6 rooms, bed & breakfast, complimentary breakfast. SGL/DBL$45-$65.

Dick and Shirley's Bed and Breakfast (4870 Triangle Rd., 95338; 966-2514) 4 rooms, bed & breakfast, complimentary breakfast. SGL/DBL$60.

The Eagle's Nest (6308 Jerseydale Rd., 95338; 966-3737) 6 rooms, bed & breakfast, complimentary breakfast. SGL/DBL$55-$70.

Granny's Garden (7333 Highway 49 North, 95538; 377-8342) 11 rooms, bed & breakfast, complimentary breakfast. SGL/DBL$65-$75.

Mariposa Hotel and Inn (5029 Highway 140; 966-4676) 34 rooms. SGL/DBL$65-$95.

Mariposa Lodge (Highway 140, 95338; 966-3607, Fax 742-7038, 800-341-8000) 37 rooms, restaurant, swimming pool, airport courtesy car, wheelchair access, no-smoking rooms. LS SGL/DBL$35-$55; HS SGL/DBL$50-$75.

Meadow Creek Ranch (2669 Triangle Rd., 95338; 966-3843) 16 rooms, bed & breakfast, complimentary breakfast. SGL/DBL$75-$95.

Miners Inn (Box 246, 95338; 742-7777, Fax 966-2343, 800-237-7277 in California) 64 rooms, restaurant, swimming pool, wheelchair access, no-smoking rooms. SGL/DBL$30-$100.

Oak Meadows Too Bed and Breakfast (5263 Highway 140 North, 95338; 742-6161) 12 rooms, bed & breakfast, complimentary breakfast. SGL/DBL$59-$69.

The Schlageter House (5038 Bullion Street, 95338; 966-2471) 8 rooms, bed & breakfast, complimentary breakfast. SGL/DBL$65-$80.

Sierra View Suites Motel (4993 Seventh Street, 95338; 966-5793, 800-627-8439) 12 rooms and suites, complimentary breakfast, in-room refrigerators, free parking, no-smoking rooms, no pets. SGL$55-$68, DBL$55-$85.

Villa Monti (4990 Eighth Street, 95338; 966-2439) 2 rooms, bed & breakfast, complimentary breakfast. SGL/DBL$50-$70.

Winsor Farms Bed and Breakfast (5636 Whitlock Rd., 95338; 966-5592) 5 rooms, bed & breakfast, complimentary breakfast. SGL/DBL$50.

Yosemite Gold Rush Inn (4994 Bullion Street, 95338; 966-4344, Fax 742-7189, 800-321-5261) 61 rooms and suites, restaurant, complimentary breakfast, swimming pool, wheelchair access, free parking. SGL/DBL$60-$175.

Markleeville

Area Code 916
Alpine County Chamber of Commerce
Box 265
Markleeville CA 96120
694-2475

Woodfords Inn (Highway 89, 96120; 694-2410) 19 rooms, restaurant, complimentary breakfast, no-smoking rooms. SGL$37, DBL$42-$47.

Martinez

Area Code 415
Martinez Area Chamber of Commerce
620 Las Juntas
Martinez CA 94553
228-2345

Super 8 Motel (4015 Alhambra Avenue, 94553; 372-5500, Fax 228-8830, 800-800-8000) 29 rooms, wheelchair access, in-room refrigerators and microwaves, fax service, no-smoking rooms, no pets. SGL/DBL$45-$55.

Marysville

Area Code 916

Yuba-Sutter Chamber of Commerce
10th and E Streets
Marysville CA 95901
743-6501

Econo Lodge (721 10th Street, 95901; 742-8586, 800-424-4777) 43 rooms, outdoor heated swimming pool, children under 18 free. SGL/DBL$30-$50.

Marysville Motor Lodge (940 E Street, 95901; 743-1513) 43 rooms, swimming pool, pets allowed. SGL$28-$30, DBL$35-$40.

McCloud

Area Code 916

Cooley's Circle 7 Guest Ranch (805 Circle Seven Rd., 96057; 964-2303) 6 cabins. SGL/DBL$45+.

McKinleyville

Area Code 707
McKinleyville Chamber of Commerce
2196 Central Avenue
McKinleyville CA 95521
839-2449

Bella Vista Motel (1225 Central Avenue; 839-1073) 20 rooms, restaurant. SGL/DBL$48-$65.

Sea View Motel (1186 Central Avenue; 839-1321) 10 cabins. SGL/DBL$35-$48.

Mendocino

Area Code 707

RENTAL SOURCES: Mendocino Coast Accommodations (1001 Main Street, 95460; 937-1913, 800-262-7801) reservation service for area bed & breakfast and private home rentals. 1BR$85-$135/$475W-$600W, 2BR$125-$175/$750W-$900W, 3BR$150-$250/$900W-$1000W. **Winning Image Properties** (Box 1883, 95460; 964-1444) rental homes. $100+.

Agate Cove Inn (11201 Lansing Street, 95460; 937-0551, 800-527-3111 in Northern California) 10 rooms, bed & breakfast, complimentary breakfast, wheelchair access. SGL/DBL$79-$175.

Blackberry Inn (44951 Larkin Rd., 95460; 937-5281) 13 rooms and efficiencies, bed & breakfast, complimentary breakfast, wheelchair access, no pets. SGL/DBL$65-$125.

Blue Heron Inn (390 Kasten Street, 95460; 937-4323) 3 rooms, bed & breakfast, complimentary breakfast. SGL/DBL$58-$90.

Headlands Inn (Box 132, 95460; 937-4431) 5 rooms, bed & breakfast, complimentary breakfast, airport courtesy car, no-smoking rooms, wheelchair access. SGL/DBL98-$150.

The Hill House (10701 Palette Drive, 95460; 937-0554, 800-422-0554 in Northern California) 44 rooms and suites, restaurant, wheelchair access. SGL/DBL$100-$175.

John Dougherty House (Box 817, 95460; 937-5266) 6 rooms, bed & breakfast, complimentary breakfast. SGL/DBL$76-$100.

Joshua Grindle Inn (44800 Little Lake Rd., 95460; 937-4143) 10 rooms, bed & breakfast, complimentary breakfast, airport courtesy car, wheelchair access, no-smoking. SGL/DBL$75-$125.

Mac Callum House (Box 206, 95460; 937-0289) 20 rooms and efficiencies, bed & breakfast, restaurant, pets allowed. SGL/DBL$65-$160.

McElroy's Inn (988 Main Street, 95460; 937-1734) 4 rooms, bed & breakfast, complimentary breakfast, swimming pool. SGL/DBL$50-$75.

Mendocino Hotel and Resort (45080 Main Street, 95460; 937-0511, Fax 937-0513, 800-548-0513) 51 rooms, restaurant, wheelchair access, free parking. SGL/DBL$50-$225.

Mendocino Village Cottages (406 Lake Street, 95460; 937-0866) 3 cottages and efficiencies, pets allowed. SGL/DBL$50-$95.

Mendocino Village Inn (44860 Main Street, 95460; 937-0246, 800-882-7029 in California) 12 rooms, bed & breakfast, complimentary breakfast, wheelchair access. SGL/DBL$59-$130.

Rachel's Inn (Box 134, 95460; 937-0088) 9 rooms, bed & breakfast, complimentary breakfast, wheelchair access, free parking. SGL/DBL$96-$165.

Sea Gull Inn (Box 317, 95460; 937-5204) 9 rooms, bed & breakfast, complimentary breakfast, wheelchair access. SGL/DBL$35-$95.

Sea Rock Inn (11101 North Lansing Street, 95460; 937-5517) 14 rooms, bed & breakfast, complimentary breakfast. SGL/DBL$65-$120.

Sears House Inn (Box 844, 95460; 937-4076) 8 rooms, bed & breakfast, complimentary breakfast, ocean view. SGL/DBL$50-$100.

Stanford Inn By The Sea (Box 487, 95460; 937-5615, 800-331-8884) 25 rooms, bed & breakfast, complimentary breakfast, swimming pool, wheelchair access, pets allowed. SGL/DBL$135-$250.

Ten Twenty-One Main Street Guest Houses (Main at Evergreen, 95460; 937-5150) 3 suites and cottages, bed & breakfast, complimentary breakfast, swimming pool. SGL/DBL$120-$150.

White Gate Inn (499 Howard Street, 95460; 937-4892) 6 rooms, bed & breakfast, complimentary breakfast, no-smoking. SGL/DBL$65-$100.

Menlo Park

Area Code 415
Menlo Park Chamber of Commerce
1100 Merrill Street
Menlo Park CA 94025
325-2818

Best Western Stanford Park Hotel (100 El Camino Real, 94025; 322-1234, Fax 322-0975, 800-368-2468) 164 rooms, restaurant, lounge, swimming pool, fireplaces, transportation to local attractions, meeting facilities, fax service, complimentary newspaper, airport courtesy car, exercise equipment, no-smoking rooms. SGL$56-$65, DBL$60-$90.

Menlo Park Motor Lodge (1315 El Camino Real, 94025; 326-7530, 800-433-1315 in California) 30 rooms and efficiencies, complimentary breakfast. SGL$40-$50, DBL$42-$56.

Mermaid Inn (727 El Camino Real, 94025; 323-9481, 800-237-4622) 39 rooms and efficiencies, complimentary breakfast, free local telephone calls, outdoor heated swimming pool, free parking, wheelchair access, no-smoking rooms, no pets. SGL$48-$72, $58-$85.

Red Cottage Inn (1704 El Camino Real, 94015; 326-9010) 30 rooms, restaurant, swimming pool, no-smoking rooms. SGL$47-$60, DBL$58-$80.

Stanford Park Hotel (100 El Camino Real, 94025; 322-1234, Fax 322-0975, 800-368-2468) 164 rooms and suites, restaurant, exercise equipment, swimming pool, meeting facilities for 150, beauty and barber shop, wheelchair access, no-smoking rooms. SGL$135-$180, DBL$145-$180.

Middletown

Area Code 707

Harbin Hot Springs (18424 Harbin Springs Rd., 95461; 989-2481, 800-622-2477 in Northern California) 65 rooms. SGL/DBL$50-$115.

Midpines

Area Code 209

The Aviary (4954 Ponderosa Way, 95345; 741-6988) 6 rooms, bed & breakfast, complimentary breakfast. SGL$65+.

Budget Host Muir Lodge (6833 Highway 140, 95345, 966-2468, Fax 966-3742) 32 rooms. SGL/DBL$45+.

Midpines (6833 Highway 140, 95345; 966-2468, Fax 966-3742) 25 rooms, swimming pool, wheelchair access, pets allowed. SGL$29-$40, DBL$40-$50.

Millbrae

Area Code 415

Best Western El Rancho Inn and Executive Suites (1100 El Camino Real, 94030; 588-8500, Fax 871-7150, 800-826-5500, 800-528-1234) 321 rooms and suites, restaurant, lounge, swimming pool, children under 18 free, whirlpool, free parking, fax service, airport courtesy car, no-smoking rooms, pets allowed. SGL$95-$105, DBL$100-$115.

Clarion Hotel San Francisco Airport (401 East Millbrae Avenue, 94030; 692-6363) 440 rooms, restaurant, swimming pool, exercise equipment, meeting facilities for 800, gift shop, beauty and barber shop, no-smoking rooms, airport courtesy car, wheelchair access, free parking. SGL/DBL$74-$115.

Comfort Inn Airport West (1390 El Camino Real, 94030; 952-3200, 800-221-2222, 800-942-2627) 99 rooms, complimentary breakfast, swimming pool, meeting facilities for 60, no-smoking rooms, wheelchair access, no pets, free parking. SGL$66, DBL$75.

Clarion Hotel Airport (401 East Millbrae Avenue, 94030; 692-6363, 800-221-2222) 435 rooms, restaurant, swimming pool, wheelchair access. SGL$105-$125, DBL$115-$135.

El Rancho Inn and Executive Suites (1100 El Camino Real, 94030; 588-2912, 800-826-5500) 321 rooms and suites, restaurant, swimming pool, meeting facilities for 100, no-smoking rooms, exercise equipment, wheelchair access, pets allowed. SGL$69+, DBL$79+.

Millwood Inn (1375 El Camino Real, 94030; 583-3835, 800-345-1375) 34 rooms and efficiencies, complimentary breakfast, free local telephone calls, free parking, fax service, in-room refrigerators and microwaves, laundry room, wheelchair access, no pets. SGL/DBL$50-$52.

TraveLodge San Francisco Airport South (110 South El Camino Real, 94030; 697-7373, 800-255-3050) 58 rooms, no-smoking rooms, airport transportation. SGL$46-$49, DBL$49-$54.

Westin San Francisco Airport (One Old Bayshore Highway, 94030; 692-3500, Fax 872-8111, 800-424-4777) 388 rooms and suites, restaurant, swimming pool, exercise equipment, wheelchair access, airport transportation, meeting facilities for 70, beauty and barber shop, gift shop, no-smoking rooms, pets allowed, free parking. SGL$99+, DBL$155.

Mill Valley

Area Code 415
Mill Valley Chamber of Commerce
85 Throckmorton Avenue
Mill Valley CA 94941
388-9700

Fountain Motel (155 Shoreline Highway, 94941; 332-1732) 27 rooms, airport transportation, no-smoking rooms. SGL/DBL$52-$78.

Howard Johnson Motor Lodge (160 Shoreline Highway, 94941; 332-5700, Fax 331-1859, 800-654-2000) 100 rooms, restaurant, swimming pool, airport transportation, no-smoking rooms. SGL/DBL$55-$90.

Mountain Home Inn (810 Panoramic Highway, 94941; 381-9000) 10 rooms, bed & breakfast, restaurant, complimentary breakfast, free parking. SGL/DBL$125+.

TraveLodge (707 Redwood Highway, 94941; 383-0340, Fax 383-0312, 800-255-3050) 52 rooms and suites, jacuzzis, restaurant. SGL/DBL$51-$66.

Milpitas

Area Code 408
Milpitas Chamber of Commerce
One Main Street
Milpitas CA 262-2613
262-2613

The Best Inn (95 Dempsey Rd., 95035; 942-1798) 76 rooms. SGL/DBL$25-$35.

Best Western Brookside (400 Valley Way, 95035; 263-5566, Fax 262-6866, 800-528-1234) 73 rooms. SGL/DBL$49-$64.

The Beverly Heritage Hotel (1820 Barber Lane, 95035; 943-9080, Fax 432-8617, 800-443-4455) 200 rooms, restaurant, complimentary breakfast, swimming pool, airport transportation, exercise equipment, wheelchair access, no-smoking rooms. SGL$145-$175, DBL$165-$195.

Comfort Inn (66 South Main Street, 95035; 262-7666, 800-221-2222) 53 rooms and suites, restaurant, complimentary breakfast, swimming pool, whirlpools, meeting facilities, wheelchair access, no pets. SGL/DBL$45-$75.

Crown Sterling Suites (901 Calaveras Blvd., 95035; 942-0400, Fax 262-8604, 800-433-4600) 267 suites, restaurant, complimentary breakfast, swimming pool, wheelchair access. SGL/DBL$135+.

Economy Inns of America (270 South Abbott Avenue, 95035; 946-8889, 800-826-0778) 124 rooms, complimentary breakfast, swimming pool. SGL$40, DBL$50.

Holiday Inn (777 Bellew Drive, 95035; 945-0800, Fax 263-4112, 800-524-2929, 800-HOLIDAY) 305 rooms and suites, restaurant, lounge, swimming pool, meeting facilities for 450, children under 18 free, exercise equipment, airport courtesy car, free parking. SGL$102-$113, DBL$113-$123.

Ooh La Lodge (1556 South Main Street, 95035; 262-3621) 34 rooms and efficiencies, wheelchair access. SGL$38+, DBL$45.

Sheraton Silicon Valley (1801 Barber Lane, 95035; 943-0600, Fax 943-0484) 290 rooms and suites, restaurant, lounge, outdoor heated swimming pool, spa, exercise equipment, meeting facilities for 250, airport courtesy car, wheelchair access, no-smoking rooms. SGL/DBL$100-$130, STS$120-$250+.

Super 8 Motel (485 South Main Street, 95035; 946-1615, Fax 262-6128, 800-800-8000) 80 rooms, restaurant, complimentary breakfast, laundry room, free local telephone calls, in-room refrigerators and microwaves, kitchenettes, wheelchair access, no-smoking rooms, no pets. LS SGL/DBL$42-$47; HS SGL/DBL$45-$60.

TraveLodge (378 West Calaveras Blvd., 95035; 263-0500, Fax 263-0416, 800-255-3050) 39 rooms and suites, restaurant, swimming pool, in-room refrigerators, fax service, no pets. SGL/DBL$47-$71.

Mineral

Area Code 916

Lassen Mineral Lodge (Box 160, 96003) 12 rooms and cabins, swimming pool. SGL/DBL$45.

Miranda

Area Code 707
Avenue of the Giants
Box 1000
Miranda CA 95553
923-2555

Miranda Gardens Resort (6766 Avenue of the Giants; 943-3011) 16 rooms, swimming pool, tennis, pets allowed. SGL/DBL$38-$135.

Whispering Pines Resort (6582 Avenue of the Giants; 943-3182) 17 rooms, swimming pool. SGL/DBL$48-$68.

Mission Hills

Area Code 818

Barrows Bed and Breakfast (Bed and Breakfast International) 1 room, complimentary breakfast, no smoking. SGL/DBL$55.

Best Western Inn (10621 Sepulveda Blvd., 91345; 891-1771, Fax 895-1446, 800-528-1234) 119 rooms, restaurant, complimentary breakfast, swimming pool, in-room refrigerators, meeting facilities, children under 12 free, no-smoking rooms, free parking, no pets. SGL$50-$60, DBL$61-$65.

Modesto

Area Code 209
Modesto Chamber of Commerce and Convention and Visitors Bureau
1114 J Street
Modesto CA 95353
577-5757

All-Star Inn (1920 West Orangeburg Avenue, 95350; 522-7271) 36 rooms. SGL/DBL$25-$35.

Best Western Mallards Inn (1720 Sisk Rd., 95350; 577-3825, Fax 577-1717, 800-528-1234) 127 rooms, restaurant, lounge, swimming pool, free local telephone calls, complimentary newspaper, meeting facilities, whirlpools, fax service, no-smoking rooms. SGL$64-$83, DBL$69-$89.

Best Western Town House Lodge (909 16th Street, 93554; 524-7261, Fax 579-9546, 800-528-1234) 59 rooms, restaurant, lounge, complimentary breakfast, swimming pool, whirlpool, no-smoking rooms, pets allowed. SGL/DBL$46-$64.

Holiday Inn (1612 Sisk Rd., 95350; 521-1612, Fax 527-5074, 800-334-2030, 800-HOLIDAY) 188 rooms and suites, restaurant, swimming pool, lighted tennis courts, exercise equipment, meeting facilities for 300, wheelchair access, no-smoking rooms. SGL/DBL$70-$90, STS$150.

Motel 6 (722 Kansas Avenue, 93531; 524-3000, 505-891-6161) 103 rooms. SGL/DBL$25-$35.

Ramada Inn (2001 West Orangeburg Avenue, 95350; 526-6000, Fax 521-9000) 128 rooms, restaurant, complimentary breakfast, swimming pool, in-room refrigerators, free parking, children under 18 free, airport transportation wheelchair access, no-smoking rooms. SGL/DBL$60-$90.

Red Lion Inn (1150 Ninth Street, 95354; 526-6000) 265 rooms and suites, restaurant, lounge, heated swimming pool, sauna, jacuzzi, gift shop, room service, meeting and convention facilities, exercise equipment, free parking, no-smoking rooms, pets allowed, airport courtesy car. SGL/DBL$90-$125.

Sundial Lodge (808 McHenry Avenue, 95350 -523-5642, Fax 521-2692) 49 rooms, restaurant, swimming pool, no-smoking rooms. SGL/DBL$50-$60.

Super 8 Motel (2025 West Orangeburg Avenue, 95359; 577-8008, Fax 575-4118, 800-800-8000) 80 rooms and suites, restaurant, complimentary breakfast, outdoor swimming pool, free local telephone calls, meeting facilities, complimentary newspaper, fax service, wheelchair access, no-smoking rooms, no pets. SGL/DBL$53-$58.

Vagabond Inn (1525 McHenry Avenue, 95350; 521-6340, Fax 575-2015) 99 rooms, restaurant, complimentary breakfast, swimming pool, wheelchair access, no-smoking rooms, pets allowed, airport transportation, free local telephone calls, no-smoking rooms, children under 18 free, fax service, complimentary newspaper. SGL$42, DBL$47-$52.

Western Host Motor Hotel (1312 McHenry Avenue, 95350; 527-1010, Fax 527-2033, 800-843-6633) 106 rooms, restaurant, lounge, outdoor heated swimming pool, jacuzzi, children under 12 free, in-room refrigerators, complimentary newspaper, free parking, laundry room, wheelchair access, no-smoking rooms, no pets. SGL/DBL$45.

Mokelumme Hill

Area Code 209

Hotel Leger (8304 Main Street, 95245; 386-1401) 12 rooms, bed & breakfast, restaurant, private baths, swimming pool. SGL$65, DBL$75.

Montara

Area Code 415

Farallone Hotel (1410 Main Street, 94037; 728-7817) 11 rooms and efficiencies. SGL$55, DBL$65.

Montebello

Area Code 213
Montebello Chamber of Commerce
1304 West Beverly Blvd.
Montebello CA 90640
721-1153

Best Star Inn (7533 Telegraph Rd., 90640; 721-3032) 47 rooms and suites, complimentary breakfast, outdoor swimming pool, wheelchair access, no-smoking rooms, located near convention center. SGL/DBL$35-$45, STS$40-$65.

Holiday Inn (7709 Telegraph Rd., 90640; 724-1400, Fax 721-4410, 800-HOLIDAY) 150 rooms, restaurant, laundry room, meeting facilities for 250, no pets. SGL/DBL$65-$79.

TraveLodge (525 West Washington Blvd., 90640; 726-8222, Fax 721-1039, 800-255-3050) 40 rooms and suites, restaurant, whirlpool, room service. SGL/DBL$37-$42.

Monte Rio

Area Code 707

Angelo's Resort (Box 277, 95462; 865-2215) 10 cabins, restaurant, no pets. SGL/DBL$50-$90.

Highland Dell Inn (21050 River Blvd., 95462; 865-1759, 800-767-1759) 10 rooms and suites, bed & breakfast, complimentary breakfast, lounge, outdoor swimming pool, no children, free parking, free local telephone calls, airport transportation, no smoking, pets allowed. SGL/DBL$65-$225.

The House Of A Thousand Flowers (Box 369, 95462; 632-5571) 12 rooms, bed & breakfast, complimentary breakfast. SGL/DBL$65-$72.

Huckleberry Springs (Box 40, 95462; 865-2683, 800-822-2683) 5 cottages, restaurant, complimentary meals, outdoor swimming pool, spa, free local telephone calls, in-room refrigerators, meeting facilities for 18, free parking, wheelchair access, no-smoking, no pets. SGL$145, DBL$175.

Northwood Lodge (19455 Highway 16, 95462; 865-1655, Fax 869-0714) 25 rooms and cabins, restaurant, swimming pool, golf, no-smoking rooms. SGL$40-$52, DBL$55-$71.

Rio Villa Beach Resort (20292 Highway 116, 95462; 865-1143) one- and two-bedroom apartments. 1BR$89, 2BR$105.

Morgan Hill

Area Code 408
Morgan Hill Chamber of Commerce
17320 Monterey Street
Morgan Hill CA 95037
779-9444

Best Western Country Inn (16525 Condit Rd., 95037; 779-0447, Fax 778-7170, 800-528-1234) 84 rooms, restaurant, complimentary breakfast, swimming pool, in-room refrigerators, fax service, laundry room, wheelchair access, no-smoking rooms. pets allowed. SGL$53-$73, DBL$58-$73.

Executive Inn Suites (16505 Condit Rd., 95037; 778-0404, Fax 778-2090, 800-626-4224) 60 rooms. SGL/DBL$65-$75.

Mountain View

Area Code 415

Best Western Mountain View Inn (2300 El Camino Real, 94040; 962-9912, Fax 962-9011) 70 rooms, restaurant, lounge, exercise equipment, whirlpool, laundry room, no-smoking rooms. SGL/DBL$64-$75.

Best Western Tropicana Lodge (1720 El Camino Real West, 94040; 961-0220, Fax 961-1471) 59 rooms, restaurant, lounge, swimming pool, whirlpool, pets allowed, fax service. SGL$55-$68, DBL$60-$74.

Mount Shasta

Area Code 916
Mount Shasta Chamber of Commerce
300 Pine Street
Mount Shasta CA 96067
926-4865

Alpine Lodge Motel (908 South Mount Shasta Blvd., 96067; 926-3145) 20 rooms, swimming pool, pets allowed. SGL/DBL$32-$80.

Best Western The Tree House Motor Inn (Lake Street, 96067; 926-3101, Fax 926-3542, 800-528-1234, 800-545-7164) 95 rooms, restaurant, lounge, swimming pool, kitchenettes, free local telephone calls, whirlpool, exercise equipment, wheelchair access, no-smoking rooms, pets allowed. SGL/DBL$60-$140.

Das Alpenhaus (504 South Mount Shasta Blvd., 96067; 926-4617) 18 rooms and efficiencies, complimentary breakfast, pets allowed. SGL/DBL$19-$56.

Evergreen Lodge (1312 South Mount Shasta Blvd., 96067; 926-2143) 20 rooms and efficiencies, complimentary breakfast, swimming pool, pets allowed. SGL/DL$24+.

Finlandia Motel (1612 South Mount Shasta Blvd., 96067; 926-5596) 14 rooms and efficiencies. SGL/DBL$20-$35.

Joanne's Bed and Breakfast (417 Lawndale Court, 96067; 926-2106) 6 rooms, bed & breakfast, complimentary breakfast. SGL/DBL$40-$50.

Mountain Air Lodge (1121 South Mount Shasta Blvd., 96067; 926-3411) 33 rooms and efficiencies, pets allowed. SGL/DBL$36-$105.

Mountain View Lodge (305 Old McCloud Rd., 96067; 926-4704) 10 rooms and efficiencies, pets allowed. SGL/DBL$22-$34.

Mount Shasta Cabins and Cottages (500 South Mount Shasta Blvd., 96067; 926-5396) 38 rooms and one-bedroom cabins and cottages, pets allowed. SGL/DBL$25-$75.

Mount Shasta House Bed and Breakfast (113 South A Street, 96067; 926-5089) 8 rooms, bed & breakfast, complimentary breakfast. SGL/DBL$55-$85.

Mount Shasta Ranch (1008 Barr Rd., 96067; 926-3870) 5 rooms, bed & breakfast, complimentary breakfast, pets allowed. SGL/DBL$55+.

Pine Needles Motel (1340 South Mount Shasta Blvd., 96067; 926-4811) 30 rooms and efficiencies, swimming pool, pets allowed. SGL/DBL$55-$75.

Shasta Lodge Motel (724 South Mount Shasta Blvd., 96067; 926-2815) 20 rooms and efficiencies, pets allowed. SGL/DBL$22-$43.

Sisson House 1904 (326 Chestnut Street, 96067; 926-6949) 8 rooms, bed & breakfast, complimentary breakfast. SGL/DBL$55+.

Stoney Brook Inn (309 West Colombero, 96067; 964-369-6118, 800-369-6118) 14 rooms and suites, bed & breakfast, complimentary breakfast, kitchenettes, hot tub, in-room refrigerators, free parking, wheelchair access, no smoking, no pets. SGL$26-$50, DBL$35-$70.

Swiss Holiday Lodge (Highway 89, 96067; 926-3446) 21 rooms and suites, swimming pool, no-smoking rooms, pets allowed. SGL/DBL$30-$85.

Timberline Motel (1142 South Mount Shasta Blvd., 96067) 15 rooms and efficiencies, pets allowed. SGL/DBL$26-$55.

Ward's Big Foot Ranch (1530 Hill Rd., 96067; 926-5170) 12 rooms, bed & breakfast, complimentary breakfast. SGL/DBL$45-$85.

Murphys

Area Code 209

RENTAL SOURCES: Forest Meadows Vacation Rentals (Highway Four, 95247; 728-3433, 800-540-6020) rental one- and two-bedroom homes and condos. 1BR$70, 2BR$115. **Gold Country Real Estate** (35 East Highway Four, 95247; 728-3448) rental homes and townhouses, two-night minimum. SGL/DBL$170-$300.

Dunbar House 1880 (Box 1375, 95247; 728-2897) 4 rooms, bed & breakfast, complimentary breakfast, private baths. SGL/DBL$105-$145.

Murphys Historic Hotel and Lodge (457 Main Street, 95247; 728-3444, Fax 728-1590) 29 rooms, restaurant, complimentary breakfast, wheelchair access, pets allowed. SGL/DBL$65-$75.

Trade Carriage House (600 Algiers Street, 95247; 728-3903) 2 rooms, restaurant, two-night minimum. SGL/DBL$75-$200.

Napa

Area Code 707
Napa Valley Conference and Visitors Bureau
1310 North San Pedro Rd.
Napa CA 94903
226-7459

RENTAL SOURCES: Bed and Breakfast Exchange (1458 Lincoln Avenue, Calistoga, 94515; 942-5900, 800-942-2924) reservation service for local bed & breakfasts. **Napa Valley Tourist Reservations** (4076 Byway East, 94558; 253-2929) reservation service for resorts, hotels, bed & breakfasts. **Napa Valley Reservations Unlimited** (1819 Tanen Street, 94559; 252-1985, 800-251-NAPA) reservation service for hotels, motels, condominiums, apartment, vacation homes and bed & breakfasts.

Arbor Guest House (1436 G Street, 94559; 252-8144) 5 rooms, bed & breakfast, complimentary breakfast, handicapped access. SGL/DBL$101-$125.

Beazley House (1910 First Street, 94559; 257-1649) 10 rooms, bed & breakfast, no-smoking rooms. SGL/DBL$101-$125+.

Best Western Inn (100 Soscol Avenue, 94559; 257-1930, Fax 255-0709, 800-528-1234) 68 rooms, restaurant, swimming pool, whirlpool, wheelchair access, no-smoking rooms, meeting facilities for 50, fax service, children under 12 free, pets allowed. LS SGL$60-$70, DBL$79-$89; HS SGL$100-$125, DBL$139-$149.

Blue Violet Mansion (443 Brown Street, 94559; 253-BLUE) 6 rooms, bed & breakfast, complimentary breakfast. SGL/DBL$101-$125.

Candlelight Inn (1045 Easum Drive, 94558; 257-3717) 3 rooms, bed & breakfast, complimentary breakfast, free parking. DBL$125-$140.

Chablis Lodge (3360 Solano Avenue, 94558; 257-1944, 800-443-3490) 34 rooms, complimentary breakfast, swimming pool, wheelchair access, pets allowed, no-smoking rooms. SGL$59-$79, DBL$64-$84.

The Chateau Hotel (4195 Solano Avenue, 94558; 253-9300, 800-253-NAPA in California) 115 rooms, restaurant, complimentary breakfast, swimming pool, wheelchair access, no-smoking rooms. SGL$70+.

Churchill Manor (485 Brown Street, 94559; 253-7733, Fax 253-8836) 10 rooms, complimentary breakfast, wheelchair access, no-smoking rooms. SGL/DBL$75-$145.

Clarion Inn Napa Valley (3425 Solano Avenue, 94558; 253-7433, Fax 252-6791, 800-221-2222) 193 rooms, restaurant, outdoor heated swimming pool, whirlpool, meeting facilities, airport transportation, wheelchair access, no-smoking rooms, pets allowed, tennis. SGL/DBL$75-$110.

Country Garden Inn (1815 Silverado Trail, 94558; 255-1197, Fax 255-3112) 11 rooms, complimentary breakfast, wheelchair access, no-smoking. SGL/DBL$120-$175.

Crown Sterling Suites (1075 California Blvd., 94559; 254-9540, Fax 253-9202, 800-433-4600) 205 rooms, restaurant, complimentary breakfast, swimming pool. SGL/DBL$120-$170.

The Elm House (800 California Blvd., 94550; 255-1831) 4 rooms, bed & breakfast, complimentary breakfast. SGL/DBL$45-$85.

Embassy Suites (1075 California Blvd., 94559; 253-9540, 800-EMBASSY) 205 rooms, restaurant, complimentary breakfast, swimming pool, free parking. SGL$99-$134, DBL$109-$159.

Hennesey House (1727 Main Street, 94559; 226-3774) 10 rooms, bed & breakfast, complimentary breakfast, free parking. DBL$80-$155.

The Inn At Napa Valley (1075 California Blvd., 94559; 253-9540, Fax 253-9202, 800-433-4600) 205 suites, restaurant, complimentary breakfast, meeting facilities, swimming pool, wheelchair access, no-smoking rooms. SGL/DBL$130-$160.

John Muir Inn (1998 Tower Avenue, 94558; 257-7220, 800-522-8999) 59 rooms, restaurant, complimentary breakfast, swimming pool, wheelchair access, no-smoking rooms. SGL/DBL$70-$150.

La Residence Country Inn (4066 St. Helena Highway, 94558; 253-0337) 23 rooms, complimentary breakfast, swimming pool, wheelchair access, no-smoking rooms. SGL/DBL$75-$125, STS$160+.

The Old World Inn (1301 Jefferson, 94559; 257-0112) 8 rooms, bed & breakfast, complimentary breakfast, no-smoking, free parking. SGL/DBL$77-$137.

Silverado Country Club and Resort (1600 Atlas Peak Rd., 94558; 257-0200, Fax 226-8449, 800-532-0500) 365 one-, two-and three-bedroom condos, three restaurants, lounge, outdoor heated swimming pool, spa, jacuzzi, golf, lighted tennis courts, in-room refrigerators and microwaves, fax service, business services, meeting facilities for 500, gift shop, laundry room, free parking, wheelchair access, no-smoking rooms, no pets. 1BR$235, 2BR$340, $465-$600.

Steele Park Resort (1605 Steele Canyon Rd., 94558; 966-2123, Fax 257-2867) 45 rooms, restaurant, swimming pool, no-smoking rooms, marina, boat rentals. SGL/DBL$75+.

Tall Timbers Mountain Chalet (1012 Darmas Lane, 94558; 252-7810) 8 cottages, bed & breakfast, complimentary breakfast, wheelchair access, no smoking, no pets, free parking. SGL/DBL$65-$125.

TraveLodge (853 Coombs Street, 94559; 226-1871, 800-255-3050) 44 rooms and suites, restaurant, lounge, swimming pool, no-smoking rooms, no pets. SGL/DBL$45-$70.

Wine Valley Lodge (200 South Coombs Street, 94558; 224-7911, 800-696-7911 in California) 35 rooms, swimming pool. SGL/DBL$45-$125.

Nevada City

Area Code 916
Nevada City Chamber of Commerce
132 Main Street
Nevada City CA 95959
265-2692

Flume's End (317 South Pine Street, 95959; 265-9665) 6 rooms, bed & breakfast, complimentary breakfast, airport courtesy car, no-smoking. SGL/DBL$75-$120.

Northern Queen Motel (400 Railroad Avenue, 95959; 265-5824) 85 rooms and cottages, restaurant, swimming pool, wheelchair access, no-smoking rooms. SGL/DBL$50-$85.

The Parsonage (427 Broad Street, 95959; 265-9478) 4 rooms, bed & breakfast, complimentary breakfast. SGL$85, DBL$95.

Piety Hill Inn (523 Sacramento Street, 95959; 265-2245) 9 rooms, bed & breakfast, complimentary breakfast. SGL$65, DBL$68.

Newark

Area Code 415

Days Inn (5977 Mowry Avenue, 94560; 795-7995, Fax 795-0295, 800-624-0085, 800-325-2525 in California) 100 rooms, restaurant, complimentary breakfast, swimming pool, wheelchair access, free parking. SGL$38-$50, DBL$45-$60.

E-Z 8 Motel (555 Cedar Court, 94560; 794-7775) 141 rooms. SGL/DBL$28-$40.

Newark-Fremont Hilton (39900 Balentine Drive, 94560; 490-8390, Fax 651-7828, 800-HILTONS) 320 rooms and suites, restaurant, swimming pool, sauna, spa, meeting facilities for 800, exercise equipment, wheelchair access, airport courtesy car, free parking. SGL$79-$104, DBL$89-$109, STS$150+.

Woodfin Suites Hotel (39150 Cedar Blvd., 94560; 795-1200, Fax 795-8874, 800-237-8811) 148 suites, restaurant, complimentary breakfast, airport transportation, pets allowed, wheelchair access. SGL$64-$84, DBL$69-$144.

Newcastle

Area Code 916
Placer County Visitor Information Center
661 Newcastle Rd.
Newcastle CA 95658
663-2061

Victorian Manor (482 Main Street, 95658; 663-3009) 4 rooms, bed & breakfast, complimentary breakfast, no children, no pets, no smoking. SGL/DBL$55+.

Nice

Area Code 707

Feather Bed Railroad Company (Box 4016, 95464; 274-8387) 9 rooms, bed & breakfast, swimming pool. SGL/DBL$75-$116.

Norden

Area Code 916

Sugar Bowl Ski Resort (Old Highway 40, 95724; 426-3651, Fax 426-3723) 29 rooms, restaurant. SGL$80-$185, DBL$110-$185.

North Highlands

Area Code 916

The Best Inn (4325 Watt Avenue, 95660; 971-9440) 89 rooms. SGL/DBL$24-$39.

Motel 6 (4600 Watt Avenue, 95660; 753-3777) 103 rooms. SGL/DBL$25-$32.

Rodeway Inn (3425 Orange Grove Avenue, 95660; 753-3600, Fax 758-8623, 800-424-4777) 145 rooms and suites, swimming pool, meeting facilities, wheelchair access, children under 18 free, no pets. SGL/DBL$45-$55.

Novato

Area Code 415

Novato Chamber of Commerce
807 DeLong Avenue
Novato CA 94948
897-1164

Alvarado Inn (250 Entrada Drive, 94949; 883-5952, 800-652-6565 in California) 70 rooms, restaurant, swimming pool, airport transportation, wheelchair access. SGL$38-$45, DBL$43-$50.

Novato Motel (8141 Redwood Blvd., 94945; 897-7111, Fax 897-8367) 60 rooms, restaurant, swimming pool, no-smoking rooms, pets allowed. SGL$36-$39, DBL$47-$55.

Quality Inn (215 Alameda del Prado, 94949, 883-4400, 800-221-2222, 800-228-5151) 104 rooms, complimentary breakfast, heated swimming pool, spa, whirlpools, meeting facilities for 100, transportation to local attractions, exercise equipment, airport transportation, wheelchair access, no pets. SGL/DBL$55-$92.

Skylark Motel (275 Alameda del Prado, 94949; 883-2406, Fax 883-3765) 30 rooms and efficiencies, restaurant, swimming pool, airport transportation, wheelchair access, no-smoking rooms. SGL/DBL$41-$65.

TraveLodge (7600 Redwood Blvd., 94945; 892-7500, Fax 898-0828, 800-255-3050) 50 rooms and suites, restaurant, lounge, complimentary breakfast, swimming pool, spa, laundry room, meeting facilities for 40, in-room refrigerators, exercise equipment, airport transportation, no-smoking rooms. SGL/DBL$59-$75.

Oakdale

Area Code 209
Oakdale District Chamber of Commerce

351 East F Street
Oakdale CA 95361
847-2244

Holiday Motel (950 East F Street, 95361; 847-7023, 800-826-0999) 32 rooms, complimentary breakfast, swimming pool, children under 12 stay free, free parking, free local telephone calls, wheelchair access, no-smoking rooms, no pets. SGL$37-$48, DBL$43-$67.

Ramada Inn (825 East F Street, 95361; 847-8181, Fax 847-9546, 800-2-RAMADA) 71 rooms, restaurant, lounge, swimming pool, children under 18 free, meeting facilities, free parking, wheelchair access, no-smoking rooms. SGL$65-$85, DBL$71-$81.

Oakland

Area Code 510
Oakland Convention and Visitors Bureau
1000 Broadway #200
Oakland CA 94607
839-9000

Apple Inn Embarcadero (1801 Embarcadero, 94606; 436-0103, Fax 533-1217) 100 rooms, restaurant, complimentary breakfast, swimming pool, wheelchair access, no-smoking rooms. airport courtesy car. SGL/DBL$54+.

Bayside Boat and Breakfast (70 Jack London Square, 94608; 444-5858) bed & breakfast aboard a boat, complimentary breakfast. SGL/DBL$115-$250.

Best Western Park Plaza Hotel (150 Hegenberger Rd., 94621; 635-5300, Fax 635-9661, 800-528-1234) 187 rooms, restaurant, lounge, swimming pool, sauna, meeting facilities for 140, free parking, wheelchair access, spa, fax service, airport courtesy car, no-smoking rooms. SGL$84-$99, DBL$94-$109.

Best Western Thunderbird Inn (233 Broadway, 94607; 452-4565, Fax 452-4634, 800-528-1234) 102 rooms, restaurant, lounge, complimentary breakfast, children under 12 free, airport transportation, swimming pool, no-smoking rooms, no pets. SGL/DBL$70-$90.

Claremont Resort Spa and Tennis Club (41 Tunnel Rd., 94623; 843-3000, Fax 843-6239, 800-323-7500) 239 rooms, restaurant, swimming pool, exercise equipment, tennis, free parking, airport transportation, lighted tennis courts, wheelchair access, no-smoking rooms. SGL/$145-$210, DBL$165-$230.

Clarion Hotel Airport (455 Hegenberger Rd., 94621; 562-6100, 800-221-2222, 800-233-1234) 335 rooms, restaurant, swimming pool, meeting facilities, airport courtesy car, wheelchair access, no pets. SGL$109-$128, DBL$119-$139.

Days Inn Airport (8350 Edes Avenue, 94621; 568-1880, Fax 569-4652, 800-325-2525) 142 rooms, restaurant, swimming pool, wheelchair access, no-smoking rooms, pets allowed, airport transportation. SGL$50-$79, DBL$55-$84.

Executive Inn (1755 Embarcadero Drive, 94606; 536-6633) 36 rooms, complimentary breakfast, swimming pool, exercise equipment. SGL/DBL$65-$90.

E-Z 8 Motel (8471 Enterprise Way, 94621; 562-4888) 101 rooms. SGL/DBL$34-$46.

Hampton Inn Airport (8465 Enterprise Way, 94621; 632-8900, Fax 632-4713, 800-950-1191, 800-HAMPTON) 151 rooms, complimentary breakfast, heated swimming pool, spa, airport transportation, meeting facilities, free local telephone calls, wheelchair access, no-smoking, pets allowed. SGL/DBL$66-$100.

Holiday Inn Airport (500 Hegenberger Rd., 94621; 562-5311, Fax 636-1539, 800-HOLIDAY) 290 rooms, restaurant, swimming pool, meeting facilities for 275, transportation to local attractions, exercise equipment, airport transportation, wheelchair access, no-smoking rooms, pets allowed. SGL/DBL$85-$115.

Hilton Oakland Airport (One Hegenberger Rd., 94615; 635-5000, Fax 635-0244, 800-HILTONS) 362 rooms, restaurant, outdoor swimming pool, airport courtesy car, meeting facilities for 1000, business service, exercise equipment, wheelchair access, no-smoking rooms. SGL$100-$125, DBL$135-$245.

Hyatt Oakland Airport (455 Hegenberger Rd., 94621; 562-6100, Fax 569-5681, 800-233-1234) 335 rooms and suites, restaurant, swimming pool, airport transportation, wheelchair access, no-smoking rooms. SGL/DBL$100+.

Hyatt Regency (1001 Broadway, 94607; 893-12324, Fax 835-3466, 800-228-9000) 488 rooms, restaurant, swimming pool, exercise equipment, wheelchair access. SGL$95-$145, DBL$115-$165.

Lake Merritt Hotel (1800 Madison Avenue, 94612; 832-2300, Fax 832-7170, 800-933-4683) 51 rooms and suites, restaurant, lounge, complimentary breakfast, children under 16 stay free, fax service, laundry room, airport transportation, wheelchair access, exercise equipment, no-smoking rooms, pets allowed. SGL/DBL$79, STS$109-$149.

London Lodge (423 Seventh Street, 94607; 451-6316) 130 rooms and efficiencies, restaurant, free parking. SGL/DBL$65.

Motel 6 (8480 Edes Avenue, 94621; 638-1180) 286 rooms. SGL/DBL$30-$36.

Motel 6 (4919 Coliseum Way, 94601; 261-7414) 96 rooms. SGL/DBL$30-$46.

Parc Oakland Hotel (1001 Broadway, 94607; 451-4000, Fax 835-3466, 800-338-1338) 488 rooms and suites, restaurant, swimming pool, airport transportation, wheelchair access, no-smoking rooms. SGL$100-$130, DBL$125-$150, STS$325+.

Park Plaza Hotel (150 Hegenberger Rd., 94621; 635-5300, Fax 635-9661, 800-635-5301) 189 rooms and suites, restaurant, lounge, outdoor heated swimming pool, jacuzzi, sauna, children under 12 free stay free, exercise equipment, valet laundry, gift shop, free parking, airport transportation, wheelchair access, no-smoking rooms, no pets. SGL$89, DBL$99, STS$81-$130.

Parkwoods Apartment Community (200 Caldecott Lane, 94618; 848-3222) one-, two- and three-bedroom condos, swimming pool. 1BR$85, 2BR$105, 3BR$125.

Thunderbird Inn (233 Broadway, 94607; 452-4565, Fax 452-4634, 800-528-1234) 101 rooms, complimentary breakfast, swimming pool, wheelchair access, no-smoking rooms. SGL$68-$78, DBL$78-$88.

Washington Inn (495 Tenth Street, 94607; 452-1776, Fax 452-4436, 800-477-1775, 800-464-1776 in California) 47 rooms and suites, restaurant, lounge, complimentary breakfast, children under 12 free, in-room refrigerators, valet laundry, fax service, airport transportation, wheelchair access, no-smoking rooms, no pets. SGL$89, DBL$99, STS$129-$218.

Waterfront Plaza Hotel (Ten Washington Street, 94607; 836-3800, Fax 832-5695, 800-729-3638) 144 rooms and suites, restaurant, swimming pool, exercise equipment, no-smoking rooms. SGL$135-$160, DBL$150-$175, STS$200+.

Occidental

Area Code 707

Heart's Desire Inn (Box 857, 95465; 874-1311) 8 rooms, bed & breakfast, complimentary breakfast, handicapped access. SGL/DBL$75-$125.

The Inn At Occidental (3657 Church Street, 95465; 874-1311, 800-551-2292) 9 rooms and suites, bed & breakfast, complimentary breakfast, no children, no smoking, no pets, free parking, wheelchair access. SGL/DBL$95, STS$175-$325.

Olema

Area Code 415
West Marin County Chamber of Commerce
Box 94
Olema CA 94950

Bear Valley Inn (Box 33, 94950; 663-1777) 3 rooms, bed & breakfast, complimentary breakfast, fireplaces, bicycle rental, no-smoking, no pets. SGL/DBL$70-$105.

Point Reyes Seashore Lodge (10021 Coastal Highway 1, 94950; 663-9000) 21 rooms and suites, bed & breakfast, complimentary breakfast. SGL/DBL$85-$175.

Roundstone Farm (Box 217, 94950; 662-1020) 4 rooms, bed & breakfast, complimentary breakfast. SGL/DBL$101-$125.

Olympic Valley

Area Code 916

RENTAL SOURCES: First Resort Property Management (203 Squaw Valley Rd., 96146) rental condos and homes. SGL/DBL$145. **Julee Rosa Realty** (305 Squaw Valley Rd., 96146) rental one- to six-bedroom condos and homes, swimming pool, pets allowed. SGL/DBL$75+. **Squaw Valley Realty** (1604 Christy Lane, 96146) rental condos and homes. SGL/DBL$90+. **Tahoe Vacation Properties** (Box 2328, 96146) rental condos and homes, pets allowed. SGL/DBL$85+.

The Hostel at Squaw Valley USA (1900 Squaw Valley Rd., 96146) 80 rooms. SGL$35+.

Christy Inn (1604 Christy Lane, 96146) 26 rooms, no pets. SGL/DBL$60+.

The Hostel at Squaw Valley (1900 Squaw Creek Rd., 96146) 80-bed hostel. SGL$35+.

Olympic Village Inn (1900 Squaw Valley Rd., 96146) 90 one-bedroom suites, swimming pool. SGL/DBL$165+.

Resort at Squaw Creek (400 Squaw Creek Rd., 96146; 583-6300, Fax 581-5407, 800-3CREEK3) 405 rooms and efficiencies, restaurant, swimming pool, exercise equipment, airport transportation, wheelchair access, no-smoking rooms. SGL/DBL$125+.

River Ranch (Alpine Meadows Rd., 96146) 16 rooms and cabins. SGL/DBL$55+.

Squaw Tahoe Resort (2000 Squaw Valley Loop Rd., 96146) one- and two-bedroom condos. SGL/DBL$65+.

Squaw Valley Inn (1920 Squaw Valley Rd., 96146; 583-1576, Fax 583-7619, 800-323-ROOM) 60 rooms and suites, restaurant, lounge, outdoor swimming pool, jacuzzis, children under 12 stay free, exercise equipment, gift shop, valet laundry, free parking, no-smoking rooms, no pets. SGL$90-$210, STS$130-$280.

Squaw Valley Lodge (201 Squaw Peak Rd., 96146; 583-5500, Fax 583-0326, 800-922-9970) 100 rooms and suites, outdoor heated swimming pool, jacuzzi, in-room refrigerators and microwave, meeting facilities for 50, laundry room, exercise equipment, tennis, wheelchair access, no-smoking rooms, no pets. SGL/DBL$100-$255, STS$100-$295.

The Tavern Inn (203 Squaw Valley Rd., 96146) 36 one- and two-bedroom condos, swimming pool. SGL/DBL$135.

Orick

Area Code 707

Prairie Creek Motel (Highway 101; 488-3841) 10 rooms, restaurant, pets allowed. SGL/DBL$30-$45.

Oroville

Area Code 916
Oroville Area Chamber of Commerce
1789 Montgomery Street
Oroville CA 95965
533-2542

Best Western Grand Manor Inn (1470 Feather River Blvd., 95965; 533-9673, Fax 533-5862, 800-528-1234) 55 rooms, complimentary breakfast, swimming pool, in-room refrigerators, whirlpool, laundry room, fax service, exercise equipment, wheelchair access. SGL/DBL$55-$90.

Villa Motel (1527 Feather River Blvd., 95965; 533-3930) 20 rooms, swimming pool. SGL/DBL$45-$50.

Pacific Grove

Area Code 408
Pacific Grove Chamber of Commerce
Forest and Central Avenues
Pacific Grove CA 93950
373-3304

Asilomar Conference Center (800 Asilomar Blvd.; 372-8016, Fax 372-7227) 320 rooms, restaurant, complimentary breakfast, swimming pool, free parking, wheelchair access. SGL$55-$65, DBL$65-$65, STS$110+.

Best Western Butterfly Trees Lodge (1150 Lighthouse Avenue, 93950; 372-0503, Fax 372-4385, 800-528-1234) 68 rooms, restaurant, complimentary breakfast, swimming pool, spa, sauna, fireplaces, fax service, meeting facilities, no-smoking rooms, wheelchair access, pets allowed. SGL$59-$99, DBL$79-$109.

Bide-A-Wee Motel (221 Asilomar Blvd., 93950; 372-2330) 17 rooms. SGL/DBL$50-$80.

Butterfly Grove Inn (1073 Lighthouse Avenue, 93950; 373-4921) 28 rooms, swimming pool, no-smoking rooms. SGL/DBL$55-$95.

Centrella Hotel (612 Central Avenue, 93950; 372-3372, 800-233-3372) 26 rooms and cottages, bed & breakfast, complimentary breakfast, wheelchair access. SGL/DBL$105-$120.

The Executive Lodge (660 Dennett Avenue, 93950; 373-8777, 800-221-9323 in California) 30 rooms, complimentary breakfast, wheelchair access, free parking. SGL/DBL$95-$150.

Gatehouse Inn (225 Central Avenue, 93950; 649-8436, 800-753-1881) 8 rooms, bed & breakfast, complimentary breakfast, wheelchair access, free parking. SGL/DBL$95-$170.

Gosby House Inn (643 Lighthouse Avenue, 93950; 375-1287) 22 rooms, bed & breakfast, complimentary breakfast, no-smoking rooms. SGL/DBL$85-$130.

Green Gables (104 Fifth Street, 93950; 375-2095) 11 rooms, complimentary breakfast, no-smoking rooms. SGL/DBL$100-$160.

Lakewood Inn (740 Crocker Avenue, 93950; 373-1114) 25 rooms. SGL/DBL$52-$72.

Lighthouse Lodge (1249 Lighthouse Avenue, 93950; 655-2111) 30 rooms, restaurant, complimentary breakfast, wheelchair access. SGL/DBL$99-$199.

Martine Inn (255 Ocean View Blvd., 93950; 373-3388) 19 rooms, bed & breakfast, complimentary breakfast, wheelchair access, no-smoking rooms, free parking. SGL/DBL$115-$225.

Old Saint Angela Inn (321 Central Avenue, 93950; 372-3246) 9 rooms, bed & breakfast, complimentary breakfast, no-smoking. SGL/DBL$75-$135.

Pacific Gardens Inn (701 Asilomar Blvd., 93950; 646-9414) 28 rooms, complimentary breakfast. SGL/DBL$70-$150.

Pacific Grove Inn (581 Pine Avenue, 93950; 375-2825) 10 rooms, bed & breakfast, complimentary breakfast, wheelchair access, no-smoking. SGL/DBL$75-$90.

Pacific Grove Motel (Lighthouse at Grove Acres, 93950; 373-3741) 20 rooms, swimming pool. SGL/DBL$40-$90.

Pacific Grove Plaza (620 Lighthouse Avenue, 93950; 373-0562) 33 rooms. SGL/DBL$120+.

Pine Acres Lodge (1150 Jewell Avenue, 93950; 372-6651, Fax 372-0392) 13 rooms. SGL/DBL$65-$175.

Quality Inn (1111 Lighthouse Avenue, 93950; 646-8885, 800-221-2222) 49 rooms, complimentary breakfast, swimming pool, sauna, whirlpools, meeting facilities, wheelchair access, no pets, free parking. SGL$70-$150, DBL$90-$190.

Rosedale Inn (775 Asilomar Avenue, 93950; 655-1000, Fax 655-0691) 28 rooms. SGL/DBL$95-$165.

Roserox Country Inn By The Sea (557 Ocean View Blvd., 93950; 373-7673) 8 rooms, bed & breakfast, complimentary breakfast, free parking. SGL/DBL$125-$205.

Seven Gables Inn (555 Ocean View Blvd., 93950; 372-4341) 14 rooms, bed & breakfast, complimentary breakfast, no-smoking. SGL/DBL$100-$185.

Sunset Motel (133 Asilomar Blvd., 93950; 375-3936) 20 rooms and suites. SGL/DBL$55-$90, STS$75-$90.

Terrace Oaks Inn (1095 Lighthouse Avenue, 93950; 373-4382) 11 rooms, complimentary breakfast. SGL/DBL$48-$73.

Wilkie's Motel (1038 Lighthouse Avenue, 92950; 372-5960, 800-439-4553 in California) 24 rooms, complimentary breakfast, no-smoking rooms. SGL/DBL$65-$85.

Pacifica

Area Code 415
Pacifica Chamber of Commerce
220 Paloma Avenue #200
Pacifica CA 94044

Best Western Lighthouse Motel (105 Rockaway Beach Avenue, 94044; 355-6300, 800-528-1234) 92 rooms, restaurant. SGL/DBL$85-$150.

Days Inn (200 Rockaway Beach, 94044; 359-7700, Fax 359-7707, 800-325-2525) 30 rooms and suites, restaurant, complimentary breakfast, swimming pool, ocean view, children under 12 free, fax service, free parking, airport transportation, wheelchair access, no-smoking rooms, no pets. SGL$50-$75, DBL$65-$85, STS$70-$110.

Lighthouse Hotel (105 Rockaway Beach, 94044; 355-6300) 90 rooms, restaurant, airport courtesy car, meeting facilities for 200, gift shop, wheelchair access, exercise equipment. SGL$75, DBL$85.

Marine View Lodge (2040 Francisco Blvd., 94044; 355-2543) 12 rooms and efficiencies, no-smoking rooms. SGL$40, DBL$50.

Nick's Sea Breeze Motel (2040 Francisco Blvd., 94044; 359-3903) 20 rooms and efficiencies. SGL/DBL$45-$48.

Pacifica Motor Inn (200 Rockaway Beach Avenue, 94044; 359-7700, 800-522-3772 in California) 30 rooms and suites, sauna, wheelchair access, exercise equipment, no-smoking rooms. SGL$42-$55, DBL$52-$62.

Seabreeze Motel (100 Rockaway Beach, 94044; 359-3903) 20 rooms, restaurant, lounge, wheelchair access. SGL$45-$55, DBL$55-$65.

Seaview Motor Lodge (2160 Francisco Blvd., 94044; 359-9494) 25 rooms and suites, no-smoking rooms, kitchenettes, wheelchair access. SGL/DBL$50-$65.

Pacific Palisades

Area Code 213
Pacific Palisades Chamber of Commerce
15304 Sunset Blvd. #204
Pacific Palisades CA 90272
454-3512

Riviera Country Club (1250 Capri Drive, 90271; 454-6591, Fax 454-8351) 32 rooms, restaurant, complimentary breakfast, tennis, wheelchair access. SGL$125+, DBL$145, STS$235+.

Palo Alto

Area Code 415

Best Western Creekside Inn (3400 El Camino Real, 94306; 493-2411, Fax 493-6787, 800-528-1234) 136 rooms, restaurant, lounge, swimming pool, fax service, meeting facilities, airport transportation, no-smoking rooms, no pets. SGL/DBL$76-$92.

Country Inn (4345 El Camino Real, 94306; 948-9154) 21 rooms, restaurant, complimentary breakfast, swimming pool. SGL/DBL$40-$55.

Cowper Inn (705 Cowper Street, 94301; 327-4475, Fax 329-1703) 14 rooms, complimentary breakfast, no-smoking. SGL/DBL$90+.

Days Inn (4238 El Camino Real, 94406; 493-4222, Fax 494-6112, 800-325-2525) 24 rooms, restaurant, complimentary breakfast, swimming pool, fax service, wheelchair access, no-smoking rooms, pets allowed. SGL$49-$75, DBL$65-$75.

Dinah's Garden Motor Hotel (4261 El Camino Real, 94306; 493-2844, Fax 856-4713, 800-227-8220) 108 rooms and suites, restaurant, swimming pool, no-smoking rooms, free parking. SGL$68-$87, DBL$70-$89.

Garden Court Hotel (520 Cowper Street, 94301; 322-9000, Fax 324-3609, 800-824-9028) 61 rooms and suites, restaurant, complimentary breakfast, exercise equipment, wheelchair access. SGL$150-$240, DBL$160-$250, STS$175-$400.

Glass Slipper Inn (3841 El Camino Real, 94306; 493-6611) 25 rooms, swimming pool. SGL/DBL$29+.

Holiday Inn Palo Alto-Stanford (625 El Camino Real, 94406; 328-2800, Fax 327-7362, 800-374-3516, 800-HOLIDAY) 334 rooms and suites, restaurant, swimming pool, meeting facilities for 450, transportation to local attractions, child care, wheelchair access, airport transportation, pets allowed. SGL$116-$136, DBL$126-$146.

Hyatt Hotels Palo Alto (4290 El Camino Real, 94306; 493-0800, Fax 493-5879) 200 rooms and suites, restaurant, lounge, swimming pool, sauna, meeting facilities, exercise equipment, lighted tennis courts, airport transportation, wheelchair access, no-smoking rooms, pets allowed. SGL/DBL$140-$155, STS$150-$175.

Hyatt Rickeys (4219 El Camino Real, 94306; 493-8000, Fax 424-0836, 800-233-1234) 347 rooms and suites, restaurant, lounge, swimming pool, meeting facilities, airport transportation, exercise equipment, wheelchair access, no-smoking rooms, pets allowed. SGL/DBL$125-$165.

Motel 6 (4301 El Camino Real, 94306; 949-0833) 71 rooms. SGL/DBL$34-$40.

Stanford Terrace Inn (532 Stanford Avenue, 94306; 857-0333, Fax 857-0343, 800-635-0554 in California) 78 rooms and suites, complimentary breakfast, swimming pool, no-smoking rooms, airport transportation, free parking. SGL$95-$120, DBL$95-$150.

The Town House Motel (4164 El Camino Real, 94306; 493-4492) 23 rooms. SGL/DBL$40-$45.

TraveLodge (3255 El Camino Real, 94306; 493-6340, Fax 424-9535, 800-255-3050) 29 rooms, restaurant, lounge, swimming pool, fax service, tours, car rental. SGL/DBL$60-$70.

Paradise

Area Code 916
Paradise Chamber of Commerce
5800 Clark Rd.
Paradise CA 95969
877-9356

The Lantern Motel (5700 Wildwood Lane, 95969; 877-5553) 16 rooms. SGL/DBL$35-$44.

Ponderosa Gardens Motel (7010 Skyway, 95969; 872-9094, Fax 872-2993) 36 rooms, swimming pool, wheelchair access, no-smoking rooms, pets allowed. SGL$45-$48, DBL$47-$57.

Pebble Beach

Area Code 408

The Inn and Links At Spanish Bay (Seventeen Mile Drive; 647-7500, Fax 647-7443, 800-654-9300) 270 rooms, restaurant, swimming pool, airport transportation, exercise equipment, wheelchair access, no-smoking rooms, pets allowed. SGL/DBL$230-$1500.

The Lodge At Pebble Beach (Seventeen Mile Drive, 93953; 624-3811, Fax 624-6357) 171 rooms, restaurant, swimming pool, wheelchair access, airport transportation, tennis, golf, exercise equipment, pets allowed. SGL/DBL$280-$1800.

Petaluma

Area Code 707
Petaluma Chamber of Commerce
314 Western Avenue
Petaluma CA 94952
762-2785

All Star Inn (1368 McDowell Blvd., 94952; 796-0333) 45 rooms. SGL/DBL$28-$34.

Best Western Petaluma Inn (200 South McDowell Blvd., 94952; 763-0994, Fax 778-3111, 800-528-1234) 75 rooms, restaurant, lounge, meeting facilities, children under 12 free, fax service, no pets, swimming pool, no-smoking rooms. LS SGL$46-$54, DBL$52-$60; HS SGL$76-$101, DBL$78-$103.

Cavanagh Inn (10 Keller Street, 94952; 756-4657) 7 rooms, bed & breakfast, complimentary breakfast. SGL/DBL$55-$95.

Motel 6 (5135 Montero Way, 94954; 664-9090) 62 rooms. SGL/DBL$30-$36.

Quality Inn (5100 Montero Way, 94954; 664-1155, Fax 664-8566, 800-221-2222) 110 rooms, restaurant, complimentary breakfast, swimming pool, whirlpool, sauna, tours, meeting facilities, airport transportation, wheelchair access, no-smoking rooms, pets allowed. SGL$54-$81, DBL$64-$94.

Seventh Street Inn (525 Seventh Street, 94952; 769-0480) 4 rooms, bed & breakfast, complimentary breakfast. SGL/DBL$76-$100.

Petrolia

Area Code 707

Mattole River Resort (42345 Mattole Rd., 95558; 629-3445, 800-845-4607) 6 cabins, pets allowed. SGL/DBL$35-$70.

Phillipsville

Area Code 707

Madrona Motel (2907 Avenue of the Giants, 95559; 943-3108) 9 rooms. SGL/DBL$25-$35.

Pico Rivera

Area Code 213
Pico Rivera Chamber of Commerce
9122 East Washington Blvd.
Pico Rivera CA 91101
795-9311

Econo Lodge (8477 Telegraph Rd., 90660; 869-9588, 800-446-6900) 45 rooms, complimentary breakfast, wheelchair access, children under 18 free, no pets. SGL/DBL$50-$100.

Rivera Motel (9118 Slauson Avenue, 90660; 948-4044) 40 rooms. SGL/DBL$35-$45.

TraveLodge (7222 Rosemead Blvd., 90660; 213-949-6648, 800-255-3050) 48 rooms, restaurant, lounge, swimming pool, jacuzzis, in-room refrigerators, no pets. SGL/DBL$42-$58.

Piercy

Area Code 707

Hartsook Country Inn (900 Highway 101; 247-3305) 64 rooms, restaurant. SGL/DBL$36-$95.

Pinole

Area Code 510

Econo Lodge (2600 Appian Way, 94564; 222-9400, 800-424-4777) 48 rooms, whirlpools, sauna, free local telephone calls, children under 18 free, wheelchair access, laundry room, no pets. SGL$40-$50, DBL$50-$60.

Motel 6 (1501 Fitzgerald Drive, 94564; 222-8174) 102 rooms. SGL/DBL$36-$42.

Placerville

Area Code 916
El Dorado County Chamber of Commerce
542 Main Street Placerville CA 95667
626-2344

Best Western Inn (Highway 50, 95667; 622-9100, Fax 622-9376, 800-528-1234) 105 rooms, restaurant, lounge, swimming pool, fireplaces, fax service, meeting facilities, wheelchair access, no-smoking rooms, pets allowed. SGL/DBL$53-$130.

Cary House (300 Main Street, 95667; 622-4271) 24 rooms. SGL/DBL$40-$65.

Days Inn (1332 Broadway, 95667; 622-3124, 800-325-2525) 45 rooms and suites, complimentary breakfast, swimming pool, free local telephone calls, children under 12 free, fax service, wheelchair access, no-smoking rooms, no pets. SGL/DBL$48-$61, STS$70-$80.

River Rock Inn (1756 Georgetown Drive, 95667; 622-7640) 4 rooms, bed & breakfast, complimentary breakfast. SGL$55, DBL$70.

Pleasant Hill

Area Code 415
Pleasant Hill Chamber of Commerce
1881 Contra Costa Blvd.
Pleasant Hill CA 94523
687-0700

Marriott Residence Inn (700 Ellinwood Way, 94523; 689-1010, Fax 689-1098, 800-331-3131) 154 rooms, restaurant, complimentary breakfast, meeting facilities for 30, in-room microwaves, wheelchair access, no-smoking rooms, pets allowed, exercise equipment. SGL/DBL$109-$139.

Pleasanton

Area Code 510
Pleasanton Chamber of Commerce
450 Main Street
Pleasanton CA 94566
846-8910

Courtyard by Marriott (5059 Hopyard Rd., 94566; 463-1414, Fax 463-0113) 159 rooms and suites, restaurant, swimming pool, exercise equipment, wheelchair access, no-smoking rooms. SGL/DBL$79-$90.

Doubletree Club Hotel Pleasanton (5990 Stoneridge Mall Rd., 94588; 463-3330, Fax 463-3330, 800-528-0444) 171 rooms and suites, restaurant, lounge, complimentary breakfast, outdoor swimming pool, spa, sauna, meeting facilities for 40, airport transportation, exercise equipment, free parking, wheelchair access. SGL$79-$99, DBL$89-$109.

Hilton Inn (7050 Johnson Drive, 94566; 463-8000, Fax 463-3330) 171 rooms and suites, complimentary breakfast, swimming pool, exercise equipment, meeting facilities for 500, business services, wheelchair access, no-smoking rooms, pets allowed. SGL/DBL$60-$100.

Holiday Inn (11950 Dublin Canyon Rd., 94588; 847-847-6000, Fax 463-2585, 800-HOLIDAY) 248 rooms and suites, restaurant, lounge, swimming pool, meeting facilities for 280, exercise equipment, airport transportation, wheelchair access, no-smoking rooms. SGL/DBL$85-$135.

Sheraton Inn Pleasanton (5115 Hopyard Rd., 94588; 501-8800, Fax 415-847-9455, 800-325-3535) 215 rooms and suites, restaurant, lounge, outdoor heated swimming pool, spa, exercise equipment, meeting facilities for 500, business services, airport transportation, wheelchair access, no-smoking rooms. SGL$75-$110, DBL$85-$120.

Super 8 Motel (5375 Owens Court, 94566; 415-463-1300, Fax 415-734-8843, 800-800-8000) 102 rooms and suites, restaurant, complimentary breakfast, outdoor swimming pool, spa, free local telephone calls, complimentary newspaper, valet laundry, wheelchair access, no-smoking rooms, no pets. SGL/DBL$63-$72.

Point Arena

Area Code 707

RENTAL SOURCES: Point Arena Lighthouse Rentals and Museum (Lighthouse Rd., 95468; 882-2777) rental lighthouses. $80-$110.

La Boube's Sea Shell Motel (135 Main Street, 94568; 882-2000) 32 rooms and efficiencies. SGL/DBL$35-$55.

Wharfmaster's Inn (785 Port Rd., 94568; 882-3171, Fax 882-2576) 26 rooms. SGL/DBL$100-$300.

Point Reyes Station

Area Code 415

RENTAL SOURCES: Cottages of Point Reyes (663-9445) reservation service for local bed & breakfasts. **Inns of Point Reyes** (663-1420) reservation service for local bed & breakfasts and inns.

Holly Tree Inn (Box 642, 94956; 663-1554) 6 rooms, bed & breakfast, complimentary breakfast, wheelchair access. SGL/DBL$101-$125.

Jasmine Cottage (Box 56, 94956; 663-1166) one room, bed & breakfast, complimentary breakfast, wheelchair access. SGL/DBL$101-$125.

Pollock Pines

Area Code 916

Pollock Pines-Camino Chamber of Commerce
6207 Pony Express Trail
Pollock Pines CA 95726
644-3970

Stagecoach Inn (5940 Pony Express Trail, 95726; 644-2029, Fax 644-6937, 800-622-8802) 26 rooms and efficiencies, complimentary breakfast, children under 8 stay free, free local telephone calls, free parking, pets allowed, wheelchair access, no-smoking rooms. SGL$45, DBL$50.

Quincy

Area Code 916
Plumas County Chamber of Commerce
500 Jackson Street
Quincy CA 95971
283-2045

Budget Host Lariet Lodge (2370 East Main Street, 95971; 283-1000, 800-999-7199) 20 rooms, swimming pool, airport transportation, no-smoking rooms. SGL/DBL$35-$50.

Feather Bed (Box 3200, 95971; 283-0102) 7 rooms, bed & breakfast, complimentary breakfast. SGL/DBL$65.

Gold Pan Motel (200 Crescent Street, 95971; 283-3686) 283-3686) 48 rooms, complimentary breakfast, swimming pool, wheelchair access, no-smoking rooms, pets allowed. SGL$32-$50, DBL$38-$59.

Ranchito Motel (2020 East Main Street, 95971; 283-2265) 30 rooms and efficiencies, wheelchair access, no-smoking rooms. SGL/DBL$39-$45.

Rancho Cordova

Area Code 619
Rancho Cordova Chamber of Commerce
11070 White Rock Rd.
Rancho Cordova CA 95670
638-8700

All Star Inn (10694 Olson Drive, 95670; 971-9440) 89 rooms. SGL/DBL$27-$33.

Best Inn (10800 Olson Drive, 95670; 638-2500) 148 rooms and suites, swimming pool, wheelchair access, no-smoking rooms. SGL/DBL$30-$50.

Best Western Heritage Inn (11269 Point East Drive, 95670; 635-4040, Fax 635-7198, 800-446-4290, 800-528-1234) 127 rooms, restaurant, lounge, swimming pool, whirlpools, meeting facilities, fax service, wheelchair access, no-smoking rooms. SGL/DBL$52-$74.

Comfort Inn (3240 Mather Field Rd., 95670; 363-3344, 800-221-2222) 112 rooms, complimentary breakfast, swimming pool, whirlpool, meeting facilities, exercise equipment, wheelchair access. SGL$59-$79, DBL$69-$89.

Courtyard by Marriott (10683 White Rock Rd., 95670; 638-3800, Fax 638-6776) 145 rooms and suites, restaurant, swimming pool, exercise equipment, wheelchair access. SGL/DBL$75-$85, STS$80-$100.

Days Inn (11131 Folsom Blvd., 95670; 635-0666, Fax 635-3297, 800-325-2525) 130 rooms, restaurant, lounge, swimming pool, whirlpool, airport courtesy car, fax service, children under 12 free, valet laundry, wheelchair access, no-smoking rooms, no pets. SGL$49-$65, DBL$55-$75.

Economy Inns of America (12249 Folsom Blvd., 95670; 351-1213, 800-826-0778) 124 rooms, complimentary breakfast, swimming pool. SGL/DBL$38-$48.

Fairfield Inn by Marriott (10713 White Rock Rd., 95670; 631-7500) 117 rooms. SGL/DBL$43+.

Motel 6 (10271 Folsom Blvd., 95670; 362-5800) 122 rooms. SGL/DBL$25-$32.

Quality Suites (11260 Point East Drive, 95742; 638-4141, 800-221-2222) 127 rooms, restaurant, lounge, complimentary breakfast, swimming pool, whirlpool, airport courtesy car, exercise equipment, wheelchair access, no-smoking rooms, no pets. SGL/DBL$65-$130.

Sheraton Rancho Cordova Hotel (11211 Point East Drive, 95742; 638-1100, Fax 638-5803, 800-325-3535) 275 rooms and suites, three restaurants, lounge, outdoor heated swimming pools, whirlpool, golf course, lighted tennis courts, meeting facilities for 4000, gift shop, exercise equipment, complimentary airport car, wheelchair access, no-smoking rooms. SGL/DBL$80-$120, STS$250-$300.

Rancho Cucamonga

Area Code 714

Best Western Heritage Inn (8179 Spruce Avenue, 91730; 466-1111, 800-528-1234) 120 rooms, restaurant, lounge, complimentary breakfast, swimming pool, spa, meeting facilities, laundry room, fax service, in-room refrigerators and microwaves, exercise equipment, no-smoking rooms. SGL$44-$75, DBL$54-$85.

Christmas House (9240 Archibald Avenue, 91730; 980-6450) 7 rooms, bed & breakfast, complimentary breakfast. SGL/DBL$75.

Red Bluff

Area Code 916
Red Bluff Chamber of Commerce
100 Main Street
Red Bluff CA 96080
527-6220

Buttons and Bows (427 Washington Street, 96090; 527-6405, 800-473-7808) 3 rooms, bed & breakfast, complimentary breakfast. SGL$53-$63, DBL$55-$65.

Friendship Kings Lodge (38 Antelope Blvd., 96080; 527-6020, Fax 527-4653, 800-426-5655) 40 rooms, swimming pool, no-smoking rooms, pets allowed. SGL/DBL$80-$120.

The Jeter Victorian Inn (1107 Jefferson Street, 96080; 527-7575) 4 rooms, bed & breakfast, complimentary breakfast. SGL$75-$140.

Lamplighter Lodge (210 South Main Street, 96080; 527-1150) 51 rooms and apartments, restaurant, complimentary breakfast, swimming pool, airport courtesy car, no-smoking rooms. SGL/DBL$85+.

Super 8 Motel (203 Antelope Rd., 96080; 527-5078, Fax 527-5078, 800-800-8000) 72 rooms, restaurant, complimentary breakfast, outdoor swimming pool, wheelchair access, fax service, free local telephone calls, no-smoking rooms, pets allowed. SGL/DBL$34-$39.

Redding

Area Code 916
Redding Convention and Visitors Bureau
777 Auditorium Drive
Redding CA 96001

225-4100

Shasta Cascade Wonderland Association
1250 Parkview Avenue
Redding CA 96001
243-2643

All Star Inn (2385 Bechelli Lane, 96001; 221-0565) 105 rooms. SGL/DBL$30-$36.

Bel Air Motel (540 Market Street, 96002; 243-5291) 46 rooms and efficiencies, swimming pool. SGL/DBL$65-$78.

Best Western Hilltop Inn (2300 Hilltop Drive, 96002; 221-6100, Fax 221-2867, 800-336-4880, 800-528-1234) 113 rooms, restaurant, lounge, complimentary breakfast, swimming pool, spa, whirlpool, meeting facilities for 100, wheelchair access, no-smoking rooms, pets allowed. SGL/DBL$65-$90.

Best Western Hospitality House Motel (532 North Market Street, 96003; 241-6464, 800-528-1234) 63 rooms, restaurant, swimming pool, meeting facilities, no-smoking rooms, pets allowed. SGL$32-$46, DBL$38-$51.

Best Western Ponderosa Inn (2220 Pine Street, 96001; 241-6300, 800-528-1234) 70 rooms, restaurant, lounge, meeting facilities, fax service, swimming pool, no-smoking rooms, tennis, pets allowed. SGL/DBL$39-$57.

Bridge Bay Resort (10300 Bridge Bay Rd., 96003; 275-3021, Fax 275-8365, 800-752-9669) 40 rooms and efficiencies, restaurant, swimming pool, pets allowed. SGL/DBL$90+.

Casa Blanca Motel (413 North Market Street, 96002; 241-3010) 63 rooms and efficiencies, swimming pool, pets allowed. SGL/DBL$50-$80.

Cedar Lodge (513 North Market Street, 96002; 244-3251) 17 rooms and efficiencies, pets allowed. SGL/DBL$50.

Colony Inn (2731 Bechelli Lane, 96002; 223-1935) 74 rooms, swimming pool, free local telephone calls, free coffee, wheelchair access. SGL/DBL$45-$63.

Days Inn (2180 Hilltop Drive, 96002; 221-8200, Fax 223-4727, 800-325-2525) 144 rooms and suites, restaurant, swimming pool, airport courtesy car, wheelchair access, no-smoking rooms. SGL/DBL$49-$89, STS$125-$150.

Econo Lodge (2010 Pine Street, 96001; 243-3336, 800-424-4777) 60 rooms and efficiencies, swimming pool, children under 18 free, pets allowed. SGL/DBL$45-$60.

Holiday Inn (1900 Hilltop Drive, 96002; 221-7500, 800-HOLIDEX) 165 rooms, restaurant, lounge, children under 18 free, swimming pool, meeting facilities for 1200, wheelchair access, airport transportation, pets allowed. SGL/DBL$64-$71.

Knotty Pine Motel (3510 Market Street, 96002; 243-3392) 16 rooms and efficiencies. SGL/DBL$38-$58.

Motel 6 (1640 Hilltop Drive, 96002; 221-1800) 80 rooms, restaurant, swimming pool, no-smoking rooms. SGL/DBL$30+.

Motel 6 (1250 Twin View Blvd., 96003; 246-4470) 97 rooms. SGL/DBL$30-$36.

Motel 99 (533 North Market Street, 96002; 241-4942) 26 rooms and efficiencies, swimming pool, wheelchair access. SGL/DBL$48-$58.

Red Lion Inn (1830 Hilltop Drive, 96001; 221-8700, 800-547-8010) 195 rooms, restaurant, swimming pool, airport courtesy car, wheelchair access, no-smoking rooms, free parking, pets allowed. SGL/DBL$69-$104.

River Inn Motor Hotel (1835 Park Marina Drive, 96001; 241-9599) 79 rooms, restaurant, heated swimming pool, sauna, water view, balconies, wheelchair access, no-smoking rooms, pets allowed. SGL$40-$50, DBL$45-$55.

Super 8 Motel (5175 Churn Creek Rd., 96002; 221-8881, Fax 221-8881, 800-800-8000) 80 rooms, restaurant, complimentary breakfast, outdoor swimming pool, spa, fax service, free local telephone calls, wheelchair access, no-smoking rooms, no pets. SGL/DBL$39-$43.

Thunderbird Lodge (1350 Pine Street, 96002; 243-5422) 66 rooms and efficiencies, swimming pool. SGL/DBL$65.

Vagabond Inn (536 East Cypress Avenue, 96002; 223-1600, Fax 221-4247, 800-522-1555) 71 rooms, restaurant, complimentary breakfast, heated swimming pool, wheelchair access, no-smoking rooms, in-room refrigerators, pets allowed, airport transportation, free local telephone calls, no-smoking rooms, children under 18 free, fax service, complimentary newspaper. SGL$48-$55, DBL$53-$55.

Redway

Area Code 707

Dean Creek Resort (4112 Redwood Drive, 95560; 923-2555) 11 rooms and efficiencies, swimming pool. SGL/DBL$50-$70.

Redwood City

Area Code 415
Redwood City-San Mateo County Chamber of Commerce
1006 Middlefield Rd.
Redwood City CA 94063
592-6282

Best Western Sundial Motel (316 El Camino Real, 94062; 366-3808, Fax 364-9380, 800-528-1234) 26 rooms, restaurant, swimming pool, children under 12 free, fax service, no-smoking rooms, no pets. SGL$50, DBL$56+.

Best Western Executive Suites (25 Fifth Avenue, 94063; 366-5794, Fax 365-1429, 800-528-1234) 26 rooms and suites, complimentary breakfast, exercise equipment, children under 12 free, whirlpools, in-room refrigerators and microwaves, fax service, no-smoking rooms, no pets. SGL/DBL$75-$150.

Capri Motel (2380 El Camino Real, 94063; 369-6221) 50 rooms, swimming pool, no-smoking rooms. SGL$32, DBL$36.

Comfort Inn (1818 El Camino Real, 94063; 800-221-2222) 52 rooms and suites, complimentary breakfast, swimming pool, whirlpool, meeting facilities, wheelchair access, no pets. SGL$55-$65, DBL$70-$85.

Continental Garden Motel (2650 El Camino Real, 94061; 369-0321, 800-556-1177, 800-453-7070 in California) 70 rooms and efficiencies, complimentary breakfast, swimming pool, no-smoking rooms. SGL/DBL$40-$45, EFF$55-$60.

Garden Motel (1690 Broadway, 94063; 366-4724) 17 rooms and efficiencies. SGL$30, DBL$35.

Howard Johnson Motor Lodge (485 Veterans Blvd., 94063; 365-5500, Fax 365-1119, 800-654-2000) 125 rooms, restaurant, lounge, swimming pool, fax service, car rental, meeting facilities for 125, child care, wheelchair access, no-smoking rooms, pets allowed, airport courtesy car. SGL$49-$64, DBL$59-$69.

Mayfair Motel (2526 El Camino Real, 94061; 365-7575) 40 rooms. SGL$32, DBL$37.

Redwood Rancho Motel (2834 El Camino Real, 94061; 366-8272) 27 rooms and efficiencies, swimming pool. SGL$37, DBL$40+.

Redwood Town House (1090 El Camino Real, 94063; 369-1731) 35 rooms, swimming pool. SGL$36, DBL$40.

Hotel Sofitel San Francisco Bay (223 Twin Dolphin Drive, 94065; 598-9000, Fax 598-0459, 800-221-4542) 350 rooms and suites, restaurant, swimming pool, meeting facilities for 750, child care, gift shop, no-smoking rooms, exercise equipment, wheelchair access, airport courtesy car, free parking. SGL$125, DBL$140.

Whipple Lodge (1225 Warren Street, 94063; 365-5000) 37 rooms and efficiencies, no-smoking rooms, wheelchair access. SGL/DBL$28+.

Reseda

Area Code 818
Reseda Chamber of Commerce
18305 Sherman Way #202
Reseda CA 91335
345-1920

Howard Johnson Lodge (7432 Reseda Blvd., 91335; 344-0324, Fax 344-7188, 800-523-4825, 800-654-2000, 800-225-0973 in California) 74 rooms and suites, complimentary breakfast, swimming pool, meeting facilities, in-room refrigerators and microwaves, wheelchair access, no-smoking rooms, no pets. SGL$54-$92, DBL$62-$102.

Richmond

Area Code 510

Days Inn (3150 Garrity Way, 94806; 262-0700, Fax 262-0927, 800-325-2525) 152 rooms and suites, restaurant, lounge, swimming pool, spa, children under 12 free, fax service, wheelchair access, no-smoking rooms, exercise equipment. SGL$59-$85, DBL$69-$95, STS$85-$125.

The Point Marina Inn (915 West Cutting Blvd., 94804; 237-3000, Fax 237-1175) 106 rooms, restaurant, swimming pool. SGL$40-$65, DBL$46-$71.

Rio Dell

Area Code 707
Rio Dell-Scotia Chamber of Commerce
715 Wildwood Avenue
Rio Dell CA 95526
764-3436

Humboldt Gables Motel (40 West Davis, 95526; 764-5609) 20 rooms. SGL/DBL$36-$40.

Rocklin

Area Code 916
Rocklin Area Chamber of Commerce
4253 Rocklin Rd.
Rocklin CA 95677
624-2548

First Choice Inn (4420 Rocklin Rd., 95677; 624-4500, Fax 624-5982, 800-462-2400) 90 rooms, efficiencies and suites, restaurant, complimentary breakfast, swimming pool, wheelchair access, airport transportation, no-smoking rooms, pets allowed. SGL/DBL$60-$75, STS$80-$90.

Rohnert Park

Area Code 707
Rohnert Park Chamber of Commerce
6020 Commerce Blvd.
Rohnert Park CA 94928
584-1415

Best Western Inn (6500 Redwood Drive, 94928; 584-7435, Fax 584-3848, 800-528-1234) 145 rooms, restaurant, swimming pool, whirlpool, fax service, children under 12 free, no-smoking rooms, pets allowed. LS SGL/DBL$40-$54; HS SGL/DBL$52-$68.

Good Night Inn (5040 Redwood Drive, 94928; 584-8180) 120 rooms, swimming pool. SGL/DBL$30-$36.

Motel 6 (6145 Commerce Blvd., 94928; 585-8888) 127 rooms. SGL/DBL$27-$33.

Red Lion Inn (One Red Lion Drive, 94928; 584-5466, 800-547-8010) 245 rooms and suites, restaurant, lounge, swimming pool, spa, room service, gift shop, meeting and convention facilities, exercise equipment, tennis, free parking, airport courtesy car. SGL/DBL$89-$110.

Roseville

Area Code 916
Roseville Area Chamber of Commerce
700 Vernon Street
Roseville CA 95678
783-8136

Best Western Inn (220 Harding Blvd., 95678; 782-4434, Fax 782-8335, 800-528-1234) 134 rooms, restaurant, lounge, complimentary breakfast, swimming pool, hot tubs, spa, no-smoking rooms, wheelchair access/room, pets allowed. SGL/DBL$48-$67.

Heritage Inn (204 Harding Blvd., 95678; 782-4466, Fax 782-4461) 101 rooms. SGL/DBL$44-$56.

Rutherford

Area Code 707

Auberge Du Soleil (180 Rutherford Hill Rd., 94573; 963-1211, Fax 963-8764) 50 rooms, restaurant, swimming pool, tennis, airport transportation, wheelchair access, pets allowed. SGL/DBL$275-$725.

Rancho Caymus Inn (1140 Rutherford, 94573; 963-1777, 800-845-1777) 26 rooms and suites, restaurant, complimentary breakfast, free local telephone calls, meeting facilities for 50, free parking, wheelchair access, no pets. SGL$95-$295.

Sacramento and West Sacramento

Area Code 916
Sacramento Convention and Visitors Bureau
131 11th Street
Sacramento CA 95814
442-5542

West Sacramento District Chamber of Commerce
1420 Merkley Avenue
West Sacramento CA 95691
371-7042

All Star Inn (1254 Halyard Drive, 95691; 372-3624) 26 rooms. SGL/DBL$60-$70.

All Star Inn (227 Jibboom Street, 95814; 441-0733) 34 rooms. SGL/DBL$28-$34.

All Star Inn (5110 Interstate, 95482; 331-8100) 32 rooms. SGL/DBL$28-$34.

Amber House (1315 22nd Street, 95816; 444-8085, 800-755-6526) 8 rooms and suites, bed & breakfast, complimentary breakfast, jacuzzi, fax service, free local telephone calls, free parking, valet laundry, airport transportation, no-smoking. SGL$75-$155, DBL$85-$195.

Aunt Abigail's (2120 G Street, 95816; 441-5007, 800-858-1568) 6 rooms, bed & breakfast, complimentary breakfast, spa, free local telephone calls, fax service, free parking, no smoking, no pets. SGL$70-$95, DBL$75-$125.

Bear Flag Inn (2814 I Street, 95816; 448-5417) 5 rooms, bed & breakfast, complimentary breakfast, no-smoking. SGL/DBL$70-$135.

The Best Inn (9646 Micron Way, 95827; 361-3131) 93 rooms. SGL/DBL$24-$39.

Best Western Harbor Inn and Suites (1250 Halyard Drive, 95691; 371-2100, Fax 373-1507, 800-528-1234) 99 rooms and suites, restaurant, swimming pool, airport courtesy car, fax service, free local telephone calls, no-smoking rooms. SGL/DBL$51-$87.

Best Western Ponderosa Motor Inn (1100 H Street, 95814; 441-1314, Fax 441-5961, 800-528-1234) 98 rooms, restaurant, lounge, complimentary breakfast, swimming pool, children under 12 free, fax service, free parking, no-smoking rooms, no pets. SGL/DBL$65-$84.

Best Western Sandman Motel (236 Jibboom Street, 95814; 443-6515, Fax 443-8346, 800-528-1234) 115 rooms, restaurant, swimming pool, airport transportation, laundry room, children under 12 free, no-smoking rooms, no pets. SGL/DBL$42-$58

Beverly Garland Hotel (1780 Tribute Rd., 95815; 929-7900, Fax 921-9147, 800-972-3976) 210 rooms and suites, restaurant, swimming pool, airport courtesy car, wheelchair access, no-smoking rooms. SGL/DBL$80-$95, STS$100-$200+.

Canterbury Inn (1900 Canterbury Rd., 95815; 927-3492) 154 rooms, restaurant, swimming pool, airport transportation, no-smoking rooms. SGL/DBL$55-$65.

Capitol Travel Inn (817 West Capitol Street, 956591; 371-6983) 38 rooms, swimming pool, no-smoking rooms. SGL$28-$32, DBL$36-$40.

Clarion Hotel (700 16th Street, 95814; 444-8000, Fax 442-8129, 800-221-2222) 239 rooms, restaurant, lounge, swimming pool, meeting facilities, airport transportation, wheelchair access, no pets. SGL$89-$99, DBL$99-$109.

Comfort Inn South (5321 Stockton Blvd., 95820; 454-5533, 800-221-2222) 93 rooms, restaurant, swimming pool, meeting facilities, wheelchair access, no pets. SGL$44-$49, DBL$52-$57.

Coral Reef Lodge (2700 Fulton Avenue, 95821; 483-6461, 800-255-1551 in California) 57 rooms and suites, restaurant, swimming pool. SGL/DBL$40-$75, STS$55-$75.

Crossroads Inn (221 Jibboom Street, 95814; 442-7777) 30 rooms. SGL/DBL$38-$45.

Days Inn Downtown (200 Jibboom Street, 95814; 448-8100, Fax 447-3621, 800-325-2525) 175 rooms, restaurant, swimming pool, meeting facilities, children under 12 free, fax service, airport transportation, wheelchair access, no-smoking rooms. SGL$38-$56, DBL$42-$68.

Discovery Motor Inn (350 Bercut Drive, 95814; 442-6971, Fax 444-2809, 800-952-5516 in California) 101 rooms and suites, restaurant, complimentary breakfast, swimming pool, airport courtesy car, wheelchair access, no-smoking rooms. SGL/DBL$60-$135, STS$100-$135.

Driver Mansion Inn (2019 21st Street, 95818; 455-5243, Fax 445-6102) 9 rooms, bed & breakfast, complimentary breakfast, no-smoking. SGL/DBL$75-$225.

Econo Lodge (1319 30th Street, 95816; 454-4400, Fax 736-2812, 800-446-6900, 800-424-4777) 83 rooms, restaurant, swimming pool, no-smoking rooms, children under 18 free, pets allowed. SGL/DBL$45-$50.

Economy Inns of America (25 Howe Avenue, 95826; 386-8404, 800-826-0778) 102 rooms, complimentary breakfast, swimming pool. SGL/DBL$35-$47.

Fountain Suites (321 Bercut Drive, 95814; 441-1444, Fax 441-6530, 800-767-1777) 200 suites, restaurant, complimentary breakfast, swimming pool, airport courtesy car, exercise equipment, wheelchair access, no-smoking rooms. STS$85-$300.

Golden Tee Inn (3216 Auburn Blvd., 95821; 482-7440) 35 rooms, swimming pool. SGL/DBL$30+.

Hartley House (700 22nd Street, 95816; 447-7829) 5 rooms, bed & breakfast, complimentary breakfast. SGL$65, DBL$85.

Hilton Inn (2200 Harvard Street, 95815; 922-4700, Fax 922-8414, 800-HILTONS) 325 rooms and suites, restaurant, outdoor swimming pool, airport courtesy car, meeting facilities for 800, exercise equipment, wheelchair access, no-smoking rooms, pets allowed. SGL/DBL$70-$130, STS$250-$450+.

Holiday Inn Northeast (5321 Date Avenue, 95841; 338-5800, Fax 334-2868, 800-HOLIDAY) 230 rooms and suites, restaurant, lounge, swimming pool, exercise equipment, wheelchair access, airport transportation. SGL/DBL$73-$99, STS$100-$165.

Holiday Inn Capitol Plaza (300 J Street, 95814; 446-0100, Fax 446-0100, 800-HOLIDAY) 370 rooms and suites, restaurant, lounge, swimming pool, gift shop, meeting facilities for 1000, concierge, children under 18 free, exercise equipment, airport transportation, wheelchair access, no-smoking rooms, pets allowed. SGL/DBL$80-$95, STS$175-$500+.

Howard Johnson Continental Inn (3343 Bradshaw Rd., 95827; 366-1266, Fax 366-1266, 800-654-2000) 126 rooms, restaurant, lounge, swimming pool, room service, meeting facilities, valet laundry, fax service, exercise equipment, wheelchair access, pets allowed. SGL$58-$63, DBL$63-$68.

Host Airport Hotel (6945 Airport Blvd., 95837; 922-8071, Fax 929-8636) 90 rooms, restaurant, swimming pool, wheelchair access, no-smoking rooms. SGL$85+, DBL$95+.

Hyatt Regency (1209 L Street, 95814; 321-6699, Fax 443-1234, 800-233-1234) 538 rooms and suites, restaurant, lounge, heated swimming pool, jacuzzi, airport transportation, exercise equipment, wheelchair access, no-smoking rooms. SGL/DBL$150-$185, STS$180-$800+.

La Quinta Inn (4604 Madison Avenue, 95841; 348-0900, Fax 331-7160, 800-531-5900) 129 rooms, restaurant, swimming pool, wheelchair access, meeting facilities, no-smoking rooms, pets allowed. SGL/DBL$55-$67.

Los Robles Lodge (2200 Auburn Blvd., 95821; 921-0200) 35 rooms, restaurant, swimming pool, pets allowed. SGL/DBL$35-$45.

Marriott Residence Inn (1530 Howe Avenue, 95825; 920-9111, Fax 921-5664, 800-331-3131) 126 rooms, airport transportation, meeting facilities for 24, in-room microwaves, exercise equipment, no-smoking rooms. SGL/DBL$125-$135.

Motel 6 (7850 College Town Drive, 95826; 383-8110, 505-891-6161) 118 rooms. SGL/DBL$30-$36.

Motel 6 (7407 Elsie Avenue, 95828; 689-6555, 505-891-6161) 122 rooms. SGL/DBL$29-$35.

Motel 6 (7780 Stockton Blvd., 95823; 689-9141, 505-891-6161) 59 rooms. SGL/DBL$30-$36.

Motel 6 (1415 30th Street, 95816; 457-0777, 505-891-6161) 94 rooms. SGL/DBL$30-$36.

Radisson (500 Leisure Lane, 95815; 922-2020, Fax 649-9463, 800-333-3333) 309 rooms and suites, restaurant, swimming pool, airport courtesy car, exercise equipment, wheelchair access, no-smoking rooms, pets allowed. SGL/DBL$95-$110, STS$170+.

Red Lion Hotel Sacramento (2001 Point West Way, 95815; 929-8855, 800-547-8010) 448 rooms and suites, restaurant, lounge, two swimming pools, gift shop, room service, meeting and convention facilities, exercise equipment, free parking, airport courtesy car, pets allowed. SGL/DBL$80-$100, STS$150-$425+.

Red Lion Inn Sacramento (1401 Arden Way, 95815; 922-8041, 800-547-8010) 378 rooms and suites, restaurant, lounge, three swimming pools, putting green, gift shop, room service, meeting and convention facilities, exercise equipment, free parking, airport courtesy car, wheelchair access, no-smoking rooms, pets allowed. SGL/DBL$70-$90, STS$90-$105.

Residence Inn by Marriott (1530 Howe Avenue, 95825; 920-9111, Fax 921-5664, 800-331-3131) 176 efficiencies, complimentary breakfast, swimming pool, airport courtesy car, wheelchair access, no-smoking rooms. SGL/DBL$95-$115.

Riverboat Delta King (1000 Front Street, 95814; 444-5464, Fax 444-5314) 45 rooms. SGL/DBL$95-$125.

Sierra Inn (2600 Auburn Blvd., 95821; 482-4770, Fax 481-7112) 180 rooms, restaurant, complimentary breakfast, swimming pool, airport transportation, exercise equipment, wheelchair access, no-smoking rooms. SGL/DBL$60-$75.

Sterling Hotel (1300 H Street, 95814; 448-1300, Fax 448-8066, 800-365-7660) 12 rooms and suites, restaurant, in-room refrigerators, meeting facilities for 175, airport transportation, free parking, exercise equipment, jacuzzis, wheelchair access, no smoking, no pets. SGL/DBL$95-$225, STS$175-$225.

Super 8 Motel (7216 55th Street, 95823; 427-7925, Fax 424-9011, 800-800-8000) 61 rooms, restaurant, outdoor swimming pool, wheelchair access, kitchenettes, fax service, no-smoking rooms, pets allowed. SGL/DBL$40-$45.

Super 8 Motel (4317 Madison Avenue, 95824; 334-7430, Fax 331-8916, 800-800-8000) 128 rooms, restaurant, complimentary breakfast, outdoor swimming pool, free local telephone calls, valet laundry, complimentary newspaper, wheelchair access, no-smoking rooms, no pets. SGL/DBL$55-$66.

Super 8 Motel (216 Bannon Street, 95814; 447-5400, Fax 447-5153, 800-800-8000) 40 rooms and suites, restaurant, complimentary breakfast, spa, sauna, laundry room, free local telephone calls, fax service, meeting facilities, wheelchair access, no-smoking rooms. SGL/DBL$52-$60.

Town and Country Inn (2060 Auburn Blvd., 95821; 922-8801) 35 rooms, restaurant, swimming pool, pets allowed. SGL/DBL$18-$45.

Traveler's Inn (3796 Northgate Blvd., 95834; 927-7117, Fax 646-1433) 132 rooms, swimming pool, wheelchair access, no-smoking rooms. SGL/DBL$65-$89.

TraveLodge (1111 H Street, 95814; 444-8800, Fax 447-7540, 800-255-3050) 71 rooms, restaurant, lounge, meeting facilities for 35, no pets. SGL/DBL$40-$55.

Vagabond Inn (909 Third Street, 95814; 446-1481, Fax 448-0364, 800-522-1555) 107 rooms, restaurant, complimentary breakfast, heated swimming pool, in-room refrigerators, wheelchair access, pets allowed, airport transportation, free local telephone calls, no-smoking rooms, children under 18 free, fax service, complimentary newspaper. SGL$52-$56, DBL$57-$66.

San Andreas

Area Code 209

Black Cart Inn and Motel (55 West St. Charles, 95249; 754-3808) 25 rooms, restaurant, meeting facilities for 275. SGL/DBL$23-$60.

Courtyard Bed and Breakfast (334 West St. Charles, 95249; 754-1518) 2 rooms, bed & breakfast, complimentary breakfast, private baths. SGL/DBL$55-$75.

Robin's News (247 West St. Charles, 95249; 754-1075) 9 rooms, bed & breakfast, complimentary breakfast, private baths. SGL/DBL$55-$95.

San Bruno

Area Code 415
San Bruno Chamber of Commerce
618 San Mateo Avenue
San Bruno CA 94066
588-0180

Courtyard by Marriott (1050 Bayhill Drive, 94066; 952-3333, 800-321-2211) 147 rooms and suites, restaurant, swimming pool, wheelchair access, no-smoking rooms. SGL$78, DBL$88.

El Patio Motel (850 El Camino Real, 94066; 589-6969) 29 rooms, airport transportation. SGL$35-$40, DBL$45-$50.

Knights Rest Motor Lodge (411 East San Bruno Avenue, 94066; 589-7535) 32 rooms and efficiencies. SGL$34-$35. DBL$35+.

Summerfield Suites Hotel (1350 Huntington Avenue, 94066; 588-0770, Fax 588-0892, 800-33-FIELD) 94 suites, complimentary breakfast, swimming pool, exercise equipment, airport courtesy car, free parking, pets allowed. SGL/DBL$119-$140.

San Carlos

Area Code 415
San Carlos Chamber of Commerce
1250 San Carlos Avenue San Carlos CA 94070
593-1068

Ho Hum Motel (1140 Morse Blvd., 94070; 595-9805) 9 rooms. SGL$20-$32, DBL$34.

San Carlos Inn (1562 El Camino Real, 94070; 591-6655, 800-554-8585 in California) 32 rooms, complimentary breakfast, wheelchair access. SGL/DBL$42-$48.

TraveLodge (26 El Camino Real, 94070; 591-5771, 800-255-3050) 29 rooms, restaurant, swimming pool, tours, complimentary newspaper, no-smoking rooms, no pets. SGL$39, DBL$54.

San Francisco and South San Francisco

Area Code 415
San Francisco Convention and Visitors Bureau
201 Third Street #90
San Francisco CA 94102
391-2000

RENTAL SOURCES:: San Francisco Reservations (1012 Darms Lane, 94558; 441-2261, 800-882-9463) rents accommodations in the San Francisco and Napa Valley areas. SGL/DBL$45-$225.

RESERVATION SERVICES: American Property Exchange (170 Page Street, 94102; 863-8484, 800-747-7784) rents condos and apartments throughout San Francisco. SGL/DBL$45-$200. **Bed and Breakfast Exchange** (1458 Lincoln Avenue, Callistoga, 94515; 707-942-5900) represents 140 bed & breakfasts and small hotels in the Napa and Sonoma

Valley, San Francisco and the North Coast. $65-$300+. **Bed and Breakfast International** (Box 282910, 94128; 696-1690, Fax 696-1699, 800-872-4500) represents bed & breakfast accommodations throughout California. Accommodations available in private home, houseboats on the Bay and inns. All rates include complimentary breakfast. SGL/DBL$50-$125. **Bed and Breakfast San Francisco** (Box 420009, 94142; 479-1913; 800-452-8249) reservation service representing bed & breakfast inns and homestays in the San Francisco, Monterey and Carmel areas. **Bed and Breakfast San Francisco** (Box 349, 94101; 931-3083) represents local bed & breakfasts. **Golden Gate Lodging Reservations** (1030 Franklin, 94109; 771-6915, Fax 771-1458, 800-423-7846) reservation service offering special rates and discounts at over 150 San Francisco and Sonoma/Napa wine country hotels. SGL/DBL$45. **Inns By Design** (Box 5098, Novato 94948; 382-1462, Fax 382-1417) represents accommodations in bed & breakfasts, boutique hotels, corporate condos and private homes. Represents properties in the San Francisco Bay area, Mendocino, Gold Country, Monterey and Carmel. **San Francisco Lodge** (421 North Point, 94133; 292-4500, 800-356-7567) reservation service for hotels, tours and rental cars. **San Francisco Reservation** (22 Second Street, 94105; 227-1500, 800-677-1550. Central hotel reservations for over 225 area hotels. No charge for services. **At Home** (4882 Cabrillo Point, Byron, 94515; 974-6937) rents 1-2-bedroom apartments in the San Francisco area. $60+.

Airport Area

Econo Lodge Airport (222 South Airport Blvd., 94080; 589-9055, 800-424-4777) 51 rooms, airport courtesy car, wheelchair access, children under 18 free, no pets. SGL$55-$75, DBL$65-$85.

Grosvenor Airport Inn (380 South Airport Blvd., 94080; 589-3200, 800-528-1234) 198 rooms, restaurant, swimming pool, airport transportation, wheelchair access, no-smoking rooms, pets allowed. SGL/DBL$75-$105.

Holiday Inn Airport (245 South Airport Blvd., 94080; 589-8500, Fax 343-1546, 800-HOLIDAY) 319 rooms, restaurant, swimming pool, gift shop, car rental, barber shop, children under 18 free, exercise equipment, wheelchair access, airport transportation, pets allowed. SGL/DBL$59-$96.

Hilton At San Francisco Airport (Box 8355, 94128; 589-0770, 800-HILTONS) 529 rooms, restaurant, outdoor swimming pool, jacuzzi, exercise equipment, business services, airport courtesy car, wheelchair access, free parking, SGL$135-$165, DBL$151-$181.

La Quinta Motor Inn (20 Airport Blvd., 94080; 583-2223, Fax 489-6770, 800-531-5900) 174 rooms, restaurant, lounge, heated swimming pool, jacuzzi, airport courtesy car, no-smoking rooms, pets allowed. SGL/DBL$62-$72.

Radisson Inn (2765 South Airport Blvd., 94080; 873-3550, 800-228-9822) 222 rooms and suites, restaurant, gift shop, airport transportation, wheelchair access, no-smoking rooms. SGL$88-$110, DBL$93-$110.

TraveLodge (326 South Airport Blvd., 94080; 583-9600, Fax 873-9392, 800-255-3050) 200 rooms and suites, restaurant, lounge, swimming pool, laundry room, airport transportation, no pets. SGL/DBL$60-$75.

Chinatown Area

Beverly Plaza Hotel (342 Grant, 94108; 781-3566, Fax 362-6298, 800-227-3823 in California) 150 rooms, restaurant, airport transportation. SGL$65-$70, DBL$74-$78.

Grant Plaza Hotel (465 Grant Avenue, 94108; 434-3883, Fax 434-3886, 800-472-6899, 800-472-6805 in California) 72 rooms and suites, fax service, wheelchair access, no-smoking rooms. SGL$39-$45, DBL$49-$52, STS$72.

Holiday Inn Financial District (750 Kearny Street, 94108; 433-6600, Fax 765-7891, 800-HOLIDAY) 566 rooms, restaurant, swimming pool, balconies, meeting facilities for 250, children under 18 free, free parking, wheelchair access. SGL$99-$139, DBL$114-$154.

Temple Hotel (469 Pine Street, 94104; 781-2565) 88 rooms, restaurant. SGL$30-$40, DBL$35-$45.

Civic Center Area

Abigail Hotel (246 McAllister, 94102; 861-9728, Fax 885-3109, 800-243-6510, 800-553-5575 in California) 62 rooms, restaurant. SGL$59-$69, DBL$69-$79.

Air Travel Hotel (655 Ellis, 94109; 771-3000, Fax 474-2871, 800-331-8999, 800-223-9889 in California) 100 rooms and suites, restaurant, lounge, fax service, meeting facilities for 60, valet laundry, free parking, wheelchair access, no-smoking rooms, no pets. SGL$39-$45, DBL$48-$59, STS$100.

American Inn Motel (760 El Camino Real, 94080; 589-0404) 17 rooms, wheelchair access. SGL$45, DBL$55.

Archbishops Mansion (1000 Fulton Street, 94117; 563-7872, 800-543-5820) 15 rooms, bed & breakfast, complimentary breakfast, free parking, private baths. SGL$115-$285.

Atherton Hotel (685 Ellis Street, 94109; 474-5720, 800-227-3608) 74 rooms, restaurant, lounge, fax service, no pets. SGL/DBL$49-$89.

Bay Bridge Motel (966 Harrison, 94107; 397-0657) 22 rooms, free parking. SGL/DBL$45-$58.

Best Western Americana (121 Seventh Street, 94103; 4495-626-0200, Fax 626-3974, 800-444-5816, 800-528-1234) 142 rooms, restaurant, lounge, swimming pool, sauna, transportation to local attractions, meeting facilities, fax service, tours, laundry room, room service, no-smoking rooms, free parking. SGL/DBL$72-$110.

Best Western Carriage Inn (140 Seventh Street, 94103; 552-8600, Fax 626-3974, 800-444-5817, 800-528-1234) 48 rooms, restaurant, lounge, complimentary breakfast, swimming pool, whirlpool, spa, tours, children under 12 free, fireplaces, room service, transportation to local attractions, wheelchair access, free parking, no-smoking rooms, no pets. LS SGL$75-$85, DBL$82-$92; HS SGL/DBL$95-$120.

Best Western Civic Center Motor Inn (365 Ninth Street, 94103; 621-2826, 800-444-5829, 800-622-0798, 800-227-4368) 57 rooms, restaurant, swimming pool, in-room refrigerators, children under 12 free, laundry room, tours, free parking, pets allowed. SGL/DBL$65-$93.

Best Western Flamingo Motor Inn (114 Seventh Street, 94103; 621-0701, Fax 623-3974, 800-444-5818, 800-528-1234) 38 rooms, restaurant, lounge, swimming pool, children under 12 free, laundry room, free parking, fax service, computer hookups, no pets. SGL$50-$65, DBL$60-$75.

Britton Hotel (112 Seventh Street, 94103; 621-7001, 800-444-5819) 79 rooms and two-bedroom suites, restaurant, children under 12 free, free local telephone calls, fax service, airport transportation, no-smoking rooms, no pets. SGL/DBL$49-$67, STS$69-$79.

Cavalier Motel (1330 El Camino Real, 94080; 589-8875) 49 rooms and efficiencies, swimming pool. SGL$41, DBL$45.

Comfort Inn (1390 El Camino Real, 94030; 952-3200, 800-221-2222) 99 rooms, restaurant, swimming pool, whirlpool, kitchenettes, fireplaces, computer hookups, wheelchair access, laundry room. SGL$68-$90, DBL$75-$100.

Comfort Inn (240 Seventh Street, 94103; 861-469, 800-544-0502) 68 rooms and suites, restaurant, meeting facilities, free parking, no pets. SGL$48-$72, DBL$55-$82.

Days Inn (465 Grove Street, 94102; 864-4040, 800-325-2525) 40 rooms and suites, restaurant, complimentary breakfast, swimming pool, in-room refrigerators and microwaves, fax service, jacuzzis, VCRs, wheelchair access, children under 12 free, no-smoking rooms, no pets. SGL$50-$75, DBL$55-$80, STS$70-$95.

Econo Lodge (825 Polk Street, 94109; 673-0411, 800-424-4777) 27 rooms, children under 18 free, no pets. SGL$52-$66, DBL$56-$72.

Embassy Motor Hotel (610 Polk, 93012; 673-1404) 84 rooms, restaurant, free parking. SGL/DBL$42-$58.

Essex Hotel (684 Ellis, 94109; 474-4664, Fax 441-1800, 800-44-ESSEX in California) 49 rooms. SGL/DBL$54-$56.

Friendship Inn Civic Center (869 Eddy, 94109; 474-4374, 800-453-4511, 800-553-2666, 800-424-4777, 800-862-8585 in California) 34 rooms, wheelchair access, whirlpools, children under 18 free, no pets, no-smoking rooms, free parking. SGL$46-$78, DBL$49-$85.

Grand Central Hotel (1412 Market, 94102; 703-9988, Fax 703-9986) 105 rooms, concierge, 24-hour room service. SGL$30-$35, DBL$40-$45.

Hotel Gotham (835 Turk, 94102; 928-7291) 114 rooms. SGL/DBL$110W-$175W.

Hallmark House Motel (800 El Camino Real, 94080; 589-6702) 13 rooms and efficiencies. SGL$38, DBL$45.

Holiday Inn Civic Center (50 Eighth Street, 94103; 626-6103, Fax 552-0184, 800-HOLIDAY) 390 rooms, restaurant, lounge, gift shop, children under 18 free, tours, car rental, meeting facilities for 150, free parking, wheelchair access, exercise equipment, no pets. SGL$84-$130, DBL$99-$155.

Hotel One (1087 Market, 94103; 861-4946, Fax 861-3337) 174 rooms, restaurant. SGL/DBL$33-$43.

Hotel One of San Francisco (587 Eddy, 94109; 775-5934, Fax 775-5666) 65 rooms, restaurant, complimentary breakfast, free parking, airport courtesy car, pets allowed, no-smoking rooms. SGL$45-$55, DBL$55-$65.

Inn At The Opera (333 Fulton, 94102; 863-2708, Fax 861-0821, 800-325-2708, 800-423-9610 in California) 48 rooms and suites, restaurant, lounge, complimentary breakfast, valet laundry, room service, children under 12 free, in-room refrigerators, fax service, complimentary newspaper, meeting facilities for 25, airport transportation, wheelchair access, no-smoking rooms, pets allowed. SGL$110-$205, DBL/STS$120-$215.

Mart Hotel (101 Ninth Street, 94103; 621-3655, Fax 621-3655) 32 rooms, free parking. SGL/DBL$45-$55.

Phoenix Inn (601 Eddy, 94109; 776-1380, Fax 885-3109) 44 rooms, restaurant, swimming pool, free parking. SGL$69-$89, DBL$79-$99.

Ramada Hotel San Francisco (1231 Market Street, 94103; 626-8000, Fax 861-1460, 800-227-4747) 460 rooms, restaurant, lounge, children under 18 free, airport transportation, beauty and barber shop, no-smoking rooms, wheelchair access. SGL$95-$135, DBL$105-$145.

TraveLodge (1707 Market Street, 94103; 621-6775, Fax 621-4305, 800-255-3050) 84 rooms and suites, restaurant, free parking, airport transportation, tours, car rental. SGL/DBL$49-$77.

TraveLodge (110 South El Camino Real, 94030; 697-7373, 800-255-3050) 58 rooms, restaurant, lounge, complimentary breakfast, swimming pool, VCRs, in-room refrigerators and microwaves, tours, car rental, airport transportation, no pets. SGL/DBL$54-$71.

TraveLodge San Francisco Center (1707 Market, 94103; 621-6775, 800-255-3050) 84 rooms, restaurant, free parking. SGL$48-$64, DBL$59-$76.

TraveLodge (790 Ellis Street, 94109; 775-7612, Fax 567-1328, 800-255-3050) 80 rooms and suites, restaurant, lounge, tours, car rental, airport transportation, no pets. SGL/DBL$52-$72.

UN Plaza Hotel (45 McAllister, 94102; 626-5200, Fax 863-7356, 800-553-1900) 135 rooms, restaurant. SGL/DBL$60-$65.

Value Inn By Nendels (1330 El Camino Real, 94080; 589-8875, Fax 387-0609, 800-547-0106) 49 rooms, restaurant, complimentary breakfast, swimming pool, free parking. SGL$50-$56, DBL$54-$60.

Embarcadero Area

Hotel Griffon (155 Stuart, 94105; 495-2100, Fax 495-3522, 800-321-2201) 62 rooms, restaurant, complimentary breakfast, swimming pool, airport transportation, exercise equipment, wheelchair access, no-smoking rooms, pets allowed. SGL/DBL$115-$135, STS$175-$250+.

Hyatt Regency San Francisco (Five Embarcadero Center, 94111; 788-1234, Fax 981-3638, 800-233-1234) 803 rooms and suites, restaurant, lounge, outdoor heated swimming pool, spa, meeting facilities, balconies, exercise equipment, wheelchair access. SGL/DBL$149-$268.

Mandarin Oriental San Francisco (222 Sansome, 94104; 885-0999, Fax 433-0289, 800-622-0404) 160 rooms, restaurant, wheelchair access. SGL$245-$475, DBL$280-$475+.

Park-Hyatt San Francisco (333 Battery, 94111; 392-1234, Fax 421-2433, 800-228-9000) 360 rooms, restaurant, lounge, meeting facilities, wheelchair access. SGL$235-$260, DBL$265-$295.

Fisherman's Wharf Area

Bayside Boat and Breakfast (Pier 39, 94133, 291-8411, 800-BOAT-BED) 8 yachts with accommodations, complimentary breakfast, free parking. SGL/DBL$140-$285.

Holiday Inn Fisherman's Wharf (1300 Columbus Avenue, 94133; 771-9000, Fax 771-7006, 800-HOLIDAY) 580 rooms, restaurant, swimming pool, children under 18 free, free parking, wheelchair access, no pets. SGL/DBL$106-$205.

Howard Johnson's Motor Lodge (580 Beach Street, 94133; 775-300, 800-654-2000, 800-652-1527 in California) 128 rooms, restaurant, free parking, wheelchair access. SGL$76-$100, DBL$84-$120.

Hyatt Fisherman's Wharf (555 North Point, 94133; 563-1234, Fax 563-2215) 315 rooms, restaurant, swimming pool, exercise equipment, free parking, wheelchair access. SGL/DBL$195.

Hyde Park Suites (2655 Hyde, 94109; 771-0200, Fax 346-8058, 800-227-3608) 24 one- and two-bedroom suites, complimentary breakfast, children under 12 free, in-room refrigerators and microwaves, fax service, laundry room, no pets. 1BR$165-$190, 2BR$220.

Ramada Hotel Fisherman's Wharf (590 Bay, 94133; 885-4700, Fax 715-771-8945, 800-228-2828) 231 rooms, restaurant, lounge, meeting facilities for 275, car rental, airport transportation, wheelchair access, children under 18 free, no-smoking rooms. SGL$79-$155, DBL$89-$165.

San Francisco Marriott Fisherman's Wharf (1250 Columbus Avenue, 94133; 775-7555, 800-228-9290) 256 rooms, restaurant, wheelchair access. SGL/DBL$128-$212.

San Remo Hotel (2237 Mason, 94133; 776-8688, Fax 776-2811) 62 rooms, restaurant. SGL$35-$45, DBL$55-$70.

Sheraton At Fisherman's Wharf (2500 Mason Street, 94133; 362-5500, Fax 956-5275, 800-325-3535) 525 rooms and suites, two restaurants, lounge, outdoor heated swimming pool, exercise equipment, meeting facilities for 300, beauty shop, travel agency, gift shop, 24-hour room service, wheelchair access, no-smoking rooms. SGL/DBL$120-$230.

TraveLodge At Fisherman's Wharf (250 Beach, 94133; 392-6700, Fax 986-7853, 800-255-3050) 250 rooms, restaurant, swimming pool, wheelchair access, free parking. SGL$105-$160, DBL$115-$170.

TraveLodge Hotel (250 Beach Street, 94133; 392-6700, 800-255-3050) 250 rooms and suites, restaurant, lounge, swimming pool, fax service, tours, car rental, free parking, tennis. no pets. SGL/DBL$89-$105.

TraveLodge (1201 Columbus Avenue, 94133; 776-7070, Fax 474-5887, 800-255-3050) 25 rooms, restaurant, lounge, fax service, tours, car rental, complimentary newspaper, tennis, no pets. SGL/DBL$65-$90.

Tuscan Inn At Fisherman's Wharf (425 North Point, 94133; 561-1100, Fax 561-1199, 800-648-4626) 199 rooms, restaurant, lounge, limousine service, concierge, room service, free parking. SGL/DL$145-$195.

The Wharf Inn (2601 Mason, 94133; 673-7411, Fax 763-5972) 51 rooms, airport transportation, free parking. SGL$73-$98, DBL$83-$108.

Japantown Area

Alamo Square Inn (719 Scott Street, 94117; 922-2055, 800-345-9888) 13 rooms, bed & breakfast, complimentary breakfast, free parking. SGL$85-$250.

Best Western Miyako Inn (1800 Sutter, 94115; 921-4000, 800-528-1234) 125 rooms, restaurant, no pets, children under 18 free, meeting facilities, fax service. SGL$73-$79, DBL$83-$89.

Edward II Bed and Breakfast Inn (3155 Scott Street, 94123; 922-3000, Fax 931-5784, 800-473-2846) 30 rooms, bed & breakfast, complimentary breakfast, restaurant, airport transportation, no-smoking rooms. SGL/DBL$67-$85+.

Miyako Hotel (1625 Post, 94115; 922-3200, Fax 921-0417, 800-533-4567) 218 rooms, restaurant, whirlpool, airport transportation, wheelchair access, no-smoking rooms. SGL$100-$160, DBL$120-$180.

Union Square Area

Adelaide Inn (5 Isadora Duncan Court, 94102; 441-2265) 16 rooms, restaurant, complimentary breakfast. SGL$32-$48, DBL$42-$46.

Alexander Inn (415 O'Farrell, 94102; 928-6800, Fax 928-3354, 800-843-8709, 800-253-9263 in California) 62 rooms and suites, complimentary breakfast, children under 12 free, fax service, meeting facilities for 35, laundry room, airport transportation, wheelchair access, no-smoking rooms, no pets. SGL$52-72, DBL$58-$72, STS$72-$92.

All Seasons Hotel (417 Stockton, 94108; 986-8737, Fax 392-0850) 48 rooms, restaurant. SGL$44-$59, DBL$49-$65.

Amsterdam Hotel (749 Taylor Street, 94108; 673-3277, Fax 673-0453, 800-637-3444) 34 rooms, bed & breakfast, complimentary breakfast, no-smoking rooms, no pets. SGL$44-$55, DBL$49-$70.

Andrews Hotel (624 Post, 94109; 563-6877, Fax 928-6919, 800-227-4742, 800-622-0557 in California) 48 rooms, restaurant, complimentary breakfast. SGL/DBL$82-$119.

Ansonia-Cambridge Hotel (711 Post, 94109; 673-2670, 800-221-6470, 800-325-1221 in California) 124 rooms, restaurant, complimentary breakfast and dinner, children under 5 free. SGL$35-$60, DBL$35-$65.

The Aston Pickwick (85 Fifth Street, 94103; 421-7500, Fax 243-8066, 800-227-3282) 190 rooms, restaurant. SGL/DBL$65-$75.

Bedford Hotel (761 Post, 94109; 673-6040, Fax 563-6739, 800-227-5642, 800-652-1889 in California) 144 rooms and suites, restaurant, lounge, fax service, meeting facilities for 80, laundry room, wheelchair access, no pets, airport transportation, no-smoking rooms. SGL/DBL$99-$155.

Bel Air Hotel (344 Jones, 94102; 771-3460) 70 rooms. SGL$33-$35, DBL$36-$38.

Beresford Arms (701 Post, 94109; 673-2600, Fax 474-0449, 800-533-6533) 102 rooms, restaurant, complimentary breakfast, kitchnettes, wheelchair access. SGL$60-$120, DBL$79-$120.

Beresford Hotel (635 Sutter, 94102; 673-9900, Fax 474-0449, 800-533-6533) 114 rooms, restaurant. SGL$69, DBL$79.

Beresford Manor (860 Sutter, 94109; 673-3330, Fax 474-0449) 87 rooms, restaurant. SGL$45-$60, DBL$55-$70.

Best Western Canterbury Hotel and Whitehall (750 Sutter, 94109; 474-6464, Fax 474-5856, 800-227-4788, 800-652-1614 in California) 275 rooms, restaurant, lounge, exercise equipment, meeting facilities, computer hookups, valet laundry, children under 18 free, no-smoking rooms. SGL$79-$109, DBL$85-$115.

Brady Acres (649 Jones, 94102; 929-8033) 25 rooms. SGL/DBL$250W-$285W.

Californian Hotel (405 Taylor, 94102; 885-2500, Fax 673-KRUG, 800-227-3346, 800-622-0961 in California) 243 rooms and suites, two restaurants, meeting facilities, barber shop, car rental, concierge. SGL$74-$94, DBL$84-$104.

Campton Place (340 Stockton, 94108; 781-5555, Fax 955-8536, 800-647-4007, 800-235-4300 in California) 126 rooms, restaurant, wheelchair access, no-smoking rooms, pets allowed. SGL/DBL$180-$300, STS$375-$750.

Carlton Hotel (1075 Sutter, 94109; 673-0241, Fax 673-4904, 800-227-4496, 800-792-0958 in California) 160 rooms and suites, restaurant, lounge, children under 10 free, wheelchair access, no-smoking rooms, no pets. SGL/DBL$77-$92, STS$200.

Cartwright Hotel (524 Sutter, 94102; 421-2865, Fax 421-2865, 800-227-3844) 114 rooms and suites, restaurant, in-room refrigerators, fax service, meeting facilities for 25, wheelchair access, no-smoking rooms, no pets. SGL$99, DBL$109, STS$140-$160.

Chancellor Hotel (433 Powell, 94102; 362-2004, Fax 362-1403, 800-428-4748) 146 rooms and suites, restaurant, lounge, airport transportation, gift shop, valet laundry, no-smoking rooms, no pets. SGL$70-$97, DBL$75-$114, STS$130-$165.

Commodore International (825 Sutter, 94109; 923-6800, 800-338-6848, 800-327-9157 in California) 113 rooms, restaurant, lounge, valet laundry, concierge.

Cornell Hotel (715 Bush Street, 94108; 421-8154, 800-232-9698) 50 rooms, restaurant, lounge, complimentary breakfast, fax service, valet laundry, no smoking, no pets. SGL$60-$70, DBL$70-$85.

Hotel David (480 Geary, 94102; 771-1600, Fax 931-5442, 800-524-1888) 50 rooms, restaurant, complimentary breakfast and dinner, airport courtesy car, wheelchair access, no-smoking rooms, no pets. SGL$79, DBL$89-$139.

Diva Hotel (440 Geary Street, 94102; 885-0200, 108 rooms and suites, restaurant, complimentary breakfast, in-room refrigerators, wheelchair access, no-smoking rooms, no pets. SGL/DBL$115+, STS$135.

The Donatello (501 Post Street, 94102; 441-7100, Fax 885-8842, 800-227-3184, 800-792-9837 in California) 125 rooms and suites, restaurant, lounge, meeting facilities for 150, fax service, no-smoking rooms. SGL$140-$200, DBL$155-$200.

Executive Suites (840 Post Street, 94109; 567-5151, Fax 776-7522) 49 condominiums, swimming pool, exercise equipment, pets allowed. SGL/DBL$90-$119.

Four Seasons Clift Hotel (495 Geary, 94102; 775-4700, Fax 441-4621, 800-332-3443) 332 rooms and suites, restaurant, exercise equipment, wheelchair access, airport transportation, no-smoking rooms, pets allowed. SGL$180-$270, DBL$180-$290.

Galleria Park (191 Sutter, 94104; 781-3060, Fax 433-4409, 800-792-9639, 800-792-9855 in California) 177 rooms, restaurant, wheelchair access. SGL/DBL$120-$130.

Gates Hotel (140 Ellis, 94102; 781-0430) 66 rooms. SGL$25-$32, DBL$32-$45.

Gaylord Hotel (620 Jones, 94102; 673-8445, 800-336-8445) 175 rooms and efficiencies, kitchenettes, no-smoking rooms. SGL$175W-$250W, DBL$200W-$300W.

Geary Hotel (610 Geary, 94102; 673-9221, Fax 928-2434, 800-227-3352, 800-828-2880 in California) 100 rooms, restaurant, no-smoking rooms, no pets. SGL$36, DBL$42.

Golden Gate Hotel (775 Bush, 94108; 392-3702, 800-835-1118) 25 rooms, bed & breakfast, complimentary breakfast, pets allowed. SGL/DBL$55-$89.

Grand Hyatt San Francisco (345 Stockton, 94105; 398-1234, Fax 391-1780, 800-233-1234) 693 rooms, restaurant, lounge, exercise equipment, meeting facilities, airport transportation, no-smoking rooms. SGL$250-$230, DBL$235-$265, STS$350-$1,700.

Grant Hotel (753 Bush, 94108; 421-7540, Fax 239-2625) 76 rooms, restaurant. SGL$40-$42, DBL$44-$46.

Handlery Union Square Hotel (351 Geary, 94102; 781-7800, Fax 781-0269, 800-223-0888) 378 rooms, restaurant, swimming pool, airport transportation, wheelchair access, no-smoking rooms, pets allowed. SGL$110-$120, DBL$120-$130.

Harcourt Residence Club Hostel (1105 Larkin, 94109; 673-7720) 92 rooms, complimentary breakfast and dinner. SGL$115W-$185W.

HoJo Inn (385 Ninth Street, 94103; 431-5131, Fax 626-5853, 800-654-2000) 22 rooms, in-room refrigerators, no-smoking rooms, no pets. SGL$65-$85, DBL$75-$95.

Holiday Inn Union Square (480 Sutter, 94108; 398-8900, Fax 989-8823, 800-HOLIDAY) 400 rooms, restaurant, lounge, gift shop, meeting facilities for 350, no pets, children under 18 free. SGL$137-$162, DBL$157-$182.

The Inn At Union Square (440 Post Street, 94102; 397-3510, 800-288-4346) 30 rooms, complimentary breakfast, wheelchair access, no smoking. SGL/DBL$110-$170.

Juliana Hotel (590 Bush, 94108; 392-2540, Fax 391-8447, 800-328-3880, 800-382-8800 in Canada) 107 rooms, restaurant, airport transportation, wheelchair access, no-smoking rooms. SGL/DBL$107-$145.

Kensington Park (450 Post, 94102; 788-6400, 800-553-1900) 90 rooms, restaurant, complimentary breakfast. SGL/DBL$110-$120.

King George Hotel (334 Mason, 94102; 781-5050, Fax 391-6976, 800-288-6005) 143 rooms, restaurant, complimentary breakfast, airport transportation, no-smoking rooms. SGL$89, DBL$99.

Lotus Hotel (580 O'Farrell, 94102; 885-8008, Fax 885-8008, 800-927-7287 in California) 70 rooms, restaurant. SGL$45-$78, DBL$65-$98.

Mark Twain Hotel (345 Taylor, 94102; 673-2332, Fax 398-0733, 800-92ASTON, 800-227-4074 in California) 116 rooms, restaurant, wheelchair access. SGL$75-$85, DBL$85-$95.

Monticello Inn (127 Ellis, 94102; 392-8800, Fax 398-2650, 800-669-7777) 91 rooms and suites, restaurant, lounge, complimentary breakfast, whirlpool, children under 12 free, meeting facilities for 10, valet laundry, complimentary newspaper, wheelchair access, no-smoking rooms, no pets. SGL$114-$200, DBL$124-$200, STS$144-$200.

Mosser Victorian Hotel of Arts and Music (54 Fourth Street, 94103; 986-4400, Fax 495-4091, 800-227-3804, 800-831-4224 in California) 168 rooms and suites, restaurant, lounge, children under 12 free, in-room refrigerators, airport transportation, no-smoking rooms, no pets. SGL/DBL$59-$69, STS$59-$99.

National 9 Inn (385 Ninth Street, 94103; 431-5131, 800-524-9999) 20 rooms, free parking. SGL$45-$85, DBL$55-$95.

Nikko San Francisco (222 Mason Street, 94102; 394-1111, Fax 421-0455, 800-NIKKO-US) 525 rooms and suites, restaurant, lounge, swimming pool, jacuzzi, hot tubs, exercise equipment, meeting facilities for 300, airport transportation, wheelchair access, no-smoking rooms, no pets. SGL$190-$230, DBL$215-$230, STS$375-$1300.

Olympic (140 Mason, 94102; 982-5010) 75 rooms, restaurant. SGL/DBL$28-$35.

Orchard Hotel (562 Sutter, 94102; 433-4434, Fax 433-3695, 800-433-4434) 96 rooms and suites, restaurant, lounge, children under 12 free, in-room refrigerators, fax service, laundry room, airport transportation, complimentary newspaper, wheelchair access, no-smoking rooms, no pets. SGL/DBL$99-$130, STS$195.

Pacific Bay Inn (520 Jones, 94102; 673-0234, 800-445-2631) 84 rooms, complimentary breakfast. SGL$65, DBL$75.

Pan Pacific Hotel San Francisco (500 Post, 94102; 771-8600, Fax 398-0267, 800-553-6465 in California) 330 rooms, restaurant, airport transportation, pets allowed, wheelchair access. SGL/DBL$185-$350.

Parc Fifty Five Hotel (55 Cyril Magnin, 94102; 392-8000, Fax 392-4734, 800-338-1338) 1003 rooms, restaurant, exercise equipment, wheelchair access. SGL$170-$220, DBL$200-$250.

Petite Auberge (863 Bush Street, 94108; 928-6000, Fax 775-5717) 26 rooms, bed & breakfast, complimentary breakfast, free parking. SGL/DBL$105-$155.

Phillip's Hotel (205 Ninth Street, 94103; 863-7652) 32 rooms, restaurant, pets allowed. SGL$25-$30, DBL$35-$40.

Hotel Pierre (540 Jones, 94102; 673-9122, 800-537-7437) 110 rooms, restaurant. SGL/DBL$35-$40.

Powell Hotel (28 Cyril Magnin Street, 94102; 398-3200, Fax 398-3654, 800-368-0700, 800-652-3399 in California) 140 rooms, restaurant, airport transportation, wheelchair access. SGL$75, DBL$85.

Powell West Hotel (111 Mason, 94102; 771-1200, Fax 398-3654, 800-368-0700, 800-652-3399) 115 rooms and suites, restaurant, lounge, children under 12 free, in-room refrigerators, fax service, meeting facilities for 50, valet laundry, wheelchair access, no pets. SGL$65, DBL$75, STS$95-$140.

Prescott Hotel (545 Post, 94102; 563-0303, Fax 563-6831, 800-283-7322) 167 rooms, restaurant, complimentary breakfast, airport transportation, wheelchair access, no-smoking rooms. SGL/DBL$155-$170.

Raphael Hotel (386 Geary, 94102; 986-2000, Fax 397-2447, 800-821-5343) 152 rooms and suites, restaurant, lounge, children under 18 free, fax service, valet laundry, airport transportation, wheelchair access, no-smoking rooms, no pets. SGL$89-$109, DBL$99-$199, STS$135-$195.

The Regis Hotel (490 Geary, 94102; 928-7900, Fax 441-8788, 800-82-REGIS) 80 rooms and suites, restaurant, lounge, complimentary breakfast, valet laundry, airport transportation, fax service, meeting facilities for 35, wheelchair access, no-smoking rooms, no pets. SGL/DBL$99-$205, STS$125-$215.

San Francisco Hilton on Hilton Square (One Hilton Square, 94102; 771-1400, Fax 923-5039, 800-HILTONS, 800-445-8667) 1907 rooms, restaurant, outdoor heated swimming pool, business services, free parking, meeting facilities for 12,500. SGL$165-$225, DBL$190-$250.

San Francisco Marriott (55 Fourth Street, 94103; 896-1600, Fax 777-2799, 800-229-9290) 1500 rooms, restaurant, swimming pool, exercise equipment, wheelchair access. SGL$119-$198, DBL$139-$228.

Savoy Hotel (580 Geary, 94102; 441-2700, Fax 441-2700, 800-227-4223) 83 rooms and suites, restaurant, lounge, complimentary breakfast, children under 16 free, in-room refrigerators, valet laundry, no-smoking rooms, no pets. SGL$89, DBL$99, STS$139-$179.

Senator Hotel (519 Ellis, 94109; 775-0506, Fax 776-0152, 800-782-0990 in California) 115 rooms, restaurant, free parking. SGL/DBL$36-$52.

Shannon Court Hotel (550 Geary, 94102; 775-5000, Fax 928-6813, 800-228-8830, 800-821-0493 in California) 173 rooms, restaurant, wheelchair access. SGL$95-$115, DBL$100-$125.

Sheehan Hotel (620 Sutter Street, 94102; 775-6500, Fax 775-3271) 61 rooms, restaurant, complimentary breakfast, swimming pool, exercise equipment, wheelchair access. SGL$40-$60, DBL$50-$70.

Sheraton Place Hotel (2 New Montgomery, 94105; 392-8600, Fax 543-0671, 800-325-3535) 550 rooms and suites, two restaurants, lounge, indoor swimming pool, whirlpool, sauna, meeting facilities for 8000, business services, exercise equipment, wheelchair access, no-smoking rooms. SGL$180-$240, DBL$200-$260.

Sir Francis Drake Hotel (450 Powell, 94102; 392-7755, Fax 391-8719, 800-227-5480 in California) 417 rooms, restaurant. SGL$120-$140, DBL$140-$210.

Sutter-Larkin Hotel (1048 Larkin, 94109; 474-6820) 34 rooms, restaurant. SGL/DBL$25-$35.

TraveLodge (790 Ellis, 94109; 775-7612, 800-255-3050) 80 rooms, restaurant, free parking. SGL$49-$62, DBL$58-$72.

Union Square Hotel (114 Powell, 94102; 397-3000, 800-553-1900) 131 rooms and suites, restaurant, complimentary breakfast. SGL/DBL$99-$129.

Villa Florence Hotel (225 Powell, 94102; 397-7700, 800-553-4411, 800-243-5700 in California) 177 rooms, restaurant, airport transportation, wheelchair access, no pets. SGL/DBL$99-$119.

Vintage Court Hotel (650 Bush, 94108; 392-4666, 800-654-1100, 800-654-7266 in California) 106 rooms, restaurant, wheelchair access, airport transportation. SGL/DBL$109-$119.

The Westin St. Francis (335 Powell, 94102; 397-7000, Fax 774-0124, 800-228-3000) 1200 rooms and suites, restaurant, exercise equipment, car rental desk, boutiques, barber and beauty shop, wheelchair access, no-smoking rooms, business service, limousine service, airline ticket office, pets allowed, 22 meeting rooms, meeting facilities for 1500. SGL$160-$280, DBL$195-$315.

The White Swan Inn (845 Bush, 94108; 775-1755, Fax 775-5717) 27 rooms, bed & breakfast, complimentary breakfast. SGL/DBL$145-$160.

York Hotel (940 Sutter, 94109; 885-6800, Fax 885-2115, 800-227-3608) 96 rooms, restaurant, complimentary breakfast. SGL/DBL$95-$175.

Lombard Area

Alfa Inn Motel (2505 Lombard, 94121; 921-2505, Fax 387-0609) 28 rooms, swimming pool, free parking. SGL/DBL$55-$75.

Art Center Bed and Breakfast (1902 Filbert Street, 94123; 567-1526, 800-821-3877) 5 rooms and suites, bed & breakfast, complimentary breakfast, free parking, in-room refrigerators, private baths, jacuzzi, airport transportation, no smoking, pets allowed. SGL/DBL$85, STS$115.

Bel Aire TraveLodge (3201 Steiner, 94123; 921-5162, 800-255-3050) 32 rooms, airport courtesy car, free parking. SGL$50-$67, DBL$53-$73.

Buena Vista Motor Inn (1599 Lombard, 94123; 923-9600) 50 rooms, free parking, wheelchair access. SGL$73, DBL$82.

Chateau Tivoli (1057 Steiner Street, 94115; 776-5462, 800-228-1647) 8 rooms and suites, bed & breakfast, complimentary breakfast, free local telephone calls, free parking, SGL$80-$100, DBL$100-$125, STS$160-$200.

Cow Hollow Motor Inn (2190 Lombard, 94123; 921-5800, Fax 922-8515) 129 rooms and suites, restaurant, exercise equipment, free parking. SGL/DBL$71-$84.

Days Inn Fisherman's Wharf (2358 Lombard Street, 94123; 922-2010, Fax 563-7958, 800-325-2525) 22 rooms, complimentary breakfast, swimming pool, wheelchair access, no-smoking rooms, no pets, children under 12 free, fax service. SGL$65-$85, DBL$70-$85.

Holland Motel (1 Richardson Avenue, 94123; 922-0810) 20 rooms, free parking. SGL$40-$60, DBL$40-$105.

Lombard Motor Inn (1475 Lombard Street, 94123; 441-6000, Fax 441-4291) 50 rooms, no-smoking rooms. SGL$78, DBL$89+.

Lombard Plaza Motel (2026 Lombard, 94123; 921-2444) 31 rooms, airport transportation, free parking, no pets. SGL/DBL$35-$69, DBL$39-$69.

Marina Motel (2576 Lombard, 94123; 921-9406) 45 rooms and suites, free parking. SGL/DBL$36-$65.

Plantation Inn Motel (3100 Webster, 94123; 921-5520) 56 rooms, swimming pool, free parking. SGL$55-$65,DBL$60-$71.

Golden Gate TraveLodge (2230 Lombard, 94123; 922-3900, 800-255-2230) 29 rooms, free parking, wheelchair access. SGL$40-$69, DBL$42-$79.

Redwood Inn (1530 Lombard, 94123; 776-3800, 800-221-6621, 800-221-2121 in California) 33 rooms, complimentary breakfast, free parking, wheelchair access. SGL$55-$70, DBL$60-$80.

Sherman House (2160 Green, 94123; 563-3600, Fax 563-1882) 15 rooms, restaurant. SGL/DBL$170-$700.

Star Motel (1727 Lombard, 94123; 441-4469) 53 rooms. SGL/DBL$62-$90.

Super 8 Motel (2440 Lombard Street, 94123; 922-0244, Fax 931-3872, 800-800-8000) 32 rooms, sauna, spa, fax service, in-room refrigerators and microwaves, wheelchair access, no-smoking rooms, no pets. SGL/DBL$60-$65.

Town House Motel (1650 Lombard, 94123; 885-5163, Fax 992-7090, 800-255-1516) 24 rooms, restaurant, complimentary breakfast, airport courtesy car, free parking. SGL/DBL$55-$85.

TraveLodge (3201 Steiner Street, 94123; 921-5162, Fax 992-9108, 800-255-3050) 32 rooms and suites, restaurant, lounge, airport courtesy car, beauty and barber shop, tours, car rental, free parking, no pets. LS SGL/DBL$60-$77; MS SGL/DBL$62-$77; HS SGL/DBL$66-$80.

Nob Hill Area

Ashley Suites (1029 Geary, 94109; 771-7396) one- and two-bedroom condominiums. SGL/DBL$250W-$750W.

Fairmont Hotel and Tower (950 Mason Street, 94108; 772-5000, Fax 772-5000, 800-527-4727) 600 rooms and suites, restaurant, exercise equipment, concierge, business services, 24-hour room service, airport transportation, wheelchair access. SGL$150-$260, DBL$180-$290, STS$450-$600.

Huntington Hotel (1075 California, 94108; 474-5400; Fax 474-6227, 800-227-4683, 800-652-1539) 143 rooms, restaurant, complimentary breakfast. SGL$160-$210, DBL$180-$230.

Hyatt San Francisco (345 Stockton Street, 94108; 398-1234, Fax 391-1780, 800-233-1234) 693 rooms and suites, restaurant, lounge, wheelchair access, no-smoking rooms, no pets. SGL/DBL$240-$265, STS$350-$1300.

Mark Hopkins Inter-Continental (One Nob Hill, 94108; 392-3434, Fax 421-3302, 800-327-0200) 391 rooms, restaurant, exercise equipment, airport transportation, wheelchair access, no-smoking rooms. SGL$180-$275, DBL$200-$305, STS$275-$1600.

Nob Hill (Bed and Breakfast International) 1 bedroom, bed & breakfast, complimentary breakfast. SGL/DBL$70.

Northpoint Executive Apartments (2211 Stockton Street; 989-6563) one-bedroom apartments, swimming pool, downtown location. 1BR$85-$115.

Ritz Carlton (California and Stockton, 94108; 296-7465, Fax 296-8559, 800-241-3333) 336 rooms, restaurant, swimming pool, airport transportation, exercise equipment, wheelchair access.SGL/DBL$175-$235.

San Francisco Residence Club (851 California, 94108; 421-2220) 84 rooms, restaurant, complimentary breakfast and dinner. SGL/DBL$175W-$425W.

Stouffer Stanford Court Hotel (905 California Street, 94108; 989-3500, Fax 391-0513, 800-227-4726, 800-HOTELS-1) 396 rooms and suites, restaurant, lounge, hot tubs, jacuzzis, children under 18 free, complimentary newspaper, laundry room, wheelchair access, no-smoking rooms, no pets. SGL$125-$185, DBL$205-$295.

Trinity Suites (845 Pine, 94108; 433-3330, Fax 477-0400) 18 suites, restaurant, wheelchair access, pets allowed, free parking. SGL/DBL$175-$275.

Washington Square Inn (1660 Stockton, 94133; 981-4220, Fax 989-0529, 800-388-0220) 15 rooms, bed & breakfast, complimentary breakfast. SGL$65-$105, DBL$75-$160.

Van Ness Area

Broadway Manor (2201 Van Ness Avenue, 94109; 776-7900, 800-727-6239) 56 rooms, restaurant, children under 16 free, fax service, meeting facilities for 25, free parking, wheelchair access, no-smoking rooms, no pets. SGL$49-$73, DBL$59-$78.

Beck's Motel Lodge (2222 Market, 94114; 621-8212, 800-227-4360) 57 rooms, in-room refrigerators, tours, fireplaces, free parking. SGL/DBL$55-$86.

Canterbury Hotel and Whitehall Inn (750 Sutter Street, 94109; 474-5856, 800-227-4788, 800-652-1614 in California) 54 rooms, restaurant, exercise equipment. SGL/DBL$79-$119.

Castle Inn Motel (1565 Broadway, 94109; 441-1155, 800-8-CASTLE) 20 rooms and efficiencies, wheelchair access, no-smoking rooms, no pets. SGL$52-$70, DBL$58-$78.

Cathedral Hill Hotel (1101 Van Ness Avenue, 94019; 776-8200, 800-227-4730, 800-622-0855 in California) 400 rooms and suites, restaurant, lounge, outdoor heated swimming pool, airport transportation, meeting facilities for 1000, no-smoking rooms, free parking. SGL$105-$170, DBL$125-$190, STS$400-$1500.

Coventry Motor Inn (1901 Lombard, 94123; 567-1200) 69 rooms, free parking, wheelchair access. SGL$71, DBL$76-$86.

Holiday Inn Golden Gate (1500 Van Ness Avenue, 94109; 441-4000, Fax 776-7155, 800-HOLIDAY) 500 rooms, restaurant, lounge, swimming pool, gift shop, car rental, meeting facilities for 800, children under 18 free, wheelchair access. SGL$95-$122, DBL$109-$123.

Holiday Lodge (1901 Van Ness Avenue, 94109; 776-4469, 800-367-8504, 800-HOLIDAY) 75 rooms, swimming pool. SGL/DBL$135-$165.

Inn San Francisco (943 South Van Ness Avenue, 94110; 641-0188, 800-359-0913) 22 rooms, bed & breakfast, complimentary breakfast, free parking. SGL/DBL$55-$95.

Kenmore Residence Club Hostel (1570 Sutter, 94109; 776-5815) 79 rooms, complimentary breakfast and dinner. SGL$115W-$220W.

Lombard Hotel (1015 Geary, 94109; 673-5232, Fax 673-9362, 800-227-3608) 100 rooms, restaurant, children under 12 free, in-room refrigerators, fax service, meeting facilities for 40, valet laundry, no-smoking rooms, no pets. SGL/DBL$77-$87.

Majestic Hotel (1500 Sutter Street, 94109; 441-1100, Fax 673-7331, 800-869-8966) 59 rooms and suites, restaurant, lounge, in-room refrigerators, fax service valet laundry, meeting facilities for 50, airport transportation, wheelchair access, no-smoking rooms, pets allowed. SGL/DBL$135-$150, STS$215-$250.

Marina Motel (2576 Lombard Street, 94123; 921-9406, 800-346-6118) 40 rooms, suites and efficiencies, in-room refrigerators, airport transportation, free parking, no pets. SGL/DBL$55-$60, STS$80-$90.

Miyako Inn (1800 Sutter Street, 94115; 921-4000, Fax 923-1064, 800-528-1234) 125 rooms and suites, restaurant, airport transportation, no-smoking. STS$130-$200.

Nob Hill Motel (1630 Pacific Avenue, 94109; 775-8160, Fax 673-8842, 800-343-6900 in California) 29 rooms, wheelchair access, no-smoking rooms, free parking. SGL$48-$65, DBL$55-$80.

Nob Hill Lambourne (725 Pine, 94108; 433-2287) 20 rooms, restaurant, complimentary breakfast, airport transportation, no-smoking rooms. SGL/DBL$175.

Pacific Heights Inn (1555 Union, 94123; 776-3310, Fax 776-8176, 800-523-1801) 40 rooms and efficiencies, complimentary breakfast, sauna, spa, complimentary newspaper, wheelchair access, free parking. SGL/DBL$69-$85.

Quality Hotel (2775 Van Ness Avenue, 94109; 928-5000, Fax 441-3990, 800-221-2222) 132 rooms, restaurant, complimentary breakfast, meeting facilities, exercise equipment, free parking, wheelchair access, no pets. SGL$67-$118, DBL$79-$120.

Queen Anne Hotel (1590 Sutter, 94109; 441-2828, Fax 775-5212, 800-262-ANNE, 800-227-3970 in California) 49 rooms, bed & breakfast, complimentary breakfast, wheelchair access. SGL/DBL$94-$125.

Hotel Richelieu (1050 Van Ness Avenue, 94109; 673-4711, Fax 673-9362, 800-227-3608) 150 rooms and suites, lounge, children under 12 free, in-room refrigerators, fax service. SGL$89-$110, DBL$99-$125.

Roadway Inn (1450 Lombard Street, 94123; 673-0691, 800-424-4777) 72 rooms, restaurant, swimming pool, free parking, children under 18 free. SGL$55-$125, DBL$65-$135.

Roadway Inn (895 Geary, 94109; 441-8220, 800-228-2000, 800-424-4777) 73 rooms, restaurant, free parking, children under 18 free, tours, no pets. SGL$60-$106, DBL$79-$116.

Royal Pacific Motor Inn (661 Broadway, 94133; 781-6661, 800-545-5574) 74 rooms and suites, sauna, in-room refrigerators, fax service, meeting facilities for 10, exercise equipment, laundry room, free parking, no-smoking rooms, no pets. SGL$72, DBL$74, STS$89.

Sea Captain Motel (2322 Lombard, 94123; 921-4980) 39 rooms, complimentary breakfast, free parking. SGL$38-$45, DBL$42-$50.

TraveLodge (2230 Lombard Street, 94123; 922-3900, Fax 921-4795, 800-255-3050) 29 rooms, restaurant, lounge, fax service, tours, car rental, free parking, no pets. SGL/DBL$54-$79.

TraveLodge (2755 Lombard Street, 94123; 931-8581, Fax 776-0904, 800-255-3050) 27 rooms, restaurant, lounge, fax service, tours, car rental, beauty shop, no pets. SGL/DBL$56-$82.

Union Street Inn (2229 Union, 94123; 346-0424) 6 rooms, complimentary breakfast, free parking. SGL/DBL$135-$145.

Vagabond Inn Midtown (2550 Van Ness Avenue, 94109; 776-7500, Fax 776-5689, 800-522-1555) 132 rooms, restaurant, lounge, heated swimming pool, wheelchair access, kitchenettes, airport transportation, free local telephone calls, no-smoking rooms, children under 18 free, fax service, complimentary newspaper. SGL$68-$89, DBL$74-$99.

Van Ness Motel (2850 Van Ness Avenue, 94109; 776-3200, 800-322-8029) 42 rooms, complimentary breakfast, free parking. SGL/DBL$42-$62.

Other Areas

Abitante 1 & II (Bed and Breakfast International) 3 rooms, complimentary breakfast, no parking. SGL/DBL$75-$85.

At Home Corporate Housing (5635 Sunfish Court, 94515; 757-5536, Fax 757-2836) studios and one- and two-bedroom apartments. SGL/DBL$60.

Beach Motel (4211 Judah, 94122; 681-6618) 20 rooms and efficiencies, free parking. SGL$35-$50, DBL$40-$55.

Best Western Grosvenor Hotel (380 South Airport Rd., 94080; 873-3200, Fax 589-3495, 800-528-1234, 800-722-7141) 204 rooms and suites, restaurant, lounge, complimentary breakfast, swimming pool, jacuzzis, fax service, airport courtesy car, no-smoking rooms. SGL/DBL$69-$86, STS$100-$125.

Casa Arguello (225 Arguello Blvd., 94118; 752-9482) 5 rooms, bed & breakfast, complimentary breakfast. SGL$65, DBL$68.

Clarion Hotel (401 East Millbrae Avenue, 94030; 692-6363, 800-221-2222) 435 rooms, restaurant, lounge, swimming pool, exercise equipment, wheelchair access. SGL$105-$125, DBL$115-$135.

Classic Suites (60 Leavenworth, 94102; 626-3662) 24 suites, restaurant. SGL$50-$60, DBL$60-$70.

Comfort Suites (121 East Grand Avenue, 94080; 589-7766, 800-221-2222, 800-228-5150) 165 rooms, restaurant, complimentary breakfast, in-room refrigerators, airport courtesy car, wheelchair access, no pets. SGL$65-$68, DBL$70-$76.

Crown Sterling Suites (250 Gateway Blvd., 94080; 589-3400, 800-433-4600). 313 suites, restaurant, swimming pool, free parking. 2BR$99-$127.

Days Inn At The Beach (2600 Sloat Blvd., 94116; 665-9000, Fax 665-5440, 800-325-2525) 33 rooms and suites, complimentary breakfast, swimming pool, in-room refrigerators and microwaves, children under 12 free, fax service, wheelchair access, no-smoking rooms, free parking, airport courtesy car, no pets. SGL/DBL$60-$95, STS$105-$130.

El Capitan Hotel (2361 Mission Street, 94110; 695-1597) 25 rooms, no pets. SGL/DBL$20-$22.

Embassy Suites South San Francisco (250 Gateway Blvd., 94080; 549-3400, Fax 876-0305, 800-EMBASSY) 313 suites, restaurant, complimentary breakfast, swimming pool, wheelchair access, free parking. SGL$120-$130, DBL$130-$140.

European Guest House Hostel (761 Minna, 94103; 861-6634) 24 rooms. SGL$10-$20.

Globe Hostel Inter-Club (10 Hallam Place, 94103; 431-0540) 30 rooms. SGL$10-$15.

Golden Gate Park (Bed and Breakfast International) 5 rental homes, bed & breakfast. SGL/DBL$45-$65.

Great Highway Motor Inn (1234 Great Highway, 94122; 731-6644) 54 rooms. SGL$58-$72, DBL$64-$74.

Hill Point Bed and Breakfast (15 Hill Point, 94117; 753-0393) 20 rooms, bed & breakfast, complimentary breakfast, airport transportation, no-smoking rooms. SGL/DBL$35-$85+.

HoJo Inn (1595 Casa Buena Drive, 94925; 924-3570, 800-654-2000) 18 rooms, restaurant, in-room refrigerators. SGL$55-$75, DBL$59-$79.

Laurel Motor Inn (444 Presidio Avenue, 94115; 567-8467, Fax 928-1866, 800-552-8735 in California) 49 rooms, restaurant, complimentary breakfast, free parking, pets allowed. SGL$70-$90, DBL$78-$98.

Le Meridien Hotel (50 Third Street, 94103; 974-6400, Fax 543-8268, 800-543-4300) 700 rooms, restaurant, airport transportation, wheelchair access. SGL$125, DBL$135+.

Mansions Hotel (2220 Sacramento Street, 94115; 929-9444, Fax 567-9391, 800-424-9444) 21 rooms, bed & breakfast, complimentary breakfast, airport transportation, tennis, pets allowed, free parking. SGL$74-$200, DBL$89-$225.

Marina Inn (3110 Octavia, 94123; 928-1000) 40 rooms, bed & breakfast, complimentary breakfast. SGL/DBL$65+.

Marriott Residence Inn (2000 Windward Way, 94404; 574-4700, Fax 572-9084, 800-331-3131) suites, kitchens, in-room refrigerators, heated outdoor swimming pool, whirlpool, spa, cable TV, free parking, laundry room, fireplaces, airport transportation, wheelchair access, no-smoking rooms, pets allowed.

Mission Sierra Motel (5630 Mission Street, 94112; 584-5020, 800-225-9646) 51 rooms and efficiencies, wheelchair access, free parking. SGL/DBL$45-$68.

Moffatt House (431 Hugo Street, 94122; 661-6210) 4 rooms, bed & breakfast, complimentary breakfast. SGL/DBL$39-$56.

Monroe Residence Club Hostel (1870 Sacramento Avenue, 94109; 474-6200) 94 rooms, complimentary breakfast and dinner. SGL$126W-$195W.

Monte Cristo (600 Presidio Avenue, 94115; 931-1875) 14 rooms, bed & breakfast, complimentary breakfast. SGL/DBL$55+.

No Name Victorian of San Francisco (847 Fillmore Street, 94117; 479-1913, Fax 921-BBSF, 800-452-8249) 6 rooms and suites, bed & breakfast, complimentary breakfast, private baths, hot tub, free parking, no smoking. SGL/DBL$65-$125.

Noe Valley Bed and Breakfast (Bed and Breakfast International) 2 rooms, complimentary breakfast, no smoking. SGL$30-$85.

Nolan House (1071 Page, 94117; 863-0384, 800-SF-NOLAN) 4 rooms and suites, bed & breakfast, complimentary breakfast, private baths, free parking, free local telephone calls, no smoking. SGL/DBL$85-$135, STS$220.

Ocean Park Motel (2690 46th Avenue, 94116; 566-7020) 24 rooms and efficiencies, free parking. SGL/DBL$44-$40.

Ocean View Motel (4340 Judah, 94122; 661-2300) 22 rooms, restaurant, free parking. SGL/DBL$38-$52.

Painted Lady Bed and Breakfast (Bed and Breakfast International) one suite, complimentary breakfast, no smoking. SGL$85.

Pine Mews Bed and Breakfast (Bed and Breakfast International) one room, complimentary breakfast, no smoking. SGL$95.

The Red Victorian (1665 Haight, 94117; 864-1978) 15 rooms, bed & breakfast, complimentary breakfast. SGL$50-$85, DBL$55-$90.

Royal Inn (120 Kickey Blvd., 94080; 755-9724) 17 rooms, wheelchair access, no pets. SGL$40-$50, DBL$50-$65.

Russian Hill Guest House (Bed and Breakfast International) 5 rooms and apartments, bed & breakfast, complimentary breakfast. SGL/DBL$125-$150.

San Francisco State University Housing Office (800 Front Blvd., 94123; 338-2872) one- and two-bedroom apartments. SGL/DBL$20-$60.

Seal Rock Inn (545 Point Lobos Avenue, 94121; 752-8000) 27 rooms and efficiencies, restaurant, ocean view, kitchenettes, free parking. SGL/DBL$66-$97.

Stanyan Park Hotel (750 Stanyan Street, 94117; 751-1000, Fax 668-5454) 36 rooms, restaurant, complimentary breakfast, wheelchair access. SGL/DBL$78-$96.

Super 8 Motel Airport (111 Mitchell Avenue South, 94080; 877-0770, Fax 871-8377, 800-800-8000, 800-843-1991) 117 rooms, continental breakfast, transportation to local attractions, complimentary newspaper, valet laundry, airport courtesy car, wheelchair access, no-smoking rooms, no pets. SGL$53-$57, DBL$61+.

Telegraph Hill I & II (Bed and Breakfast International) 3 rooms, bed & breakfast, complimentary breakfast. SGL/DBL$58-$68.

Value Inn By Nendels (900 Franklin, 94109; 885-6865, Fax 474-1652, 800-843-4021, 800-223-9626 in California) 59 rooms, restaurant, exercise equipment, free parking, wheelchair access. SGL/DBL$69-$76.

Hotel Verona (317 Leavenworth, 94102; 771-4242, Fax 771-3355, 800-422-3646 in California) 65 rooms, restaurant, complimentary breakfast, wheelchair access. SGL$30-$36, DBL$35-$47.

Victorian Inn On The Park (301 Lyon Street, 94117; 931-1830, 800-435-1967) 12 rooms, bed & breakfast, complimentary breakfast. SGL/DBL$88-$144.

The Westin Hotel Airport (One Old Bayshore Highway, 94030; 692-3500, Fax 872-8111, 800-228-3000) 388 rooms, Executive Club Level, two restaurants, lounge, indoor heated swimming pool, whirlpool, sauna, exercise equipment, 24-hour room service, computer hookups in rooms, business services, pets allowed, free parking, wheelchair access/room, no-smoking rooms, airline ticket office, boutiques, cable TV. SGL/DBL$135, STS$375-$465.

Wye Motel (100 Hickey Blvd., 94080; 755-9556) 20 rooms. SGL$35, DBL$42.

San Gregorio

Area Code 415

Rancho San Gregorio (Box 54, 94074; 747-0810) 4 rooms, bed & breakfast, complimentary breakfast. SGL$55-$85, DBL$60-$85.

San Jose

Area Code 408
San Jose Convention and Visitors Bureau
One Paseo de San Antonio
San Jose CA 95150
295-9600

Airport Plaza Inn (2118 The Alameda, 95126; 243-2400, Fax 243-5487) 40 suites, restaurant, complimentary breakfast, swimming pool, airport courtesy car, wheelchair access, no-smoking rooms. STS$65-$100+.

Alameda Motel (1050 The Alameda, 95126; 295-7201) 21 rooms. SGL$36-$40, DBL$40-$50.

Best Western Gateway Inn (2585 Seaboard Avenue, 95131; 435-8800, Fax 435-8879, 800-437-8855, 800-528-1234) 148 rooms, restaurant, lounge, complimentary breakfast, heated swimming pool, sauna, in-room refrigerators, fax service, meeting facilities, laundry room, airport courtesy car, wheelchair access. SGL/DBL$59-$78.

Best Western Inn (455 South Second Street, 95113; 298-3500, Fax 298-2477, 800-528-1234) 72 rooms, restaurant, complimentary breakfast, swimming pool, exercise equipment, free parking, no-smoking rooms. SGL/DBL$48-$68.

Best Western San Jose Lodge (1440 North First Street, 95112; 453-7750, Fax 437-9519, 800-528-1234) 75 rooms, restaurant, lounge, swimming pool, fax service, children under 12 free, no-smoking rooms, pets allowed. SGL$54-$60, DBL$56-$65.

Briar Rose (897 East Jackson Street, 95112; 279-5999) 5 rooms, bed & breakfast, complimentary breakfast. SGL/DBL$65-$125.

Comfort Inn Airport (1310 North First Street, 95112; 453-1100, 800-221-2222, 800-228-5150) 56 rooms, restaurant, complimentary breakfast, heated swimming pool, whirlpool, airport courtesy car, wheelchair access, no pets. SGL$59-$69, DBL$65-$75.

Comfort Inn Executive Suites (1215 South First Street, 95110; 280-5300, 800-221-2222, 800-228-5150) 59 rooms and suites, restaurant, whirlpool, VCRs, wheelchair access, no pets. SGL$53-$75, DBL$55-$80.

De Anza Hotel (233 West Santa Clara Street, 95113; 286-1000, Fax 286-0500, 800-843-3700) 101 rooms and suites, restaurants, lounge, complimentary breakfast, in-room refrigerators, fax service, meeting facilities for 100, gift shop, laundry room, wheelchair access, no-smoking rooms, no pets. SGL/DBL$120-$155, STS$250.

Executive Inn Suites (3930 Monterey Rd., 95111; 281-8700, 800-453-7755, 800-292-7667) 25 rooms. SGL$80, DBL$72-$85.

E-Z 8 Motel (1550 North First Street, 95112; 453-1830) 81 rooms. SGL/DBL$34-$46.

E-Z 8 Motel (2050 North First Street, 95131; 436-0636) 88 rooms. SGL/DBL$33-$45.

Fairmont Hotel (170 South Market Street, 95113; 998-1900, Fax 280-0394, 800-527-4727) 541 rooms and suites, restaurant, swimming pool, exercise equipment, airport transportation, wheelchair access, no-smoking rooms. SGL$135-$175, DBL$150-$195, STS$400-$1500.

Friendship Inn (2188 The Alameda, 95126; 248-8300, 800-424-4777) 30 rooms, restaurant, lounge, children under 18 free. SGL/DBL$35-$45.

Gum Tree Motel (4170 Monterey Rd., 95111; 224-4122) 32 rooms, complimentary breakfast, swimming pool. SGL/DBL$50-$65.

The Hensley House (456 North Third Street, 95112; 298-3537, Fax 298-4676, 800-634-2567) 5 rooms, bed & breakfast, complimentary breakfast, airport courtesy car, free parking. SGL/DBL$75-$125.

Holiday Inn Airport (1355 North Fourth Street, 95112; 453-5340, 800-HOLIDAY) 194 rooms, restaurant, lounge, swimming pool, airport courtesy car, meeting facilities for 250, children under 18 free, wheelchair access, no-smoking rooms, pets allowed. SGL/DBL$75-$100.

Holiday Inn Park Center Plaza (282 Alameda Blvd., 95113; 998-0400, Fax 289-9081, 800-HOLIDAY) 230 rooms and suites, restaurant, lounge, swimming pool, meeting facilities for 1000, children under 18 free, airport transportation. SGL/DBL$65-$105.

Homewood Suites Hotel (10 West Trimble Rd., 95131; 428-9900, Fax 428-0222, 800-CALL-HOME) one- and two-bedroom suites, restaurant, complimentary breakfast, swimming pool, transportation to local attractions, no-smoking rooms. STS$99-$119, 2BR$129-$149.

Howard Johnson Lodge (1755 North First Street, 95112; 453-3133, Fax 453-3133, 800-654-2000) 94 rooms, swimming pool, valet laundry, car rental, meeting facilities for 85, airport courtesy car, no-smoking rooms. SGL/DBL$59-$124.

Hyatt Regency Airport (1740 North First Street, 95112; 993-1234, Fax 453-0259, 800-233-1234) 470 rooms and suites, restaurant, lounge, swimming pool, whirlpool, exercise equipment, airport courtesy car, wheelchair access, no-smoking rooms. SGL/DBL$140-$165, STS$300-$600.

Le Baron Hotel (1350 North First Street, 95112; 453-6300, Fax 437-9693, 800-538-6818, 800-662-9898 in California) 327 rooms and suites, restaurant, swimming pool, airport courtesy car, exercise equipment, wheelchair access, no-smoking rooms. SGL/DBL$105-$135, STS$135-$500+.

Motel 6 (2081 North First Street, 95131; 436-8180, 505-891-6161) 75 rooms. SGL/DBL$33-$39.

Motel 6 (2560 Fontaine Rd., 95121; 270-3131, 505-891-6161) 202 rooms. SGL/DBL$31-$37.

Mother Olson's Inn (72 North Fifth Street, 95112; 998-0223) 32 rooms. SGL/DBL$100-$160.

Oasis Motel (5340 Monterey Rd., 95111; 225-0320) 60 rooms, complimentary breakfast, swimming pool, pets allowed. SGL/DBL$45-$51.

President Inn (3200 Monterey Rd., 95111; 972-2200, Fax 972-2632) 55 rooms, swimming pool, exercise equipment. SGL/DBL$65-$85.

Radisson Plaza Hotel (1471 North Fourth Street, 95112; 452-0200, Fax 437-8819, 800-333-3333) 186 rooms and suites, restaurant, swimming pool, exercise equipment, airport courtesy car, wheelchair access, no-smoking rooms. SGL/DBL$110-$135, STS$275+.

Red Lion Hotel (2050 Gateway Place, 95110; 453-4000, Fax 437-9507, 800-547-8010) 76 rooms, restaurant, complimentary breakfast, swimming pool, airport transportation, no-smoking rooms, pets allowed. SGL$135-$150, DBL$150-$165, STS$400-$600.

Rodeway Inn (2112 South Monterey Highway, 95112; 294-1480, 800-424-4777) 95 rooms, restaurant, swimming pool, wheelchair access, children under 18 free, no pets. SGL$48-$80, DBL$52-$85.

The San Jose Inn (1860 The Alameda, 95112; 293-9361, 800-331-9361) 56 rooms and suites, restaurant, lounge, outdoor heated swimming pool, children under 18 free, fax service, meeting facilities for 50, kitchenettes, free parking, wheelchair access, no-smoking rooms, pets allowed. SGL$38, DBL$43, STS$45.

Summerfield Suites Hotel (1602 Crane Court, 95112; 436-1600, Fax 436-1075, 800-833-4353) 98 suites. SGL/DBL$129-$159.

TraveLodge (1041 The Alameda, 951226; 295-0159, Fax 998-5509, 800-255-3050) 63 rooms and suites, restaurant, lounge, swimming pool, in-room refrigerators, meeting facilities for 30, airport transportation. SGL/DBL$42-$58.

TraveLodge (1415 Monterey Rd., 95110; 993-1711, Fax 993-8744, 800-255-3050) 26 rooms and suites, restaurant, lounge, whirlpool, no pets. SGL/DBL$45-$60.

Vagabond Inn (1488 North First Street, 95112; 453-8822, Fax 453-0559, 800-522-1555) 76 rooms, restaurant, heated swimming pool, laundry room, wheelchair access, pets allowed, airport transportation, free local telephone calls, no-smoking rooms, children under 18 free, fax service, complimentary newspaper. SGL$54, DBL$59-$64.

San Juan Bautista

Area Code 408
San Juan Bautista Chamber of Commerce
201 Third Street
San Juan Bautista CA 95045
623-2454

San Juan Inn (410 Alameda Street, 95045; 623-4380) 42 rooms, restaurant, swimming pool, no-smoking rooms. SGL/DBL$40-$60.

San Leandro

Area Code 510

San Leandro Marina Inn (68 San Leandro Marina, 94577; 895-1311, 800-786-7783) 131 rooms, complimentary breakfast, swimming pool, airport transportation, wheelchair access, no-smoking rooms. SGL/DBL$82-$87, STS$95-$99.

San Mateo

Area Code 415

Best Western (2940 Norfolk Street, 94403; 341-3300, Fax 341-9999, 800-528-1234) 103 rooms, restaurant, exercise equipment, airport transportation, fax service, whirlpool, no-smoking rooms, no pets. SGL/DBL$62-$82.

Dunfey's San Mateo (1770 South Amphlett Blvd., 94402; 573-7661, Fax 573-0533, 800-843-6664, 800-238-6339 in California) 290 rooms and suites, restaurant, swimming pool, airport courtesy car, exercise equipment, wheelchair access, no-smoking rooms, pets allowed. SGL$85-$117, DBL$100-$127.

Firestone Lodge Motel (2175 El Camino Real, 94403; 341-5671) 47 rooms and efficiencies, wheelchair access. SGL$30, DBL$35.

Hillsdale Inn (477 East Hillsdale Blvd., 94403; 341-3461) 88 rooms, swimming pool. SGL$41, DBL$47.

Hollywood Motel (480 North Bayshore Blvd., 94401; 340-7141) 40 rooms and efficiencies. SGL/DBL$30-$38.

Los Prados Inn-TraveLodge (2940 South Norfolk Street, 94403; 341-3300, 800-341-1234) 116 rooms restaurant, swimming pool, wheelchair access, no-smoking rooms. SGL$52, DBL$57-$75.

Marriott Residence Inn (2000 Windward Way, 94404; 574-4700, Fax 572-9084, 800-331-3131) 160 rooms, heated swimming pool, whirlpool, airport transportation, exercise equipment, wheelchair access, meeting facilities for 65, in-room microwaves and VCRs, no-smoking rooms, pets allowed. SGL$104-$109, DBL$129-$139.

Villa Hotel (4000 South El Camino Real, 94403; 341-0966, Fax 573-0164, 800-341-2345) 300 rooms and suites, restaurant, swimming pool, airport courtesy car, wheelchair access, no-smoking rooms, pets allowed. SGL$65-$79, DBL$73-$87.

San Rafael

Area Code 415
Marin County Chamber of Commerce and Visitors Bureau
30 North San Pedro Rd.
San Rafael CA 94903
472-7470

RENTAL SOURCES: Seashore Bed and Breakfasts of Marin (Old Creamery Building; 663-9373) reservation service for local bed & breakfasts. SGL/DBL$50-$200.

Colonial Motel (1735 Lincoln Avenue, 94901; 453-9188) 18 rooms, free parking, in-room refrigerators, wheelchair access, no-smoking rooms, free parking, tours. SGL$48-$52, DBL$45-$54.

Dominican College of San Rafael (1520 Grand Avenue, 94901; 485-3228) 240 rooms, restaurant, swimming pool, free parking. SGL/DBL$40-$55.

Embassy Suites Hotel (101 McInnis Parkway, 94903; 499-9222, Fax 499-9268, 800-EMBASSY, 800-458-5848 in California) 236 suites, indoor and outdoor restaurant, complimentary breakfast, meeting facilities for 500, gift shop, indoor swimming pool, whirlpool, exercise equipment, free parking, no-smoking rooms, transportation to local attractions, conference and meeting facilities, wheelchair access. SGL$114, DBL$129.

Friendship Inn (1600 Lincoln Avenue, 94901; 456-4975, 800-424-4777) 60 rooms, restaurant, swimming pool, whirlpools, kitchenettes, meeting facilities, wheelchair access, children under 18 free, no-smoking rooms, pets allowed. SGL$53-$68, DBL$56-$73.

Holiday Inn Marin (1010 Northgate Drive, 94903; 479-8800, 800-HOLIDAY) 224 rooms, restaurant, lounge, swimming pool, airport transportation, exercise equipment, wheelchair access, meeting and banquet facilities for 300, free parking, pets allowed. SGL$79-$112, DBL$89-$125.

National 9 Inn (855 Francisco Blvd., 94901; 456-8620, 800-524-9999) 18 rooms, wheelchair access, no-smoking rooms. SGL$40-$45, DBL$45-$55.

Panama Hotel (4 Bayview Street, 94901; 457-3993) 17 rooms and suites, restaurant, complimentary breakfast. SGL/DBL$40-$150.

San Rafael Inn (865 Francisco Blvd., 94901; 454-9470, 800-422-9470) 32 rooms, swimming pool. SGL$46-$60, DBL$52-$65.

Thirty Nine Cypress (39 Cypress, 94901; 663-1709) 3 rooms, bed & breakfast, complimentary breakfast. SGL/DBL$90-$100.

Villa Inn (1600 Lincoln Avenue, 94901; 456-4975) 60 rooms and efficiencies, restaurant, meeting facilities, laundry room, wheelchair access, no-smoking rooms. SGL/DBL$56-$85.

Santa Clarita

Area Code 805

Hampton Inn (25259 The Old Rd., 91381; 253-2400, Fax 253-1583, 800-426-7866) 130 rooms, restaurant, swimming pool, wheelchair access, no-smoking rooms. SGL$65-$70, DBL$70-$75.

TraveLodge of Santa Clarita (17843 Sierra Highway, 91351; 252-1716, 800-255-3050). 54 rooms, outdoor heated swimming pool, jaccuzzi, free parking. SGL/DBL$55-$65.

Santa Nella

Area Code 208

Best Western Andersen's Inn (12637 South Highway 33, 95322; 209-826-5534, Fax 827-1448, 800-528-1234) 94 rooms, restaurant, lounge, complimentary breakfast, swimming pool, balconies, spas, laundry room, no-smoking rooms, wheelchair access, pets allowed. SGL/DBL$52-$68.

Holiday Inn (13070 South Highway 33, 95322; 209-826-4444, Fax 826-8071, 800-HOLIDAY) 159 rooms, restaurant, swimming pool, meeting facilities for 300, wheelchair access, no-smoking rooms, pets allowed. SGL$40-$60, DBL$50-$65.

LaFontaine TraveLodge (28976 West Plaza Drive, 95322; 826-8282, Fax 826-9039, 800-255-3050) 100 rooms, restaurant, lounge, complimentary breakfast, swimming pool, whirlpool, in-room refrigerators, laundry room, meeting facilities for 100, fax service, exercise equipment, wheelchair access, no-smoking rooms. SGL$59, DBL$66.

Santa Rosa

Area Code 707
Sonoma County Convention and Visitors Bureau
637 First Street
Santa Rosa CA 95404
545-1420

All Star Inn (3145 Cleveland Avenue, 95401; 525-9010) 34 rooms. SGL/DBL$28-$34.

Astro Motel (323 Santa Rosa Avenue, 95404; 545-8555) 30 rooms. SGL/DBL$30-$50.

Best Western Garden Inn (1500 Santa Rosa Avenue, 95404; 546-4031, 800-334-9596) 78 rooms, restaurant, two swimming pools, wheelchair access, no-smoking rooms, pets allowed. SGL/DBL$50-$60.

Best Western Hillside Inn (2901 Fourth Street, 95409; 546-9353, 800-528-1234) 35 rooms, restaurant, swimming pool, kitchenettes, children under 12 free, laundry room, pets allowed. SGL/DBL$55-$110.

Coopers Grove Ranch Guest House (5763 Sonoma Mountain Rd., 95401; 571-1928) 4 rooms and cottages, complimentary breakfast, swimming pool. SGL/DBL$86-$150.

Days Inn (175 Railroad Street, 95401; 573-9000, Fax 573-0272, 800-325-2525) 135 rooms and suites, restaurant, lounge, swimming pool, spa, gift shop, children under 12 free, fax service, valet laundry, meeting facilities, wheelchair access, no-smoking rooms, no pets. SGL$49-$90, DBL$59-$105, STS$85-$125.

Doubletree Hotel (3555 Round Barn Blvd., 95403; 523-7555, Fax 545-2807, 800-528-0444) 250 rooms and suites, restaurant, lounge, outdoor heated swimming pool, whirlpool, spa, meeting facilities for 350, airport transportation, free parking, wheelchair access, no-smoking rooms. SGL/DBL$70-$110, STS$150-$200+.

Econo Lodge (1800 Santa Rosa Avenue, 95407; 523-3480, 800-424-4777) 43 rooms, restaurant, children under 18 free, wheelchair access, no-smoking rooms, pets allowed. SGL/DBL$35-$60.

El Rancho Tropicana Resort Hotel and Convention Center (220 Santa Rosa Avenue, 95407; 542-3655, Fax 576-1033,

800-654-4401, 800-248-4747) 300 rooms, restaurant, three heated swimming pools, banquet and conference facilities, tennis courts, airport courtesy car, exercise equipment, wheelchair access, free parking. SGL$55-$70, DBL$60-$90.

Flamingo Resort Hotel (4th and Farmer's Lane, 95404; 545-8530, 800-848-8300) 137 rooms and suites, restaurant, heated swimming pool, meeting facilities for 600, airport transportation, exercise equipment, tennis. LS SGL/DBL$62-$82, STS$92-$142; HS SGL/DBL$66-$68, STS$87-$176.

Fountaingrove Inn (101 Fountaingrove Parkway, 95403; 578-6101; Fax 544-3126, 800-222-6101 in California) 83 rooms and suites, restaurant, complimentary breakfast, swimming pool, airport courtesy car, wheelchair access, no-smoking rooms, pets allowed. SGL/DBL$75-$85, STS$125-$160.

The Gables Inn (4257 Petaluma Hill Rd., 95404; 585-7777) 6 rooms, bed & breakfast, complimentary breakfast, wheelchair access, no-smoking. SGL/DBL$95-$115.

Gee-Gee's (7810 Sonoma Highway 12, 95409; 833-6667) 4 rooms, bed & breakfast, complimentary breakfast, swimming pool. SGL/DBL$75-$100.

Heritage Inn (870 Hopper Avenue, 95404; 533-1255) 95 rooms, swimming pool. SGL/DBL$37+.

Holiday Inn (3345 Santa Rosa Avenue, 95407; 579-3000, Fax 544-1408, 800-545-1224, 800-HOLIDAY) 100 rooms, restaurant, swimming pool, exercise equipment, wheelchair access, pets allowed. SGL$62-$67, DBL$72-$77.

Hotel La Rose (308 Wilson Street, 95401; 579-3100, Fax 579-3247, 800-LA-ROSE8) 57 rooms and suites, restaurant, wheelchair access, no smoking, airport transportation. SGL/DBL$50-$100, STS$125+.

Los Robles Lodge (925 Edwards Avenue, 95401; 545-6330, Fax 575-5826, 800-235-6330, 800-522-1001 in California) 105 rooms, restaurant, swimming pool, jacuzzi, rooms service, in-room refrigerators, airport courtesy car, no-smoking rooms, pets allowed. SGL/DBL$70-$90.

Melitta Station Inn (5850 Melitta Rd., 95401; 538-7712) 6 rooms, bed & breakfast, complimentary breakfast. SGL/DBL$65-$90.

Motel 6 (2760 Cleveland Avenue, 95403; 546-1500, 505-891-6161) 100 rooms. SGL/DBL$30-$36.

Northwood Lodge (19455 Highway 116, 95462; 865-1655) 25 rooms. SGL/DBL$52-$65.

Pygmalion House (351 Orange Street 95407; 526-3407) 5 rooms, bed & breakfast, complimentary breakfast, no-smoking. SGL/DBL$50-$70.

The Sandman Motel (3421 Cleveland Avenue, 95403; 544-8570, Fax 544-8710) 112 rooms, restaurant, swimming pool, no-smoking rooms. SGL/DBL$42-$50.

Super 8 Lodge (2632 Cleveland Avenue, 95403; 542-5544, Fax 578-9376, 800-800-8000) 100 rooms and restaurant, complimentary breakfast, outdoor swimming pool, free local telephone calls, fax service, complimentary newspaper, wheelchair access, no-smoking rooms, no pets. SGL/DBL$38-$48.

TraveLodge (1815 Santa Rosa Avenue, 95407; 542-3472, 800-255-3050) 31 rooms and suites, restaurant, lounge, swimming pool. SGL/DBL$50-$60.

TraveLodge Downtown (635 Healdsburg Avenue, 95401; 544-4141, 800-255-3050) 44 rooms and suites, restaurant, lounge, swimming pool, sauna, tennis, airport transportation. SGL/DBL$35-$52.

Vintners Inn (4350 Barnes Rd., 95403; 575-7350, Fax 575-1426, 800-421-2584 in California) 44 rooms and suites, restaurant, swimming pool, airport transportation, wheelchair access, no-smoking rooms. SGL/DBL$108-$185.

Saratoga

Area Code 408
Saratoga Chamber of Commerce
20460 Saratoga-Los Gatos Rd.
Saratoga CA 95071
867-0753

The Inn At Saratoga (20645 Fourth Street, 95070; 867-5020, Fax 741-0981, 800-338-5020) 46 rooms and suites, restaurant, complimentary breakfast, swimming pool, exercise equipment, wheelchair access, no-smoking rooms. SGL/DBL$145-$400+, STS$300-$500.

Saratoga Motel (14626 Big Basin Way, 95070; 867-3307) 20 rooms. SGL/DBL$55-$75.

Sausalito

Area Code 415
Sausalito Chamber of Commerce
333 Caledonia Street
Sausalito CA 94966
332-0505

RENTAL SOURCES: J. Andrew Paulson Realty (201 Squaw Creek Rd., 94965) rents studio apartments. SGL/DBL$72+.

Alta Mira Hotel (125 Bulkley Avenue, 94965; 332-1350) 35 rooms and cottages, restaurant, free parking. SGL/DBL$70-$170.

Casa Madrona Hotel (801 Bridgeway, 94965; 332-0502, Fax 332-2537, 800-288-0502) 34 rooms and 2 cottages, bed & breakfast, restaurant, complimentary breakfast, wheelchair access, no-smoking rooms. SGL/DBL$90-$140, STS$145-$300.

Golden Gate AYH Hostel (Building 941, Fort Barry, 94965; 331-2777) 66 rooms, kitchen. SGL$8+.

Sausalito Hotel (16 El Portal, 94965; 332-4155) 15 rooms, bed & breakfast, complimentary breakfast, free parking. SGL/DBL$65-$125+.

Scotia

Area Code 707

Scotia Inn (Box 248, 95565; 764-5683) 11 rooms, bed & breakfast, complimentary breakfast. SGL/DBL$50-$75.

Scotts Valley

Area Code 408

Best Western Inn (6060 Scotts Valley Drive, 95066; 438-6666, Fax 439-8752, 800-528-1234) 58 rooms, restaurant, swimming pool, spa, meeting facilities, wheelchair access, fireplaces, balconies, hot tubs, children under 12 free, laundry room, fax service, no-smoking rooms, pets allowed, free parking. LS SGL/DBL$55-$125; HS SGL/DBL$70-$125.

Sea Ranch

Area Code 707

RENTAL SOURCES: Rams Head Realty (Box 123, 95497; 785-2427) represents 120 private home rentals. **Sea Ranch Escapes** (Box 238, 95497) rents private homes. **Sea Ranch Vacation Rentals** (Box 123, 95497; 785-2427).

Sea Ranch Lodge and Golf Links (Box 44, 95497; 785-2371, Fax 785-2917, 800-842-3270) 20 rooms, restaurant, swimming pool, tennis, golf. SGL/DBL$115+.

Shell Beach

Area Code 805

Shell Beach Motel (653 Shell Beach Rd., 93449; 773-4373) 9 rooms, swimming pool, no-smoking rooms. SGL/DBL$68-$75.

Spyglass Inn (2705 Spyglass Drive, 93449; 773-4855, 800-824-2612) 83 rooms, restaurant, complimentary breakfast, airport transportation, wheelchair access, no-smoking rooms, pets allowed.

Sierra City

Area Code 916

Butte's Resort Motel (Box 234, 96125; 862-1170) 12 rooms and efficiencies. SGL/DBL$35-$110.

Herrington's Sierra Pines (Box 235, 96125; 862-1151) 20 rooms and efficiencies, restaurant. SGL/DBL$49+.

High Country Inn (Box 7, 96125 -862-1530) 4 rooms, bed & breakfast, complimentary breakfast. SGL/DBL$70.

Packer Lake Lodge (Box 237, 96125; 862-1221) 14 rooms and efficiencies, restaurant. SGL/DBL$48-$98/$307W-$646W.

Sardine Lake Resort (Box 216, 96125; 862-1196) 9 cabins. SGL$40, DBL$45.

Sierra Chalet Motel (Box 455, 96125; 862-1110) 4 rooms and efficiencies. SGL/DBL$40+.

Yuba River Inn (Box 236, 96125; 862-1122) 9 cabins, swimming pool. SGL/DBL$30+.

Sierraville

Area Code 916

Canyon Ranch Resort (Old Truckee Rd., 96126; 994-3340) 8 cabins, swimming pool. SGL/DBL$45+.

Skyforest

Area Code 714

Storybook Inn (Box 362, 92385; 336-1483, 800-554-9208) 11 rooms and suites, bed & breakfast, complimentary breakfast, hot tub, free local telephone calls, free parking, wheelchair access, no-smoking rooms, no pets. SGL/DBL$98, STS$98-$200.

Smith River

Area Code 707

Best Western Ship Ashore Resort (12370 Highway 101N, 95567; 487-3141, Fax 487-7070, 800-528-1234) 54 rooms, restaurant, lounge, fax service, whirlpools, kitchenettes, airport transportation, beach, pets allowed. LS SGL/DBL$38-$46; HS SGL/DBL$46-$55.

Somerset

Area Code 209

Fitzpatrick Winery and Lodge (7740 Fairplay Rd., 95648; 245-3248) 4 rooms, bed & breakfast, complimentary breakfast. SGL/DBL$60.

Somesbar

Area Code 916

Young's Ranch Resort (Highway 96, 95568; 469-3322) 11 cabins, restaurant. SGL/DBL$37-$100.

Sonoma

Area Code 707
Sonoma Valley Visitors Bureau
453 First Street
Sonoma CA 95476
996-1090

RENTAL SOURCES: Bed and Breakfast Exchange (1458 Lincoln Avenue, Calistoga, 94515; 942-5900) reservation service for local bed & breakfasts. **Bed and Breakfast International** (Box 282910, San Francisco 94128; 415-696-1960) represents bed & breakfasts in the Sonoma Valley Area.

Best Western Sonoma Valley Inn (550 Second Street West, 95476; 938-9200, Fax 938-0935, 800-334-5784, 800-528-1234) 75 rooms, restaurant, lounge, complimentary breakfast, swimming pool, jacuzzis, meeting facilities, fax service, wheelchair access, no-smoking rooms. LS SGL/DBL$70-$75; HS SGL/DBL$100-$145.

El Dorado Hotel (405 First Street West, 95476; 996-3030, Fax 996-3148, 800-289-3031) 27 rooms, restaurant, complimentary breakfast, heated swimming pool, wheelchair access, pets allowed, free parking. SGL/DBL$85-$130.

El Pueblo Motel (896 West Napa Street, 95476; 996-3651) 38 rooms, swimming pool. SGL/DBL$55+.

The Hidden Oak (214 East Napa, 95476; 996-9863) 3 rooms, bed & breakfast, complimentary breakfast, fireplaces, bicycles. SGL/DBL$85-$105.

Magiliulo's Inn (691 Broadway, 95476; 996-1031) 5 rooms, bed & breakfast, complimentary breakfast, restaurant, wheelchair access, no-smoking. SGL/DBL$70-$80.

Mission Inn and Spa (Box 1447, 95476; 938-9000, Fax 938-4250) 173 rooms. SGL/DBL$135+.

Sonoma Chalet (18935 Fifth Street, 95476; 938-3129) 7 rooms, bed & breakfast, complimentary breakfast, free parking. SGL/DBL$75-$110.

Sonoma Hotel (100 West Spain Street, 95476; 996-2996) 17 rooms, bed & breakfast, complimentary breakfast, airport transportation, no pets. SGL/DBL$62-$115.

Sonoma Mission Inn and Spa (Box 1447, 95476; 938-9000, Fax 938-4250, 800-358-9022) 170 rooms and suites, restaurant, swimming pool, exercise equipment, airport transportation, lighted tennis courts, wheelchair access, free parking. SGL/DBL$140-$290.

Sonoma Valley Inn (550 Second Street West, 95476; 938-9200, 800-334-KRUG) 75 rooms, complimentary breakfast, swimming pool, wheelchair access, free parking. SGL/DBL$75-$130.

Thistle Dew Inn (171 West Spain Street, 95476; 938-2909) 6 rooms, bed & breakfast, complimentary breakfast, wheelchair access. SGL/DBL$80-$100.

The Trojan Horse Inn (19455 Sonoma Highway, 95476; 996-2430) 6 rooms, complimentary breakfast, wheelchair access, no-smoking. SGL/DBL$74-$130.

Victorian Garden Inn (316 East Napa Street, 95476; 996-5339) 4 rooms, bed & breakfast, complimentary breakfast, swimming pool. SGL/DBL$79-$135.

Vineyard Inn (23000 Arnold Drive, 95476; 938-2350) 9 rooms, bed & breakfast, complimentary breakfast. SGL/DBL$55-$135.

Westerbeke Ranch (2300 Grove Street, 95476; 996-7546) 50 beds. SGL/DBL$58-$76.

Sonora

Area Code 209
Tuolumne County Visitors Bureau
16 West Stockton
Sonora CA 95370
533-4420

Aladdin Motor Inn (14260 Mon Way, 95370; 533-4971, Fax 532-1522) 60 rooms. SGL/DBL$45+.

Barretta Gardens Inn (700 South Barretta Street, 95370; 532-6039) 5 rooms, complimentary breakfast, no-smoking rooms. SGL/DBL$79+.

Best Western Oaks Motor Hotel (19551 Hess Avenue, 95370; 533-4400, Fax 532-1964, 800-528-1234) 71 rooms and suites, restaurant, swimming pool. LS SGL/DBL$54-$69; HS SGL/DBL$55-$73, STS$100-$120.

The City Hotel (Main Street, 95310; 532-1479) 9 rooms. SGL/DBL$60-$85.

Gunn House Motel (2876 South Washington Street, 95370; 532-3421) 25 rooms, restaurant, complimentary breakfast, swimming pool. SGL/DBL$55-$75.

La Casa Inglesa (18047 Lime Kiln Rd., 95370; 532-5822) 5 rooms and suites, complimentary breakfast, no-smoking. SGL/DBL$70-$100.

Ryan's House (153 South Shepherd Street, 95370; 533-3445, 800-831-4897) 3 rooms, bed & breakfast, complimentary breakfast, private baths. SGL$80, DBL$85.

Serenity (15305 Bear Club Drive, 95370; 533-1441) 4 rooms, bed & breakfast, complimentary breakfast. SGL/DBL$65-$105.

Sonora Aladdin Motor Inn (14260 Mono Way, 95370; 533-4971, Fax 522-1522) 60 rooms, restaurant, swimming pool, airport transportation, wheelchair access, no-smoking rooms, pets allowed. SGL$37-$50, DBL$42-$60.

Sonora Inn (1260 South Washington Street, 95370; 532-7468, Fax 532-4542, 800-321-5261) 63 rooms, restaurant, complimentary breakfast, swimming pool, free parking. SGL$38-$50, DBL$45-$55.

Soquel

Area Code 408

Blue Spruce Inn (2815 Main Street, 95063; 464-1137) 5 rooms, bed & breakfast, complimentary breakfast, free parking. SGL/DBL$80-$115.

Stanton

Area Code 714

Best Western Cypress (7161 West Katella Avenue, 90680; 527-6680, Fax 527-7737, 800-528-1234) 72 rooms, restaurant, complimentary breakfast, swimming pool, spa, sauna, children under 12 free, laundry room, in-room refrigerators, wheelchair access, no-smoking rooms. SGL$45-$85, DBL$51-$92.

Comfort Inn (11632 Beach Rd., 90608; 891-7688, 800-221-2222) 38 rooms, restaurant, heated swimming pool, spa, wheelchair access, no pets. LS SGL$36-$46, DBL$40-$46; HS SGL$42-$54, DBL$46-$54.

Days Inn (10301 Beach Blvd., Stanton, 90680; 826-6060, 800-325-2525) 28 rooms suites, complimentary breakfast, wheelchair access, VCRs, free local telephone calls, in-room refrigerators and microwaves, tours, no-smoking rooms. SGL$42-$58, DBL$46-$42.

Daystop (10301 Beach Blvd., 90680; 826-6060) 32 rooms. SGL/DBL$42-$65.

Motel 6 (7450 Katella Avenue, 90680; 891-7521) 207 rooms. SGL/DBL$25-$31.

Tahiti Motel (11850 Beach Blvd., 90680; 893-7521) 15 rooms. SGL/DBL$26-$40.

Saint Helena

Area Code 707
Saint Helena Chamber of Commerce
1080 Main Street
Saint Helena CA 94574
963-4456

Bartels Ranch and Country Inn B&B (1200 Conn Valley Rd., 94574; 963-4001) 3 rooms, bed & breakfast, complimentary breakfast, wheelchair access, free parking. SGL/DBL$125+.

Chestelson House (1417 Kearney Street; 963-2238) 4 rooms, complimentary breakfast, no-smoking. SGL/DBL$60-$100.

El Bonita Motel (195 Main Street, 94574; 963-3216, 800-541-3284 in California) 22 rooms, restaurant, swimming pool, no-smoking rooms. SGL/DBL$61-$85.

Elsie's Conn Valley Inn (726 Rossie Rd., 94574; 963-4614) 3 rooms, bed & breakfast, complimentary breakfast, fireplaces, in-room refrigerators. SGL/DBL$75-$95.

Harvest Inn (One Main Street, 94574; 963-9463, Fax 963-4402, 800-950-8466) 54 rooms, complimentary breakfast, swimming pool, free parking, pets allowed. SGL/DBL$105-$300.

Judy's Bed and Breakfast (2036 Madrona Avenue, 94574; 963-3081) 1 room, bed & breakfast, complimentary breakfast, swimming pool. SGL/DBL$75-$100.

Harvest Inn (One Main Street, 94574; 963-6493, Fax 963-4402, 800-950-8466) 54 rooms, complimentary breakfast, lounge, outdoor heated swimming pool, jacuzzi, fax service, meeting facilities for 40, airport transportation, wheelchair access, free parking, pets allowed. SGL/DBL$100-$325.

La Residence Country Inn (4066 St. Helena Highway, 94558; 253-0337) 20 rooms, bed & breakfast, complimentary breakfast, swimming pool, wheelchair access, free parking. SGL/DBL$95-$125.

Meadowood Resort Hotel (900 Meadowood Lane, 94574; 963-3646, Fax 963-3532, 800-458-8080) 70 rooms, restaurant, swimming pool, wheelchair access, tennis, golf. SGL/DBL$200-$395.

Oliver House (2970 Silverado Trail, 94574; 963-4089) 4 rooms, bed & breakfast, complimentary breakfast, no-smoking. SGL/DBL$125+.

Rancho Caymus Inn (Box 78, 94573; 963-1777) 26 suites and efficiencies, restaurant, complimentary breakfast, wheelchair access. STS$85-$160, EFF$225-$300.

Shady Oaks Country Inn (399 Zinfandel Lane, 94574; 963-1190) 4 rooms, bed & breakfast, complimentary breakfast, wheelchair access, free parking. SGL/DBL$60-$125.

Hotel St. Helena (1309 Main Street, 94574; 963-4388, Fax 963-5402) 17 rooms, restaurant, complimentary breakfast. SGL/DBL$85-$135.

Villa St. Helena (2727 Sulphur Springs Avenue, 94574; 963-2514) 3 rooms, complimentary breakfast, swimming pool, no children allowed. SGL/DBL$185-$235.

White Sulphur Springs Resort (3100 White Sulphur Springs Rd., 94574; 963-8588) 33 rooms, complimentary breakfast, swimming pool, free parking. SGL/DBL$45-$55.

The Wine Country Inn (1152 Lodi Lane, 94574; 963-7077) 25 rooms, bed & breakfast, complimentary breakfast, swimming pool. SGL/DBL$101-$125+.

Stinson Beach

Area Code 415

Casa Del Mar (37 Belvedere Avenue; 868-2124) 35 rooms and suites. SGL/DBL$90-$120.

Stockton

Area Code 209
Stockton-San Joaquin Convention and Visitors Bureau
46 West Fremont Street
Stockton CA 95202
943-1987

All Star Inn (6717 Plymouth Rd., 95207; 951-8120) 36 rooms. SGL/DBL$27-$33.

All Star Inn (817 Navy Drive, 95206; 473-2000) 122 rooms. SGL/DBL$30-$45.

Best Western Charter Way Inn (550 West Charter Way, 95206; 948-0321, Fax 463-1638, 800-528-1234, 800-528-1800) 80 rooms, restaurant, no-smoking rooms, fax service, pets allowed. SGL/DBL$45-$60.

Best Western Stockton Inn (4219 East Waterloo Rd., 95215; 931-3131, Fax 931-0423, 800-528-1234, 800-528-1800) 141 rooms and suites, restaurant, lounge, heated swimming pool, whirlpool, airport courtesy car, fax service, meeting facilities, no-smoking rooms, no pets. SGL/DBL$61-$77, STS$150-$160.

Eden Park Inn (1005 North El Dorado; 466-2711, Fax 465-6126) 88 rooms, restaurant, swimming pool, within walking distance of the Stockton Civic Auditorium, conference meeting facilities, wheelchair access, no-smoking rooms. SGL/DBL$85-$125.

Econo Lodge (2210 Manthey Rd., 95206; 466-5741, 800-424-4777) 69 rooms, restaurant, swimming pool, laundry room, kitchenettes, children under 18 free, wheelchair access, no-smoking rooms, no pets. SGL$32-$45, DBL$37-$44.

Hilton Hotel (2323 Grand Canal Blvd., 95207; 957-9090, Fax 473-8908, 800-444-9094 in California) 200 rooms and suites, restaurant, lounge, outdoor swimming pool, convention and meeting facilities for 800, business services, jacuzzi, airport transportation, exercise equipment, wheelchair access, no-smoking rooms, pets allowed. SGL/DBL$75-$125, STS$250+.

Holiday Inn Plum Tree Plaza Hotel (111 East March Lane, 95207; 474-3301, Fax 474-7612, 800-HOLIDAY) 203 rooms, restaurant, lounge, swimming pool, spa, jacuzzi, meeting facilities for 300, children under 18 free, exercise equipment, wheelchair access, airport transportation, pets allowed. SGL$85-$95, DBL$100-$105.

La Quinta Inn (2710 West March Lane, 95207; 952-7800, Fax 472-0732, 800-531-5900) 153 rooms, restaurant, swimming pool, meeting facilities, exercise equipment, wheelchair access, no-smoking rooms, pets allowed. SGL$50-$56, DBL$58-$64.

Motel 6 (1625 French Camp Turnpike, 95206; 467-3600, 505-891-6161) 185 rooms. SGL/DBL$22-$28.

Motel 6 (4100 Waterloo Rd., 95202; 831-9511, 505-891-6161) 60 rooms. SGL/DBL$28-$34.

The Sixpence Inn (2717 West March Lane, 95207; 477-5576) 167 rooms. SGL/DBL$27-$38.

Travelers Inn (2654 West March Lane, 95205; 478-4300, Fax 478-1872, 800-833-8300) 124 rooms and suites, restaurant, swimming pool, wheelchair access, no-smoking rooms. SGL/DBL$45-$50, STS$75+.

Vagabond Motor Hotel (22 North Center Street, 95202; 948-6151, Fax 948-1220, 800-522-1555) 100 rooms, restaurant, complimentary breakfast, heated swimming pool, wheelchair access, pets allowed, airport transportation, free local telephone calls, no-smoking rooms, children under 18 free, fax service, complimentary newspaper. SGL$35-$40, DBL$45-$50.

Sunnyvale

Area Code 408
Sunnyvale Chamber of Commerce
499 South Murphy Avenue
Sunnyvale CA 94086
736-4971

Ambassador Business Inn (910 East Fremont Avenue, 94087; 738-500, Fax 245-4167, 800-538-1600) 305 rooms and suites, complimentary breakfast, swimming pool, exercise equipment, wheelchair access, no-smoking rooms. SGL/DBL$72-$86, STS$105-$125.

Best Western Inn (940 Weddell Drive, 94089; 734-3742, Fax 734-1462, 800-528-1234) 88 rooms, restaurant, lounge, swimming pool, children under 12 free, fax service, free local telephone calls, no-smoking rooms. SGL/DBL$50-$64.

Best Western Sunnyvale (940 Weddell Drive, 94089; 734-3742, 800-528-1234) 88 rooms, restaurant, swimming pool, airport courtesy car. SGL$65-$75, DBL$75-$85.

Captain's Cove Motel (600 North Mathilda Avenue, 94086; 735-7800, 800-322-2683) 102 rooms and efficiencies, complimentary breakfast, free parking. SGL$55, DBL$59.

Comfort Inn (595 North Mathilda Avenue, 94086; 749-8000, 800-221-2222) 52 rooms, restaurant, complimentary breakfast, whirlpool, sauna, in-room refrigerators and microwaves, VCRs, complimentary newspaper, wheelchair access, no pets. SGL$67-$87, DBL$72-$92.

Co-Z 8 Executive Inn (170 South Sunnyvale Avenue, 94086; 244-1040, 800-882-1984) 106 rooms and efficiencies. SGL/DBL$48+.

Days Inn (590 North Mathilda Avenue, 94086; 737-1177, 800-367-5618, 800-537-0056 in California) 36 rooms and efficiencies, complimentary breakfast. SGL/DBL$56.

Econo Lodge (385 Weddell Drive, 94089; 734-9700, 800-424-4777) 34 rooms, restaurant, complimentary breakfast, swimming pool, wheelchair access, no-smoking rooms, no pets. SGL/DBL$45-$56.

Friendship Inn (958 El Camino Real, 94087; 733-8800, 800-424-4777) 42 rooms, restaurant, meeting facilities, children under 18 free, wheelchair access, no-smoking rooms, no pets. SGL$39-$55, DBL$49-$65.

Hilton Inn (1250 Lakeside Drive, 94086; 738-4888, Fax 737-7147, 800-445-8667) 372 rooms and suites, restaurant, complimentary breakfast, outdoor swimming pool, jacuzzi, sauna, meeting facilities for 800, business services, wheelchair access, airport courtesy car. SGL/DBL$110-$170, STS$150-$250.

Holiday Inn (1217 Wildwood Avenue, 94089; 245-5330, Fax 732-2628, 800-888-3899, 800-HOLIDAY) 200 rooms and suites, restaurant, lounge, swimming pool, meeting facilities for 250, wheelchair access, no-smoking rooms, airport courtesy car, no pets. SGL/DBL$99-$134.

Maple Tree Inn (711 El Camino Real, 94087; 720-9700, 800-423-0243) 179 rooms, complimentary breakfast, swimming pool, no-smoking rooms. SGL/DBL$70-$85.

Marriott Residence Inn (1080 Stewart Drive, 94086; 720-8893, Fax 720-8749, 800-331-3131) 232 rooms and suites, complimentary breakfast, swimming pool, airport transportation, meeting facilities for 12, in-room microwaves, exercise equipment, wheelchair access, room service, car rental, pets allowed. SGL/DBL$120-$150.

Marriott Residence Inn Silicon Valley (750 Lakeway Drive, 94086; 720-1000, Fax 737-9722, 800-331-3131) 233 rooms and suites, swimming pool, meeting facilities for 60, room service, car rentals, airport courtesy car. SGL/DBL$124-$154.

Motel 6 (806 Ahwanee Avenue, 94086; 720-1222, 505-891-6161) 59 rooms, swimming pool. SGL/DBL$36-$42.

Motel 6 (777 North Mathilda Avenue, 94086; 736-4595, 505-891-6161) 135 rooms. SGL/DBL$33-$39.

Quality Inn (1280 Persian Drive, 94089; 744-0660, 800-221-2222) 72 rooms, restaurant, complimentary breakfast, outdoor heated swimming pool, meeting facilities, wheelchair access, no pets. SGL/DBL$50-$68.

Radisson Haus Inn (1085 East El Camino Real, 94087; 247-0800, 800-333-3333) 137 rooms and suites, restaurant, complimentary breakfast, swimming pool, free parking, airport courtesy car, wheelchair access, no-smoking rooms. SGL/DBL$110-$150, STS$140+.

Royal Executive Inn (820 East El Camino Real, 94087; 245-2520) 100 rooms, restaurant, swimming pool. SGL/DBL$35-$66.

Sheraton Inn Sunnyvale (1100 North Mathilda Avenue, 94089; 745-6000, Fax 734-8276, 800-325-3535) 174 rooms and suites, three restaurants, lounge, outdoor swimming pool, spa, exercise equipment, meeting facilities for 200, business services, airport courtesy car, wheelchair access, no-smoking rooms. SGL/DBL$90-$120.

Summerfield Suites (900 Hamlin Court, 94086; 745-1515, Fax 745-0540, 800-833-4354) 138 rooms and one- and two-bedroom suites, complimentary breakfast, swimming pool, airport courtesy car, no-smoking rooms, exercise equipment. SGL/DBL$129-$159.

Sundowner Inn (504 Ross Drive, 94089; 734-9900, Fax 747-0580, 800-223-9901) 105 rooms and suites, restaurant, complimentary breakfast, swimming pool, exercise equipment, no-smoking rooms, pets allowed. SGL$50-$75, DBL$60-$85+.

The Vagabond Inn (816 Ahwahnee Avenue, 94086; 734-4607, Fax 734-1675, 800-522-1555) 60 rooms, restaurant, swimming pool, in-room refrigerators, pets allowed, airport transportation, free local telephone calls, no-smoking rooms, children under 18 free, fax service, complimentary newspaper. SGL$45-$55, DBL$50-$65.

Valu Inn (852 West El Camino Real, 94087; 773-1234, Fax 773-0420, 800-527-2810) 59 rooms, restaurant, complimentary breakfast, wheelchair access, no-smoking rooms. SGL/DBL$50-$60.

Woodfin Suites (635 El Camino Real, 94087; 738-1700, Fax 738-0840, 800-237-8811) 88 suites, restaurant, complimentary breakfast, swimming pool, airport courtesy car, wheelchair access, pets allowed. STS$110-$145.

Wyndham Garden Hotel (1300 Chesapeake Terrace, 94089; 747-0999, Fax 745--759, 800-822-4200) 180 suites, restaurant, lounge, outdoor heated swimming pool, whirlpool, exercise equipment, wheelchair access, no-smoking rooms, meeting facilities for 135, airport courtesy car. SGL/DBL$99-$199.

Sunset Beach

Area Code 714

Best Western Inn (17205 Pacific Coast Highway, 90742; 840-2431, Fax 592-4093, 800-528-1234) 50 rooms and suites, restaurant, lounge, complimentary breakfast, beach, fax service, children under 12 free, in-room refrigerators, no pets. SGL/DBL$79-$139.

Harbour Inn (Box 1439, 90742; 592-4770) 23 rooms, bed & breakfast, complimentary breakfast, wheelchair access. SGL/DBL$69-$109.

Ramada Inn (16555 Pacific Coast Highway, 90742; 597-1993, Fax 597-1664, 800-2-RAMADA) 27 rooms, swimming pool, spa, in-room refrigerators and microwaves, meeting facilities for 15, wheelchair access. SGL/DBL$70+.

Susanville

Area Code 916

Best Western Trailside Inn (2785 Main Street, 96130; 257-4123, Fax 257-2665, 800-528-1234) 70 rooms and suites, restaurant, lounge, swimming pool, meeting facilities, fax service, spa, wheelchair access, no-smoking rooms, pets allowed. LS SGL/DBL$40-$52; HS SGL/DBL$50-$84, STS$50-$72.

Sutter Creek

Area Code 209

Foxes Inn Sutter Creek (Box 159, 95685; 267-5882) 6 rooms, bed & breakfast, complimentary breakfast, free parking, no-smoking. SGL$85-$125, DBL$90-$130.

Gold Quartz Inn (15 Bryson Drive, 95685; 267-9155, 800-752-8738) 24 rooms and suites, bed & breakfast, complimentary breakfast, wheelchair access, free parking, no-smoking. SGL$64-$95, DBL$72-$110.

Hanford House (61 Hanford Street, 95685; 267-0747) 9 rooms, bed & breakfast, complimentary breakfast, wheelchair access, no-smoking. SGL/DBL$75-$100+.

Sutter Creek Inn (75 Main Street, 95685; 267-5606) 19 rooms, bed & breakfast, complimentary breakfast, no-smoking rooms. SGL/DBL$50-$135.

Sylmar

Area Code 818
Sylmar Chamber of Commerce
13251 Gladstone Avenue
Sylmar CA 91342
367-1177

Friendship Inn (17283-87 San Fernando Rd., 91342; 367-1223, 800-424-4777) 32 rooms, swimming pool, whirlpool, wheelchair access, children under 18 free, no pets. SGL/DBL$36-$47.

Tahoe City

(See also **Lake Tahoe**)

Area Code 916
Greater North Lake Tahoe Chamber of Commerce
950 North Lake Blvd.
Lake Tahoe CA 95730
583-2371

Tahoe North Visitors and Convention Bureau
Box 5578
Lake Tahoe CA 95730
583-3494

RENTAL SOURCES: Alpine Meadows Realty (Box 1176; 583-1545). **Alpine Place** (Box 5206; 583-1890). **Coldwell Banker** (475 North Lake Blvd., 96145; 583-3793, 800-899-2662) rental condos, cabins and homes. SGL/DBL$70+. **ERA/Tahoe Escape** (245 North Lake Blvd., 96145; 583-0223, 800-488-2177) rental condos, cabins and homes. SGL/DBL$65+. **Hauserman Real Estate** (Box 1901, 96145; 583-3793, 800-899-2662). **Lake Pine Realty** (2825 Hillcrest Avenue, 96145) rental cottages. SGL/DBL$45+. **O'Niel Associates** (1877 North Lake Blvd., 96145) rental condos and homes. **Phillip Marcus Realty** (Box 459, 96145) rental townhouses. SGL/DBL$80+. **Tahoe Park Realty** (Box 966, 96145; 583-6942, 800-800-6942). **Tahoe Timberline Properties** (505 West Lake Blvd., 96145) rental condos and homes. SGL/DBL$75. **Tahoe Vacation Properties** (Box 2328, 96146) rental condos. SGL/DBL$120.

The Captain's Alpenhaus (6941 West Lake Blvd., 96142; 525-5000) 33 rooms and efficiencies, bed & breakfast, complimentary breakfast, swimming pool, pets allowed. SGL/DBL$65+.

Cedar Glen Lodge (6589 North Lake Blvd., 96148; 546-4281) 26 rooms and efficiencies, swimming pool. SGL/DBL$52.

Charmey Chalet (6549 North Lake Blvd., 96148; 546-2529) 10 cabins, swimming pool. SGL/DBL$45+.

The Chaney Guest House (4725 West Lake Blvd., 96145; 525-7333) 26 rooms and efficiencies, bed & breakfast, complimentary breakfast. SGL/DBL$85+.

Chinquapin Lakefront Resort (3600 North Lake Blvd., 96145; 583-6991) one- to four-bedroom townhouses, swimming pool, tennis courts, boat dock. SGL/DBL$100.

Cottage Inn At Lake Tahoe (1690 West Lake Blvd., 96145; 581-5073) 8 cottages, complimentary breakfast. SGL/DBL$90+.

Cottonwood Lodge (6542 North Lake Blvd., 96148; 546-2220) 16 cottages, swimming pool. SGL/DBL$49+.

Dunes Resort (6780 North Lake Blvd., 96148; 546-2196) 28 cottages. SGL/DBL$48+.

Edgelake Beach Club (7680 North Lake Blvd., 96148; 546-5974) 23 studios and three-bedroom apartments. SGL/DBL$50+.

Fire Lite Lodge (7035 North Lake Blvd., 96148; 546-7222) swimming pool. SGL/DBL$40+.

Granlibakken Resort (Granlibakken Rd., 96145; 583-4242, Fax 583-7641, 800-543-3221) 36 one- , two- and three-bedroom condos, swimming pool, tennis. SGL/DBL$75+.

Granlibakken Ski and Racquet Resort (1690 West Lake Blvd., 583-4242, Fax 583-7641) 156 rooms. SGL/DBL$80-$335.

Holiday House (7276 North Lake Blvd., 96148; 546-2369) one-bedroom apartments, pets allowed. SGL/DBL$75-$115.

Lake of the Sky (955 North Lake Blvd., 96145; 583-3305) 35 rooms and efficiencies, swimming pool. SGL/DBLE$66+.

The Mayfield House (236 Grove Street, 96145; 583-1001) 5 rooms, bed & breakfast, complimentary breakfast. SGL/DBL$70+.

Mourelatos Lakeshore Resort (6834 North Lake Blvd., 96148; 583-5334) 38 rooms and efficiencies. SGL/DBL$57+.

Northstar at Tahoe (Highway 267, 96160; 562-1113) one- to four-bedroom condos and private homes. SGL/DBL$108+.

Peppertree Inn (645 North Lake Blvd., 96145; 800-624-8590, 800-824-5342 in California) 36 rooms and efficiencies, swimming pool. SGL/DBL$59+.

Red Wolf Lakeside Lodge (7630 North Lake Blvd., 96134; 546-3952) 55 rooms and efficiencies, swimming poll. boat dock. SGL/DBL$50+.

River Ranch (Highway 89 and Alpine Meadows Rd., 96145; 583-4264) 12 rooms. SGL/DBL$55+.

Rocky Ridge (1877 North Lake Blvd., 96145; 583-3723) one- to three-bedroom condos, swimming pool. $125-$225.

Stanford Alpine Chalet (2000 Chalet Rd., 96145; 583-4625) 12 rooms, bed & breakfast, complimentary breakfast. SGL$50.

Tahoe City Inn (790 North Lake Blvd., 96145; 581-3333) 18 rooms. SGL/DBL$35+.

Tahoe Vista Inn and Marina (7220 North Lake Blvd., 96148; 546-7662, Fax 546-7963, 800-662-3433) 162 rooms and suites, pets allowed. SGL/DBL$152+.

Tamarack Lodge (2311 North Lake Blvd., 96145; 583-3350) 22 rooms and efficiencies. SGL/DBL$49+.

Tatami Cottage Resort (7449 North Lake Blvd., 96148; 546-3523) 18 cottages, pets allowed. SGL/DBL$49+.

Thornley Lodge (7630 North Lake Boulvard, 96148; 546-3952) 39 rooms, suites and cabins. SGL/DBL$30+.

TraveLodge (455 North Lake Blvd., 96145, 800-255-3050) 47 rooms, restaurant, swimming pool, no-smoking rooms. SGL/DBL$53+.

Villa Vista Resort (6750 North Lake Blvd., 96148; 546-3333) 32 rooms and cottages, swimming pool. SGL/DBL$60+.

VIsta Shores Resort (6731 North Lake Blvd., 96148; 546-3635) 65 rooms and one- to three-bedroom cottages and suites, swimming pool. SGL/DBL$45+.

The White House (1620 North Lake Blvd., 96145; 583-5800) rental home. SGL/DBL$130.

Woodvista Lodge (7699 North Lake Blvd., 96148; 583-3839) 25 rooms and cabins, pets allowed. SGL/DBL$40+.

Tiburon

Area Code 415

Tiburon Lodge and Conference Center (1651 Tiburon Blvd., 94920; 435-3133, Fax 435-2451, 800-762-7770, 800-842-8766 in California) 96 rooms, restaurant, swimming pool, wheelchair access, no-smoking rooms, free parking. SGL$65+, DBL$80+, STS$125-$175/$700W-$795W.

Trinidad

Area Code 707
Trinidad Chamber of Commerce
Box 356
Trinidad 95570

Bishop Pine Lodge (1481 Partricks Point Drive ; 677-3314) 13 one- and two-bedroom cottages, exercise equipment, in-room refrigerators and microwaves, hot tubs, airport courtesy car, no children, no pets. SGL/DBL$60-$100, EFF$65-$105.

Driftwood Motel (3602 Patricks Point Drive; 677-3483) 10 rooms. SGL/DBL$45-$65.

The Lost Whale Bed and Breakfast Inn (3452 Patricks Point Drive; 677-3425) 4 rooms, bed & breakfast, complimentary breakfast, no-smoking. SGL$80-$100+, DBL$90-$120.

Ocean Grove Lodge Motel (480 Patricks Point Drive; 677-3543) 9 rooms, restaurant. SGL/DBL$50-$75.

Shadow Lodge (687 Patricks Point Drive; 677-0532) 8 cabins, pets allowed. SGL/DBL$65-$85.

Shannon's Sea Cliff Motel (875 Patricks Point Drive; 677-9988) 4 rooms. SGL/BL$28-$38.

Trinidad Bay Bed and Breakfast Inn (560 Edwards Street; 677-0840) 18 rooms and suites, bed & breakfast, complimentary breakfast, airport transportation, no-smoking, no pets. SGL/DBL$105-$145.

Trinidad Inn (1170 Patricks Point Drive; 677-3349) 9 rooms and efficiencies, no-smoking rooms. SGL/DBL$40-$60.

View Crest Lodge (3415 Patricks Point Drive; 677-3393) 7 rooms. SGL/DBL$65+.

Trinity City

Area Code 916

Coffee Creek Ranch (Coffee Creek Rd., 96091; 266-3343) 14 rooms. SGL/DBL$115-$225.

Truckee

Area Code 916
Truckee-Donner Chamber of Commerce
Highway 267
Truckee CA 95734
587-2757

Best Western Truckee-Tahoe Inn (11331 Highway 267, 96161; 587-6385, Fax 587-8173, 800-824-6385, 800-528-1234) 100 rooms, complimentary breakfast, swimming pool, sauna, laundry room, wheelchair access, exercise equipment, no-smoking rooms. SGL/DBL$53-$92.

Blue House Inn (7660 Highway 89, 06162) 6 rooms, complimentary breakfast. SGL/DBL$85+.

Donner Lake Village Resort (15695 Donner Pass Rd., 96161; 587-6081) 54 rooms and efficiencies, complimentary breakfast. SGL/DBL$60+.

Northstar At Tahoe (Highway 267, 96191; 587-0200, Fax 587-0215, 800-533-6787) 183 townhouses, swimming pool, tennis, golf, exercise equipment, no-smoking rooms. SGL/DBL$110-$175, STS$145-300+.

Richardson House (101545 High Street, 96160) 12 rooms, bed & breakfast, complimentary breakfast. SGL/DBL$$85+.

Star Hotel (10015 West River Street, 96160; 587-3007) 17 rooms, restaurant, complimentary breakfast, wheelchair access, pets allowed. SGL/DBL$56+.

Super 8 Motel (11506 Deerfield Drive, 95737; 587-8888, 800-800-8000) 43 rooms, restaurant, complimentary breakfast, spa, sauna, free local telephone calls, fax service, wheelchair access, no-smoking rooms, pets allowed. LS SGL$51, DBL$57; HS SGL$71, DBL$80.

Truckee Hotel (Commercial Row, 96190) 37 rooms, complimentary breakfast. pets allowed. SGL/DBL$57.

Truckee Tahoe Inn-Best Western (11331 Highway 267, 800-528-1234) 66 rooms, swimming pool, complimentary breakfast. SGL/DBL$62+.

Tujunga

Area Code 818
Tujunga Chamber of Commerce
10110 Commerce Avenue
Tujunga CA 91402
352-4433

Tujunga-Glendale Travel Inn (7254 Foothill Blvd., 91042; 352-5951) 28 rooms and efficiencies, restaurant. SGL$50, DBL$60.

Turlock

Area Code 209

Best Western Orchard Inn (5025 North Golden State Blvd., 95380; 667-2827, Fax 634-6588, 800-521-5025, 800-528-1234) 72 rooms, restaurant, lounge, swimming pool, meeting facilities for 30, whirlpool, fax service, wheelchair access, no-smoking rooms, pets allowed. LS SGL/DBL$47-$60; HS SGL/DBL$66-$85.

Best Western Inn (1119 Pedras Rd., 95380; 634-9351, Fax 632-0231, 800-528-1234) 95 rooms and suites, restaurant, lounge, swimming pool, fax service, children under 12 free, no-smoking rooms. SGL/DBL$46-$95.

Ukiah

Area Code 707
Greater Ukiah Chamber of Commerce
495 East Perkins Street
Ukiah CA 95482
462-4705

Mendocino County Convention and Visitors Bureau
Box 244
Ukiah CA 95482
462-3091

Best Western Inn (601 Talmage Rd., 95482; 462-8868, 800-528-1234) 40 rooms, complimentary breakfast, swimming pool, meeting facilities, no pets, no-smoking rooms, fax service. SGL$38, DBL$42.

Cottage Inn Motel (755 South State Street, 95482; 462-8509) 30 rooms and efficiencies, swimming pool, airport transportation, no-smoking rooms, pets allowed. SGL$22, DBL$28.

Discovery Inn (1340 North State Street, 95482; 462-8873, Fax 462-1249) 154 rooms and suites, restaurant, heated swimming pool, sauna, whirlpool, meeting and banquet facilities, tennis, wheelchair access, no-smoking rooms. SGL$46-$48, DBL$48-$55.

Econo Lodge (750 South State, 95482; 462-7536, 800-424-4777) 31 rooms, restaurant, lounge, swimming pool, children under 18 free, wheelchair access, no-smoking rooms, no pets. SGL/DBL$35-$50.

Garden Court Motor Inn (1175 South State Street, 95482; 462-5646) 10 rooms and efficiencies. SGL$28, DBL$32.

Holiday Lodge (1050 South State Street, 95482; 462-2906, 800-341-8000) 44 rooms, restaurant, swimming pool, no-smoking rooms. SGL/DBL$26-$32.

Lantern Inn (650 South State Street, 95482; 462-6601) 29 rooms. SGL$25, DBL$28-$33.

Manor Inn Motel (950 North State Street, 95482; 462-7584; 800-922-3388) 57 rooms, restaurant, heated outdoor swimming pool, waterbeds, airport transportation, wheelchair access, no-smoking rooms, pets allowed. SGL$32, DBL$38.

Oak Knoll Bed and Breakfast (858 Sanel Drive, 95482; 462-8322) 4 rooms, bed & breakfast, complimentary breakfast. SGL/DBL$50-$60.

Sanford House (306 South Pine Street, 95482; 462-1653) 4 rooms, bed & breakfast, complimentary breakfast. SGL$80, DBL$85.

Super 8 Motel (1070 South State Street, 95482; 462-6657, 800-800-8000) 31 rooms, restaurant, outdoor swimming pool, free local telephone calls, wheelchair access, no-smoking rooms, no pets. SGL$32, DBL$35-$48.

TraveLodge (406 South State Street, 95482; 462-8611, 800-255-3050) 40 rooms and suites, restaurant, swimming pool, airport transportation, no pets. SGL$38-$50, DBL$40-$60.

Vichy Springs Resort (2605 Vichy Springs Rd., 95482; 462-9515) 14 rooms and cottages, swimming pool. SGL$65, DBL$85, 1BR$115, 2BR$125.

Western Traveler Motel (693 South Orchard, 95482; 468-9167) 56 rooms, restaurant, swimming pool. SGL/DBL$46-$68.

Union City

Area Code 510

Best Western Wellix Inn (31140 Alvarado-Niles Rd., 94587; 475-0600, Fax 475-0919, 800-528-1234) 76 rooms, restaurant, swimming pool, spa, meeting facilities, children under 12 free, fax service, complimentary breakfast, wheelchair access, no-smoking rooms, no pets. SGL/DBL$45-$69.

Holiday Inn (32083 Alvarado Niles Rd., 94587; 415-489-2200, 800-HOLIDAY) 267 rooms and suites, restaurant, lounge, swimming pool, exercise equipment, gift shop, car rental, meeting facilities for 700, wheelchair access, airport transportation. tennis. SGL$59-$85, DBL$59-$90, STS$150-$180.

Vacaville

Area Code 707
Vacaville Chamber of Commerce
400 East Monte Vista Avenue
Vacaville CA 95688
448-6424

Best Western Heritage Inn (1420 East Monte Vista Avenue, 95688; 448-8453, Fax 447-8649, 800-528-1234) 41 rooms, restaurant, lounge, complimentary breakfast, swimming pool, fax service, no-smoking rooms, pets allowed. SGL/DBL$41-$50.

Brigadoon Lodge (1571 East Monte Vista Avenue, 95688; 448-6482, 800-548-4949) 87 rooms and efficiencies, restaurant, complimentary breakfast, swimming pool, wheelchair access, no-smoking rooms. SGL$40-$50, EFF$55-$75.

Quality Inn (950 Leisure Town Rd., 95687; 446-8888, 800-221-2222) 120 rooms, restaurant, lounge, complimentary breakfast, swimming pool, whirlpool, exercise equipment, wheelchair access, no pets. SGL$44-$69, DBL$49-$74.

Super 8 Motel (101 Allison Court, 95688; 449-8884, Fax 449-9132, 800-800-8000) 53 rooms, restaurant, complimentary breakfast, outdoor swimming pools, free local telephone calls, fax service, wheelchair access, no-smoking rooms, pets allowed. SGL/DBL$40-$51.

TraveLodge (995 Merchant Street, 95688; 448-6964, 800-255-3050) 32 rooms and suites, restaurant, swimming pool, no pets. SGL/DBL$35-$49.

Vallejo

Area Code 707
Vallejo Chamber of Commerce and Convention and Visitors Bureau
Two Florida Street
Vallejo CA 94590
644-5551

All Star Inn (597 Sandy Beach Rd., 94590; 552-2912) 33 rooms. SGL/DBL$28-$34.

All Star Inn (1455 Sears Point Rd., 94590; 643-7611) SGL/DBL$32-$37.

Best Western Heritage Inn (1955 East Second Street, 94590; 746-0401, 800-327-9321 in California) 100 rooms and efficiencies, complimentary breakfast, swimming pool, wheelchair access, no-smoking rooms. SGL/DBL$45-$75.

Best Western Royal Bay (44 Admiral Callaghan Lane, 94591; 643-1061, Fax 643-4719, 800-528-1234) 78 rooms and suites, restaurant, swimming pool. SGL/DBL$65-$85, STS$95+.

Comfort Inn (1185 Admiral Callaghan Lane, 94591; 648-1400, Fax 552-8623, 800-228-5150, 800-424-4777, 800-824-1039) 80 rooms, restaurant, complimentary breakfast, swimming pool, whirlpool, exercise equipment, airport courtesy car, free parking. SGL$42-$85, DBL$44-$90.

Gateway Motor Hotel (2070 Solano Avenue, 552-1600, Fax 644-3419, 800-824-1039) 61 rooms and efficiencies, restaurant, complimentary breakfast, swimming pool, airport transportation, exercise equipment, pets allowed. SGL$32-$49, DBL$39-$59, EFF$42-$65.

Holiday Inn Marine World (1000 Fairgrounds, 94589; 644-1200, 800-HOLIDAY, 800-533-5753) 168 rooms, restaurant, lounge, swimming pool, meeting facilities for 250, wheelchair access, airport transportation, no pets, free parking. SGL$63-$67, DBL$67-$77.

Motel 6 (458 Fairgrounds, 94589; 642-7781) 97 rooms. SGL/DBL$23-$29.

Motel 6 (101 Maritime Academy Drive, 94590; 557-0777) 101 rooms. SGL/DBL$23-$29.

Ramada Inn (1000 Admiral Callaghan Lane, 94591; 643-2700, Fax 642-1148, 800-228-2828) 131 rooms and suites, restaurant, complimentary breakfast, swimming pool, children under 18 free, in-room refrigerators, airport transportation, free parking, wheelchair access, no-smoking rooms. SGL$55-$85, DBL$65-$90, STS$85-$120+.

Regency Inn (4326 Sonoma Blvd., 94585; 643-4150) 48 rooms and efficiencies, free parking. SGL$35-$45, DBL$40-$50, EFF$45-$55.

The Royal Bay Inn (44 Admiral Callaghan, 94591; 643-1061) 48 rooms and suites, restaurant, complimentary breakfast, swimming pool, airport transportation, pets allowed. SGL/DBL$36-$60.

Super 8 Motel (1596 Fairgrounds Drive, 94589; 554-9655, Fax 554-3951, 800-800-8000) 117 rooms, restaurant, complimentary breakfast, outdoor heated swimming pool, spa, laundry room, free local telephone calls, kitchenettes, meeting facilities, fax service, airport transportation, wheelchair access, no-smoking rooms, pets allowed. SGl/DBL$45-$55

TraveLodge (160 East Lincoln, 94590; 552-7220, Fax 647-3419, 800-322-2428, 800-262-4557) 60 rooms, restaurant, lounge, swimming pool, whirlpool, laundry room, fax service, meeting facilities, kitchenettes, tennis, pets allowed. SGL$38-$48, DBL$$55-$65.

Valu Inn (300 Fairgrounds Drive, 554-8000, 800-666-8899) 49 rooms. SGL/DBL$32-$70.

Walnut Creek

Area Code 415
Walnut Creek Chamber of Commerce
1501 North Blvd. #419
Walnut Creek CA 94596
934-2007

Comfort Suites (1170 Fairway Drive, 91789; 594-9999, 800-888-5757) 92 suites, swimming pool, exercise equipment, free parking. SGL$49-$75, DBL$59-$85.

Diablo Mountain Inn (2079 Mount Diablo Blvd., 94596; 937-5050) 24 rooms, complimentary breakfast, swimming pool. SGL$49-$54, DBL$55-$60.

Doubletree Hotel (2355 North Main Street, 94596; 934-2000, Fax 934-6374, 800-528-0444) 338 rooms and suites, restaurant, lounge, outdoor heated swimming pool, spa, meeting facilities for 500, free parking, airport transportation, wheelchair access, no-smoking rooms, pets allowed. SGL/DBL$105-$140, STS$150-$500.

Embassy Suites (1345 Treat Blvd., 94596; 934-2500, Fax 256-7233. 800-EMBASSY) 249 rooms and suites, restaurant, indoor swimming pool, sauna, whirlpool, meeting and banquet facilities for 266, gift shop, car rental, business services, room service, exercise equipment, no-smoking rooms, free parking. SGL/DBL$129-$144.

Holiday Inn (1170 Fairway Drive, 91789; 594-9999, Fax 594-9343, 800-HOLIDAY) 92 rooms, restaurant, lounge, complimentary breakfast, swimming pool, in-room refrigerators and microwaves, meeting facilities for 100, exercise equipment, wheelchair access, airport transportation, no pets. SGL$59-$85, DBL$90+.

Mansion at Lakewood (1056 Hacienda Drive, 94598; 945-3600, 800-477-7898) 7 rooms, bed & breakfast, complimentary breakfast. SGL/DBL$85-$155.

Motel 6 (2389 North Main Street, 94596; 935-4010, 505-891-6161) 71 rooms. SGL/DBL$36-$42.

Walnut Creek Inn (1475 South Main Street, 94596; 935-3220, Fax 945-8302, 800-633-8937) 74 rooms and suites, restaurant, swimming pool, airport transportation, wheelchair access, no-smoking rooms. SGL/DBL$60-$65, STS$75-$80.

Walnut Creek Motor Lodge (1960 North Main Street, 94596; 932-2811, 800-824-0334 in California) 71 rooms and suites, restaurant, SGL/DBL$45-$55, STS$70-$80.

Watsonville

Area Code 408
Watsonville Area Chamber of Commerce
444 Main Street
Watsonville CA 95076
724-3849

RENTAL SOURCES: Pajaro Dunes (2661 Beach Rd., 95076; 722-4671, 800-564-1771) rentals source for homes and condos.
Best Western Inn (740 Freedom Blvd., 95076; 724-3367, Fax 761-1785, 800-528-1234) 42 rooms, restaurant, complimentary breakfast, heated swimming pool, spa, whirlpool, fax service, in-room refrigerators, no-smoking rooms, wheelchair access, pets allowed. SGL$42-$52, DBL$48-$72.

Econo Lodge (972 Main Street, 95076; 724-8881, 800-446-6900) 23 rooms and efficiencies. SGL/DBL$43+.

El Rancho Motel (976 Salinas Rd., 95076; 722-2766) 11 rooms and efficiencies. SGL/DBL$45-$58.

Motel 6 (125 Silver Leaf Drive, 95076; 728-4144, 505-891-6161) 124 rooms, swimming pool, wheelchair access, no-smoking rooms. SGL/DBL$55-$65.

National 9 Motel (One Western Drive, 95076; 724-1116) 18 rooms and suites, swimming pool, wheelchair access, pets allowed. LS SGL/DBL$29-$55; HS SGL/DBL$53-$75.

Pajaro Dunes Conference and Vacation Center (2661 Beach Rd., 95076; 722-4671, Fax 728-7444, 800-564-1771) 105 condominiums and private homes, tennis, wheelchair access, free parking. SGL/DBL$140-$505.

Wawona

Area Code 209

RENTAL SOURCES: Redwoods (Box 2085, 95389; 375-6666) rental service for one- to five-bedroom private homes.

The Redwoods Guest Cottages (Chilnaualna Falls Rd., 95389; 375-6666, Fax 375-6400) 89 cottages, wheelchair access, no-smoking rooms, pets allowed. SGL/DBL$68-$200+.

Weed

Area Code 916
Weed Chamber of Commerce
Box 366
Weed CA 96094
938-4624

Hi-Lo Motel (88 South Weed Blvd., 96094; 938-2731) 36 rooms, pets allowed. SGL$30, DBL$36.

Lake Shastina Golf Resort (5925 Country Club Drive, 96094; 800-358-GOLF) 36 one- to four-bedroom condo and town houses, restaurant, lounge, outdoor swimming pool, spa, tennis, golf, children under 14 free, kitchenettes, fax service, meeting facilities, free parking, no-smoking rooms, pets allowed. 1BR$98, 2BR$148.

Motel 6 (466 North Weed Blvd., 96094; 938-4101) 118 rooms, swimming pool, pets allowed, no-smoking rooms. SGL$30, DBL$36.

Shastina Golf Inn (550 Shastina Drive, 96094; 938-4227) 18 rooms, free parking, pets allowed. SGL/DBL$24-$28.

Sis-Q-Inn Motel (1825 Shastina Drive, 96094; 938-4194) 22 rooms, airport transportation, wheelchair access, pets allowed, no-smoking rooms. SGL$33, DBL$40.

Stewart Mineral Springs (4617 Stewart Springs Rd., 96094) five-bedroom private home. $300 per day.

Townhouse Motel (157 South Highway, 96094; 938-4431) 20 rooms and suites, pets allowed. SGL$26, DBL$32-$35.

Y Ranch House Motel (90 North Weed Blvd., 96094; 938-4481) 22 rooms, restaurant, swimming pool, airport transportation, pets allowed. SGL$20-$30, DBL$23-$33.

Weott

Area Code 707

Sequoia Motel (Box 111; 946-2276) 10 rooms, swimming pool, pets allowed. SGL/DBL$50-$60.

Westley

Area Code 209

Days Inn (7114 McCracken Rd., 95387; 894-5500, Fax 894-3291, 800-325-2525) 33 rooms, restaurant, complimentary breakfast, swimming pool, spa, fax service, whirlpools, laundry room, wheelchair access, no-smoking rooms, pets allowed. SGL$40-$42, DBL$45-$48.

Westport

Area Code 707

Bowen's Pelican Lodge (38921 Highway 1, 95488; 964-5588) 8 rooms, bed & breakfast, complimentary breakfast. SGL/DBL$45-$80.

Dehaven Valley Farm (39247 North Highway 1, 95488; 961-1660) 8 rooms, bed & breakfast, complimentary breakfast. SGL/DBL$84-$125.

Howard Creek Ranch (40501 North Highway 1, 95488; 964-6725) 7 rooms and suites, bed & breakfast, complimentary breakfast, pets allowed, swimming pool, SGL/DBL$50-$95.

Wesport Inn (37040 North Highway 1, 95488; 964-5135) 6 rooms, bed & breakfast, complimentary breakfast, swimming pool. SGL/DBL$38-$40.

Williams

Area Code 916

Comfort Inn (400 C Street, 95987; 473-2381, 800-221-2222) 61 rooms, restaurant, complimentary breakfast, swimming pool, whirlpool, wheelchair access. SGL$39-$48, DBL$44-$53.

Willits

Area Code 707
Willits Chamber of Commerce
15 South Main Street
Willits CA 95490
459-4113

The Holiday Lodge Motel (1540 South Main Street, 95490; 459-5361) 16 rooms, restaurant, swimming pool, pets allowed, no-smoking rooms. SGL/DBL$38-$52.

The Lark Motel (1411 South Main Street, 95490; 459-2421) 22 rooms and suites, swimming pool, no-smoking rooms. SGL/DBL$36-$38, STS$45-$55.

Willows

Area Code 916
Glenn County Chamber of Commerce
West Wood and Murdock Streets
Willows CA 95998
934-7994

Best Western Golden Pheasant Inn (249 North Humboldt Avenue, 95988; 934-4603, Fax 934-4275, 800-528-1234) 104 rooms, restaurant, lounge, complimentary breakfast, two heated swimming pools, fax service, no-smoking rooms, wheelchair access, pets allowed. SGL/DBL$45-$69.

Cross Roads West (452 North Humboldt, 95988; 934-7026) 41 rooms, restaurant, swimming pool, pets allowed. SGL$25, DBL$35.

Super 8 Motel (457 Humboldt Avenue, 95988; 934-2871, 800-800-8000) 41 rooms, restaurant, complimentary breakfast, outdoor swimming pool, free local telephone calls, wheelchair access, no-smoking rooms, pets allowed. SGL/DBL$33-$40.

Wilmington

Area Code 213

Quality Inn (1402 West Pacific Coast Highway, 90744; 834-3400, 800-221-2222) 72 rooms, complimentary breakfast, swimming pool, whirlpools, free parking, wheelchair access, no pets. SGL$45-$90, DBL$51-$110.

Windsor

Area Code 707

Country Meadow Inn (11360 Old Redwood Highway, 95492; 431-1276) 5 rooms, complimentary breakfast, swimming pool. SGL/DBL$89-$109.

Wishon

Area Code 209

Miller's Landing (37976 Rd. 222, 93669; 642-3633) 10 rooms and efficiencies, wheelchair access, pets allowed. SGL/DBL$30-$80.

Yosemite and Yosemite National Park

Area Code 209

RENTAL SOURCES: Yosemite West Condominiums (Box 821; 454-2033) 1BR$78-$108. **Yosemite West Reservations** (Box 36, 95389; 642-2211) reservation service for local accommodations.

Ahwahnee Hotel (Highway 140, 95389; 252-4848) 290 rooms and cabins, restaurant, swimming pool, tennis, wheelchair access, no-smoking rooms. SGL$195+, DBL$200+.

Curry Village (Highway 41, 95389; 252-4848) 200 rooms and cabins, restaurant, swimming pool, exercise equipment. SGL/DBL$73-$100.

Days Inn (40662 Highway 41, 93644; 642-2525, Fax 658-8481, 800-325-2525) 41 rooms and suites, restaurant, swimming pool, hot tubs, children under 12 free, fax service, wheelchair access, no-smoking rooms, no pets. SGL$35-$45, DBL$40-$65, STS$75-$125.

Wawona Lodge (Box 2005, 95389; 252-4848) 104 rooms, restaurant, swimming pool, tennis, no-smoking rooms. SGL/DBL$60-$80.

Yosemite Lodge (Yosemite National Park, 95389; 252-4848, Fax 372-1433) 485 rooms, restaurant, swimming pool, wheelchair access, no-smoking rooms. SGL/DBL$27-$92.

Yountville

Area Code 707
Yountville Chamber of Commerce
Box 2064

Yountville CA 94599
944-1559

Napa Valley Tourist Bureau
Box 3240
Yountville CA 94599
258-1957

Best Western Napa Valley Lodge (94599; 944-2468, Fax 944-9362, 800-528-1234) 55 rooms, restaurant, complimentary breakfast, swimming pool, sauna, in-room refrigerators, balconies, meeting facilities, fireplaces, complimentary newspaper, fax service, no-smoking rooms, exercise equipment. LS SGL$112-$122, DBL$122-$132; HS SGL/DBL$175-$195.

Bordeaux House (6600 Washington Street, 94599; 944-2855, 800-677-6370 in California) 6 rooms, bed & breakfast, complimentary breakfast, free parking. SGL/DBL$95-$120.

Burgundy House (6711 Washington Street, 94599; 944-0889) 5 rooms, bed & breakfast, complimentary breakfast, private baths. SGL/DBL$100-$110.

Magnolia Hotel (6529 Yount Street, 94599; 944-2056) 12 rooms, complimentary breakfast, swimming pool, no-smoking rooms. SGL/DBL$89-160.

Napa Valley Lodge (Box 1, 94599; 944-2468, 800-368-2468) 43 rooms and one-bedroom suites, complimentary breakfast, swimming pool, exercise equipment. SGL/DBL$68-$113, STS$130.

Napa Valley Railway Inn (6503 Washington Street, 94599; 944-2000) 9 rooms. SGL/DBL$95-$105.

Vintage Inn Napa Valley (6541 Washington, 94599; 944-1112, Fax 944-1617, 800-982-5539) 80 rooms, complimentary breakfast, swimming pool, whirlpool, fireplaces, airport transportation, tennis, wheelchair access, pets allowed, free parking. SGL$124-$189, DBL$134-$189.

Yreka Area

Area Code 916
Yreka Chamber of Commerce
1000 South Main Street
Yreka CA 96097, 842-1649

Best Western Miner's Inn (122 East Miner Rd., 96097; 842-4355, Fax 842-4480, 800-528-1234) 135 rooms, restaurant, swimming pool, fax service, pets allowed. SGL$42, DBL$53.

Gold Pan Motel (801 North Main Street, 96097; 842-9918) 19 rooms. SGL/DBL$35-$45.

Heritage Inn (306 North Main Street, 96097; 842-6835) 25 rooms. SGL/DBL$65.

Klamath Motor Lodge (1111 South Main Street, 96097; 842-2751) 28 rooms, swimming pool, no-smoking rooms. SGL/DBL$35-$40.

Motel Orleans South (1804B Fort Jones Rd., 96097; 842-1612) 53 rooms. SGL/DBL$45-$65.

Thunderbird Lodge (526 South Main Street, 96096; 842-4404, 800-554-4339 in California) 44 rooms, swimming pool, no-smoking rooms. SGL/DBL$75+.

Wayside Inn (1235 South Main Street, 96096; 842-4412, 800-767-4148) 44 rooms and suites, restaurant, outdoor heated swimming pool, spa, free local telephone calls, in-room refrigerators, free parking, wheelchair access, no-smoking rooms, pets allowed. SGL$30-$68, DBL$38-$76, STS$135-$150.

Yuba City

Area Code 916

Best Western Bonanza Inn (1001 Clark Avenue, 95991; 674-8824, Fax 674-0563, 800-528-1234) 125 rooms and suites, restaurant, swimming pool, airport transportation. SGL$60-$66, DBL$65-$75.

Moore Mansion Inn (560 Cooper Avenue, 95991; 674-8550) 5 rooms, bed & breakfast, complimentary breakfast. SGL/DBL$65.

Motel 6 (700 North Polora, 95991; 674-1710) 50 rooms. SGL/DBL$28-$34.

Twin Palms Motel (2129 Live Oak Blvd., 95991; 674-9670) 11 rooms and efficiencies, wheelchair access. SGL$25, DBL$30.

Vada's Motel (545 Colusa Avenue, 95991; 671-1151) 40 rooms, restaurant, airport transportation, no-smoking rooms. SGL/DBL$43-$46.

ADDITIONAL RESOURCES

WHERE TO STAY IN SOUTHERN CALIFORNIA

The most complete source available anywhere for every type of accommodation: B&Bs, country inns, condos and cottages for rent, hotels and motels. Over 3,500 places described, with prices, phones, special offers. 5 3/8 x 8 paperback/320 pp/$12.95/1-55650-573-6.

THE FLORIDA WHERE TO STAY BOOK

More than 4,000 places to stay in the #1 vacation destination in the country – condos for rent, inns, motels, hotels, even beach houses for rent by the week or month. Prices, descriptions, all details. 5 3/8 x 8 paperback/448 pp/$12.95/1-55650-539-6

THE GREAT AMERICAN WILDERNESS: TOURING AMERICA'S NATIONAL PARKS

The 41 most scenic parks, from Acadia to Yosemite, and how to see them: main access routes, where to stay, where to eat, which roads are most crowded or most beautiful, how much time to allow, what you can safely skip and what you must not miss. Special sections tell how to tour each park if you have only limited time – or if time is not a factor – and 11 detailed itineraries suggest ways to combine visits to several scenic areas in a single trip. Maps of each park included, showing all surrounding access roads. 5 3/8 x 8 paperback/288 pp/$11.95/1-55650-567-1

USA BY RAIL

Details what you will encounter on the 28 long-distance trains that criss-cross North America, describing points of interest along the way and spots where the trips can be broken. Station information, sightseeing, where to stay, route maps, excursions. Over 500 destinations, including 37 major cities, are covered. 5 3/8 x 8 paperback/320 pp/$15.95/1-55650-521-3

ADVENTURE GUIDE TO THE ALASKA HIGHWAY

A complete guide to what you will find along the highway, plus all worthwhile side-trips and approaches, such as the Alaska-Marine Highway, Klondike Highway, Top-of-the-World Highway. Maps & color photos. 5 3/8 x 8 paperback/288 pp/1-55650-457-8

ADVENTURE GUIDE TO BAJA CALIFORNIA 2nd Edition

Thorough update of this classic tourguide to the peninsula, from Tijuana and Mexicali to Cabo San Lucas at the tip. The best driving routes, fascinating history, hotels, restaurants, all practical details. 5 3/8 x 8 paperback/288 pp/$13.95/1-55650-590-6

CANADIAN ROCKIES ACCESS GUIDE

The ultimate guide to outdoor adventure, from Banff to Lake Louise to Jasper National Park. Walking and canoeing routes, climbs, cycling itineraries. Maps, photos. 6 x 9 paperback/360 pp/$15.95/0-919433-92-8

HAWAII: A WALKER'S GUIDE

Walking the awesome Na Pali cliffs and climbing the Kilauea Volcano are just a few of the unforgettable adventures detailed here. Each hike is graded for difficulty, from multi-day excursions to scenic strolls. Detailed maps, color photos. 5 3/8 x 8 paperback/224 pp/$14.95/1-55650-215-X

THE GOLF RESORT GUIDES

Two updated volumes (EAST and WEST editions) describe the most rewarding golf resorts in every state, plus Canada, Mexico (in Western Edition), and the Caribbean (in Eastern Edition). All facilities are described and rated: golf courses, pro shop, tennis, ski, lodging, special packages offered, fees, restaurants, directions for arrival. Maps. 5 3/8 x 8 paperbacks/448 pp each/$13.95 each/EASTERN 1-55650-568-X; WESTERN 1-55650-569-8.

CALIFORNIA INSIDER'S GUIDE

Packed with stunning photographs and extensive historical & cultural background, combined with rich practical detail, the famous Insider's Guides cover the world. The California guide tells you where to stay, where to eat, what to see, how to get around, region-by-region. Large fold-out map included. Hundreds of color photos. 5 5/8 x 8 3/4 paperback/256 pp/$14.95/1-55650-163-3

MEXICO INSIDER'S GUIDE
5 5/8 x 8 3/4 paperback/320 pp/$17.95/1-55650-454-3

CANADA WEST INSIDER'S GUIDE
5 5/8 x 8 3/4 paperback/256 pp/$17.95/1-55650-580-9

ADVENTURE GUIDE TO COSTA RICA
Biggest, most detailed guide on the market. Exhaustive coverage of history, people, customs, uniques wildlife, restaurants, transport, where to stay. The best hiking trails, the national parks, a complete guide to San José and all other towns, with maps and photos. Offbeat, unusual adventure possibilities as well. 5 3/8 x 8 paperback/360 pp/$16.95/1-55650-456-X

ADVENTURE GUIDE TO BELIZE
Second edition. With some of the best diving in the world, 1000-foot waterfalls, virgin rainforest, 500 bird species, this is a naturalist's paradise. The latest and best color guide available. Hotels, food, maps, color photos. 5 3/8 x 8 paperback/288 pp/$14.95/1-55650-493-4

ADVENTURE GUIDE TO THE DOMINICAN REPUBLIC
Miles of pristine beaches, jungles, soaring mountains and Old Santo Domingo, first Spanish capital of the Americas. A complete practical guide to every aspect of the island, from food to hiking, luxury hotels to budget travel bargains, shopping and trabsport. Maps. 5 3/8 x 8 paperback/256 pp/$13.95/1-55650-537-X

⁊⋆

Write Hunter Publishing, Inc., 300 Raritan Center Parkway, Edison NJ 08818 or call (908) 225 1900 for our complete free color catalog describing these and over 1,000 other unisial travel guides and maps to all parts of the world – from Africa to South America, from Europe to Asia. Find them in the best bookstores or you can order direct by sending your check to the address above (add $2.50 to cover shipping / handling).